STRATEGY

DAVID T. KOLLAT

TABLE OF CONTENTS

Part IV
Developing Annual Plans

Part V
Evaluating Strategies and Plans

LIST OF FIGURES

PREFACE

This book is written for people who are interested in strategy. The focus is on *how* to develop business and corporate strategies, rather than simply what they are. The reader is provided analytical frameworks, concepts, processes, techniques, and templates that can be used to develop strategies and plans, and/or evaluate those that already exist.

The basis for this book is the author's 40 plus years of experience in a wide variety of businesses. Following seven years as a college professor, this includes 11 years as a senior executive at Limited Brands, 31 years as a business consultant, and over three decades serving on boards of directors of more than 15 companies, including six NYSE and Nasdaq listed corporations.

This exposure has been supplemented with a broad review of books, journal articles, consulting reports in the public domain, and business periodical and magazine articles.[1] Much of this literature review has occurred over the past four years in preparation for writing this book, and has focused on ideas, processes, and concepts that have practical usefulness in a real business setting.[2]

This book views business and corporate strategy as a continuous dynamic process of anticipation, adjustments, and refinements, in response to changing market, environmental, and competitive developments, on the one hand, and the company's actual results on the other. Strategy is an ongoing *work in progress*, and it involves much more than the static perspective of a concept and structure point of view that characterizes most discussions of it.

Strategy is the critical component of a strategic management system. Strategic management systems integrate the long-term strategy into an annual operating plan for the corporation, and for each of its operating divisions, if it is a multi-division organization. Further, the system links the achievement of financial results with both long term and annual incentive compensation, and provides for the proper oversight and approval by the board of directors. Properly executed, with reasonable earnings-per-share, profitability objectives and other explicit metrics tied directly to incentive cash and stock compensation levels, this system aligns the interests of executives, shareholders, and other stakeholders of the company.

Companies with well-developed strategy formulation and strategic management systems may want to compare their approach with the one presented here to see if there are opportunities for improvement. For companies with less well developed processes, the templates presented here may be useful in designing an approach that makes sense for their businesses. Companies or executives that need to develop strategies, and have little or no experience with the process, may find the discussion informative in developing their approach.

Board members may find this book valuable in fulfilling their fiduciary responsibilities. Does the company have an acceptable strategy? Is it well thought out? Are the right things being considered? Is the business moving too fast, or too slow? Are the results acceptable, or should they be better? How much better? Hopefully the discussion, particularly Chapters 23 and 24, is an informative source in making these and similar kinds of judgments.

Business students, particularly MBA and other graduate students, should find this book valuable. It presents analytical frameworks, concepts, processes, and templates that are used by well-managed companies. This book is not a theoretical discussion, but rather an attempt to present best practices in the real world of business. Students will use these perspectives in their careers, and will be expected to be proficient with them.

Some business professors might also find this book useful, not only as a text book or resource book for the class room, but also as a framework for meaningful research. For the last several decades we have been in a regrettable and unconscionable position. Text books and research by academicians are disregarded by many business people as being *irrelevant*. Business books, written by executives and consultants, are viewed by many academicians as lacking *rigor*. There needs to be a new *rigor/relevance paradigm* that is both rigorous and relevant. This book is intended to be a step in that direction, and hopefully it provides a partial roadmap for, and will stimulate, academic research that is useful in the business community.

I would like to thank my administrative associate, Lisa Adrion, and my research associate, Andra Gillum for their assistance and understanding. Their contributions have been valuable, and their attitude always positive and uplifting. Most importantly, I have been able to spend more time with them which is the most important thing to me since they are also my daughters.

Finally, I would like to express my appreciation to my mentors: W. Arthur Cullman; William R. Davidson; Alton F. Doody; Bert C. McCammon; John K. Pfahl; Ronald P. Willett; and Leslie H. Wexner. I have been very fortunate in my professional life, and they are the primary reason.

Miami Beach, FL
January 2008

PART I

INTRODUCTION

CHAPTER 1

STRATEGIC MANAGEMENT

"Executives are continuously confronted
with the need to answer two questions:
'Are we doing things right?'
'Are we doing the right things?'"

Peter F. Drucker

Strategy and execution are the twin determinants of business success. Both are equally important. A great strategy will not produce exciting results if the execution is poor. Alternatively, great execution will generally not produce great results over an extended time period if the strategy is weak. Achieving and maintaining excellence in both strategy and execution is extraordinarily difficult, and shortfalls are common. Consider:

- Coca-Cola is the world's largest beverage company selling more than 400 brands in 200 countries. For years Coke has enjoyed a significant lead in market share over its rivals, including Pepsi. Yet, over the past five years Coke has been able to increase its earnings-per-share by only 6.9 percent per year, compared to 17.8 percent for Pepsi. And, over the same five years, Coke's total stock return to shareholders has compounded at 6 percent per year, compared to 14.5 percent per year for Pepsi. Despite a market share disadvantage, and the fact that it is 44 percent larger than Coke, Pepsi has outperformed what may be the strongest brand name in the world.
- For years Gap was the dominant retailer of casual apparel for men, women and children. In recent years, Gap's preeminence has been eclipsed by Abercrombie & Fitch. Abercrombie has been able to achieve a 27 percent compound annual return to shareholders over the last five years, compared to 6 percent for Gap. A&F's average return on assets

over the last five years has been 20 percent, compared to Gap's 9.5 percent. Gap lost momentum, A&F gained momentum.

- Kellogg and General Mills are the dominant players in the breakfast cereal business, both are among the largest packaged goods companies in the United States, and both are about the same size, at $11.1 and $12.2 billion, respectively. Kellogg, however, earns a return on assets about 50 percent higher than General Mills, and has been growing its earnings-per-share at 16.3 percent per year over the past five years compared to only 4.9 percent for GM. Kellogg is more profitable and faster growing.
- Best Buy is the largest specialty retailer of consumer electronics in North America with about 900 stores in the United States. Circuit City is a distant second with sales of $12.3 billion compared to Best Buy's $37 billion. Best Buy has continuously dominated Circuit City, achieving a ten year compounded annual stock total return to investors of 40 percent compared to CC's 3 percent, and earning a return on assets eight times greater than CC's.

This book focuses primarily on strategy, and after completing it, you should be able to explain the strategic reasons for the differences in performance. More importantly, you should be able to apply the insights to develop and/or improve the strategies of your business, and/or ones you are involved with.

Strategy is part of what is generally called strategic management. The components of strategic management depend on the complexity of the business. Single-unit businesses generally have a less complex system than enterprises consisting of multiple operating divisions.

A SINGLE BUSINESS UNIT ENTERPRISE

Figure 1.1 presents a generic management system for a single business unit enterprise. This would be a business that has one brand, or one division, or one retail concept if it is a retail business. Examples of this type of business would include Coach, Peet's Coffee & Tea, and Panera Bread.

The starting point in the system is the development or revision a long-term business strategy. Long-term means multi-year . . . 3 years or 5 years being the most common. In publicly-held companies, this long-term business strategy is reviewed and approved, or approved with modifications, by the board of directors. Some businesses have some part of their compensation systems devoted to long-term performance, and for those who do, it would be common for the long-term strategy to be used to set performance targets for these compensation plans.

Figure 1.1 A generic strategic management system for a single business unit enterprise

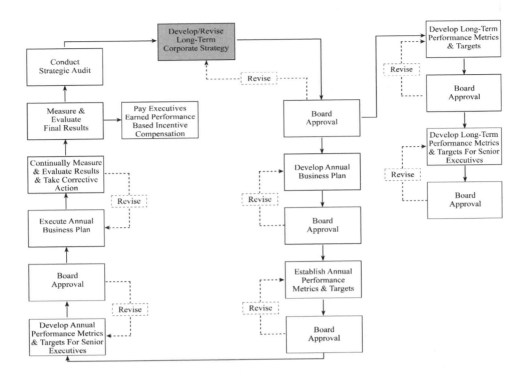

The long-term strategy also provides the principal basis for, and input into, the annual business plan. Effective annual business plans articulate what part of the long-term strategy the business intends to execute during the coming fiscal year so that the long-term strategy can be achieved. Like the long-term strategy, the annual business plan is also reviewed by the board and accepted, or, more commonly, accepted with modifications. Sometimes the plan is rejected. The annual plan that is accepted by the board then serves as the basis for the annual bonus compensation plan for senior executives.

Throughout the fiscal year, the annual business plan is implemented, results are measured, and corrective action is taken. At the end of the fiscal year, the final results determine whether senior executives receive annual bonuses, and the amount of these bonuses. The final results can also impact whether executives earn partial credit toward the long-term bonus program.

Continuing with Figure 1.1, the annual results for the fiscal year also become part of the strategic audit, a critical process that assesses and evaluates what the enterprise has accomplished, and where it has not been successful. This analysis, when combined with forecasts about various relevant dimensions of the businesses' future . . . like economic trends, environmental and technological trends, competitive developments and trends . . . constitute the strategic audit which provides input into the next version of the long-term business strategy of the enterprise.

The concepts, structure and processes diagramed in Figure 1.1, and described above, constitute strategic management. Most well-managed and well-governed businesses have a system similar to this one. The concepts may have different names, and/or the process sequence may vary, and/or the time periods may be different, but professionally-managed companies have a management system that resembles this one. The management system integrates long-term strategy, annual business plans, and the bonus component of compensation systems, provides the proper oversight by the board of directors, and helps align the interests of executives, the board, and shareholders.

A MULTI-UNIT BUSINESS ENTERPRISE

This type of enterprise consists of more than one operating division, generally several divisions, and occasionally more than 100 divisions. Examples of this type of business include General Electric, Estee Lauder, Microsoft, and Goldman Sachs. As Figure 1.2 indicates, the generic management system for a multi-unit business is more complex; however, it is designed to accomplish the same objectives as the one for businesses with single operating units.

The process involves a series of interacting "top down"-"bottoms-up" . . . and 'bottoms-up"-"top-down" iterations. Usually the process begins with the development or revision of a long-term strategy for the entire corporation that, in the simplest terms, describes what the enterprise is trying to accomplish and how it proposes doing it. As before, the time frame will vary, but it is most often 5 years, sometimes less, and occasionally more.

The long-term corporate strategy provides general direction for possible corporate acquisitions and divestitures. The input for acquisitions will include the industries, market segments, and product/service scopes that are of potential interest as well as size and scale requirements, competitive advantage expectations, synergy requirements, and so on. The divestiture component identifies which products, services, businesses, and operating divisions are candidates for elimination because they are no longer appropriate to the company's business portfolio. For obvious reasons, the divestiture components may remain confidential, or confined to a very limited audience.

Equally importantly, the long-term corporate strategy provides guidelines for the operating divisions to use in developing or revising their long-term business strategies. These inputs generally include economic forecasts and various planning

Figure 1.2 A generic strategic management system for a multiple business unit enterprise

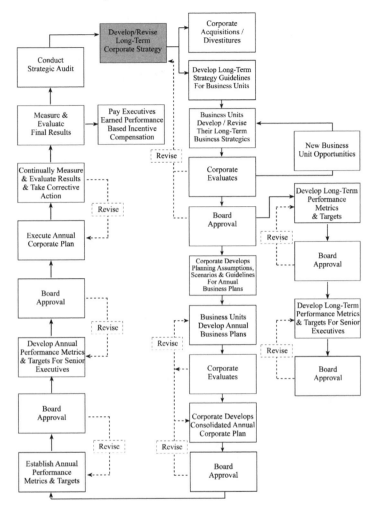

assumptions as well as specific sales, operating profit, return-on-investment, market share, and other requirements that each division should attain over the time period so that the corporation as a whole can meet its objectives, and hence satisfy or exceed shareholder and other stakeholder expectations.

With this input, each operating division develops or revises its long-term business strategy. These strategies are reviewed and critiqued by the CEO and his executive team, and the appropriate changes, often "negotiated" changes, are made to each operating divisions' long-term strategy. This process often surfaces new business opportunities which may be added to the strategic agenda of the operating division in question, or some other operating division, or be "housed" for the time being with some group at the corporate level.

The revised operating division strategies are consolidated into the long-term corporate strategy. Revisions to the original corporate strategy are made. Additional growth initiatives that do not involve any existing operating divisions may be added. Strategic initiatives that span several operating divisions may be consolidated at the corporate level for emphasis and execution efficiency, and additional strategic initiatives not involving any existing divisions may be added. Organizational structures and development programs may be changed and/or added.

The consolidated long-term corporate strategy that reflects the thinking of the CEO is then presented to the board of directors. The plan is approved, or approved with modifications, or occasionally rejected.

Approved long-term corporate and business strategies may serve as the basis for long-term incentive compensation plans for selected corporate executives and operating division personnel. These plans specify the long-term bonus compensation that each participant will receive based on certain results, generally some level of operating income, and/or net profit before or after taxes, some measure of return-on-investment, market share, and so on that is achieved over the time span of the long-term strategy. These compensation plans will be reviewed and approved by the compensation committee of the board of directors, or by the entire board.

The approved long-term corporate strategy will also be used by executives to formulate the annual corporate plan and the annual operating plans of the operating divisions. The process typically begins at the corporate level by reviewing current results; analyzing key trends in consumer and/or customer markets; forecasting the most likely economic scenarios; identifying most likely moves of major competitors; and so on. The process will also identify sales, earnings-per-share, return-on-investment, and other targets that the enterprise hopes to achieve during the next year. Based on this work, the corporate group will issue planning assumptions and scenarios, other guidelines, and sales, operating income, and return-on-investment targets for each operating division.

Using this input, each operating division will analyze its own business, assess its own environmental and competitive space, and its approved long-term strategy, and develop its annual operating plan. The CEO and his team will review the proposed annual plans of each of the operating divisions, and changes that are agreed to will be incorporated into revised annual plans. These revised plans will be consolidated into an annual corporate plan. Revisions to the original corporate plan will be made, and various growth and strategic initiatives might be modified and/or added, and relevant organizational changes may be made.

The consolidated annual corporate plan including pro-forma financial statements will be presented to the board of directors for approval. This approval process may produce additional changes which will be incorporated into a revised consolidated plan. This final annual corporate plan becomes the road map for the following year. Typically, it should also be used to set bonus targets for the CEO and his staff as well as the executive teams of the operating divisions. This annual incentive compensation plan will also be reviewed and approved by the compensation committee of the board of directors, and recommended to the entire board for approval.

The annual corporate plan is implemented, results are measured, and corrective action is taken. At the end of the fiscal year, each executive in the annual bonus plan is paid the bonus amount stipulated in the plan previously approved by the board.

The annual results also become an input into the strategic audit. Actual results are combined with analyses of new trends and developments, and collectively provide input into the next revision of the long-term strategy. The process is then repeated for the next year.

This type of system, or some variation of it, is used by professionally-managed, multi-division enterprises. Although it is more complex that the system used in single division businesses, it accomplishes the same purposes. Specifically, it integrates the long-term strategy into the annual operating plan for the corporation and for each of its operating divisions, links precisely the achievement of financial results with both long-term and annual incentive compensation, and provides for the proper oversight and approval by the board of directors. Properly executed with reasonable earnings-per-share and profitability objectives and other explicit metrics tied directly to bonus compensation levels, this system aligns the interests of executives, the board of directors, and shareholders and other stakeholders of the company.

LOGIC AND OVERVIEW

Formulating strategy is a never-ending, dynamic, process of anticipation, adjustments and refinements . . . in response to changing market, environmental, and competitive developments, on the one hand, and the company's actual results on the other. Strategy is always a *work in progress*, and it involves much more than the static perspective of a concept and structure point of view that characterizes most discussions of it.

The organization of the remainder of this book is simple and straightforward. Part II, consisting of Chapters 3–9, presents a process and template for developing long-term business strategies in single-unit businesses, and in individual operating divisions of multi-division enterprises.

Part III, consisting of Chapters 12–20, presents a process and framework for developing long-term corporate strategies in multi-division enterprises. The steps in the processes in Part II and III are identical, but the scope and content differ.

Part IV focuses on developing annual business plans. Chapter 21 is concerned with a single-unit business annual business plan, while Chapter 22 considers developing annual business plans for corporations consisting of multiple operating divisions. Both of these chapters deal with how to translate long-term strategies into annual business plans so that the latter make the necessary contribution to the achievement of the long-term strategy.

Finally, Part V, consisting of Chapters 23 and 24, deal with evaluating business strategies and plans for single-unit businesses, and evaluating corporate strategies and plans for multi-division enterprises, respectively.

CHAPTER 2

STRATEGIC PERSPECTIVES

"I have this idea in mind. All of us get 15 percent better each year."

James McNerney, CEO
Boeing

There are several points of view that shape our approach to business and corporate strategy. These perspectives are derived from the experiences of organizations that have been extraordinarily successful over a long period of time. They are:

- Consumer/customer orientation.
- Life cycle insights.
- Innovation challenge.
- Profitability mandate.
- Earnings-per-share growth mandate.
- Operating in multiple time frames.
- Thinking in the right scale.
- Overcoming functional myopia.
- Dealing with corporate distortion.
- Inclusion and collaboration.
- Being both aggressive and conservative.
- Maintaining an anticipatory and flexible posture.

These form the framework for our discussion in this chapter and establish the foundation for the remainder of the book. As will become apparent, working harder is a necessary, but not sufficient condition for exceptional performance.

Consumer/Customer Orientation

The purpose of a business should be to satisfy consumer/customer needs, wants, desires, and problems at a profit to the customer and the company. The customer must be willing to say that they would rather have the product or service that the company is providing, rather than the money that they are charging . . . that is the "profit to the customer." Simultaneously, the company must sell the product or service at a price that, on average pays for the cost of the product, covers operating expenses and overhead, and provides a return to the owners of the business.

Sometimes a business deals directly with the ultimate consumer. In other cases, the business sells to someone (customer) who in turn sells to the ultimate consumer or user. In all cases, the customer and consumer must be satisfied, hopefully "delighted," so that they want to repeat the transaction the next time the situation presents itself.

All of the resources of the business should be organized to satisfy the customer needs, wants, desires, and problems the company chooses to address. All resources, processes, capabilities and assets of the business should be evaluated in terms of whether and how they "add value" to the customers' experience.

Successful business strategies are generally consumer/customer driven. Successful multi-division businesses are comprised of operating divisions with products and services that each satisfy selected consumer/customer needs. It is bewildering that such a simple and obvious insight can be overlooked by companies who, for whatever reasons, become focused on themselves, competitors, or others, and lose sight of the basic reality that their raison de etre is to satisfy the selected needs of their customers/consumers.

Life Cycle Insights

Like people, all products and services have a life cycle. The "product life cycle" is a generalized model of sales and profit trends for a product, product class, or category over a period of time. (Figure 2.1)

The *development phase* is the period of time before the product or service is brought to the market. Consumer and customer needs are analyzed, product concepts tested, engineering and production techniques developed, and marketing strategies and programs are designed. The period of time that is involved in this phase varies widely depending on the product, but can range from a few months to several decades.

The *introduction phase* begins when the new product or service is first brought to market. Sales are typically modest, and increase at a relatively slow rate. The

Figure 2.1 A generic product life-cycle model

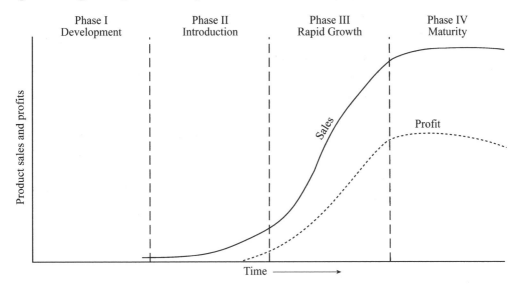

marketing effort required to introduce the product usually eliminates profit margins until the latter part of this stage.

During the *growth phase* demand begins to accelerate and the size of the total market expands rapidly. Other companies enter the market with competing products. The nature of the company's problems shifts from trying to persuade customers to try the product, to getting them to prefer his brand. The number and types of retailers or other customers handling the product generally increase, and they each build inventory in anticipation of sales. This often causes manufacturers' sales to increase more rapidly than retail sales, which in turn creates an exaggerated illusion of profit potential, and thereby attracts additional competitors.

Market saturation is the first sign of the *maturity phase* of the life cycle. Most prospective customers own the product, and the rate of sales increase declines, often to a parity with population growth. Price competition intensifies, and competitive efforts focus on increasingly finer differentiations in the product, customer services, and advertising claims.

When market maturity ends, the product enters the final stage of the life cycle—*decline*. The product begins to lose customer appeal. Overcapacity becomes endemic, and prices and margins continue to decline. Eventually, the product is replaced by better products or by substitutes.

There is a great deal of variation in the length of the cycle and its various stages. Some products, like women's fashions, have a short and pronounced life cycle, while others, like men's shoes, have a life cycle that remains in the maturity stage for generations, with per-capita consumption neither rising nor falling. In other cases, a product experiences a gradual, but steady decline in per-capital con-sumption, as in the case of beer and carbonated soft drinks.[3] Generally, product and service life cycles are compressing in time, and the time that is available to develop new ones is also shrinking. In other words, the pace of change is accelerating.

The product/service life cycle has several valuable insights for business and corporate strategies:

- All products and services have a finite, limited life. Unless management takes appropriate action, the sales and profit margins of all products eventually decline and disappear.
- The death of products can be postponed in many instances through effective business strategies.
- In multi-product enterprises, individual products are in differing stages of their life cycles, and it is important to consider those stages in develop-ing strategies of the individual products and businesses that are involved.
- It is critical to architect and maintain a balanced product life-cycle port-folio mix. Specifically, in any multi-product business experiencing a nor-mal rate of growth, the sales of any product will eventually reach a peak. An effective business and corporate strategy will predict with reasonable accuracy when that peak will occur, have developed and tested life-cycle extension strategies, and/or have additional products ready to market, and/or in the introduction phase of their life-cycle.[4]

Having a robust pipeline of new products, services and businesses that will satisfy future earnings-per-share growth and profitability objectives is a critical de-terminant of the success of business and corporate strategies.

THE INNOVATION CHALLENGE

Despite the importance of having a balanced product life-cycle portfolio, the fact is that historically most product and institutional innovations have been made by outsiders. The businesses that would appear most likely to develop new products or institutional concepts generally do not develop them. For example:

- Why didn't a coffee manufacturer, like Folgers (Proctor&Gamble) or Maxwell House (General Foods) invent Starbucks? Why haven't they reacted more effectively after it was invented?
- Why didn't a supermarket chain like Kroger or Publix invent Whole Foods?

- Why didn't a mattress manufacturer, like Sealy, Serta, or Simmons, invent foam or air mattresses?
- Why was the iPhone invented by Apple rather than Nokia or Motorola?

The apparent explanation for these and other similar events is that, for most companies, strategic innovation is a painful and unnatural process. Unfortunately, it is often subordinated to other activities, regardless of whether a company is successful or is having problems. Success itself is often the justification for continuing the practices, policies and patterns that brought it. On the other hand, when a company experiences difficulties, current problems generally enjoy the highest priority and occupy the attention of senior executives.

Moreover, the reward structures of many companies ensures that current operations have a higher priority than development activities. Executive evaluations, bonuses, equity grants, and other forms of compensation are usually based almost entirely on current results rather than on major innovations.

There are many other reasons for the absence of innovation, but it is sufficient at this point to recognize the problem, realize that the lack of planned systematic innovation is unacceptable, and recognize the need to develop structures, processes, and reward systems to promote and ensure the type of innovation that is required.

PROFITABILITY MANDATE

From an accounting perspective, profit is a residual; that is, profit is what is left after you subtract from sales, the cost of sales, operating expenses, and taxes. From this vantage point, shareholders or owners of the business get whatever is left over after everything has been paid for.

In developing high-yield strategies, it is more useful to take the opposite point of view. Profitability is a requirement, not a residual. Effective strategies are designed to satisfy consumer/customer needs *and achieve a target level and rate of profitability*. This performance-driven perspective is a central component of our approach to strategy.

EARNINGS-PER-SHARE GROWTH

REQUIREMENTS

From one point of view, earnings growth is an *ex post* measure of what an organization has accomplished over some period of time like a year, or five years. The opposite perspective is most useful in developing high-yield strategies. That is, earnings-per-share growth targets are one of the principal objectives of business organizations, and strategies should be designed to achieve these objectives so that owners receive the proper return on their investment.

Combining the last two perspectives, strategies should be designed to achieve targeted rates of EPS growth and profitability. Earnings growth and profitability are the two most important drivers of strategy, at both the business and corporate level, and over multiple years as well as annually.

MULTIPLE TIME FRAMES

In order to achieve maximum effectiveness, it is imperative to think in four different, but related, time frames (Figure 2.2):

- **T0.** Is the current fiscal year.
- **T1.** Is the next fiscal year, which is also the first year of a multi-year strategic plan. Here we assume that it is a 5 year plan.
- **T2.** Is the remainder of the multi-year plan; in this case years 2–5.
- **T3.** Is the relevant time span beyond T2.

The focus, intensity, and specificity of thinking should vary by time period, moving from high to lower. The most focus, intensity and specificity should be on

Figure 2.2 Multiple time frames for long-term business and corporate strategies

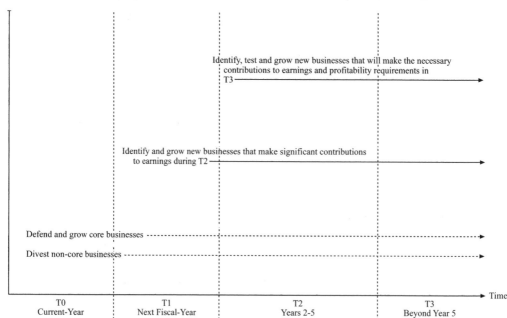

16

T0, and achieving the objectives and initiatives for the current fiscal year. Simultaneously, appropriate attention must be paid to T1, the next fiscal year and simultaneously the first year in the multi-year plan that is assumed here. At the same time, a lesser focus, intensity and specificity should be on T2, the remainder of the multi-year plan, in this case years 2–5. Finally, very limited focus, intensity, and specificity . . . but some, nonetheless . . . needs to be directed to the relevant time period beyond the current multi-year plan (T3), to do those things that need to be done now in order to be successful in the future.

In addition to focus, intensity and specificity, it is important to achieve the proper *balance* in time and attention to these four time frames. Spending too much time with T0 issues may jeopardize the future. Alternatively, spending too much time on T1, T2, and T3, can cause a company to miss performance objectives in the current fiscal year. The right balance varies from one company to another, and for the same company the right balance can change depending on the circumstances it faces.

The T3 time frame is the one most commonly overlooked or under analyzed. This is the time frame *beyond* the current multi-year plan, and may stretch 10 or more years into the future. To differentiate this from normal multi-year planning, we call this "scoping." By scoping out EPS growth requirements for 10 or even 20 years, and then translating those targets into sales and net income goals, executives can gain a better understanding not only of future requirements, but also of the scale and type of strategies that are needed in the interim in order to build a base that is sufficiently large and properly dimensioned. This type of scoping needs to be done infrequently, and is generally best confined to the Chairman, CEO, and their close team.

As the pace of environmental and competitive change has accelerated and becomes more disruptive, response time requirements have shortened and become more multi-dimensional. Revisions need to be made more frequently, and planning documents need to be more precise and concise. General Electric, for example, uses what they refer to as "playbooks" rather than lengthy planning documents. Some technology companies use planning "rules" and "guidelines" rather than more elaborate plans. These circumstances are real and must be accommodated, but the fact is that it is still important . . . in fact, even more important . . . to think and plan in the four time frames.

THINKING IN THE RIGHT SCALE

A major reason why the rate of EPS growth generally declines as a business becomes larger is because, in the absence of scoping, executives tend to think in the same scale that they are operating in. The T3 scoping exercise raises the issue of how the business is going to find the sales and profit requirements that it needs to meet its objectives. The current scale of thinking is often not appropriate; rather it is critical to think in a larger scale.

Larger scale means products, services, and businesses . . . and acquisitions, if they are appropriate . . . that are larger in sales and profit potential, and/or faster in growth trajectory. Larger scale also means thinking in terms of creating growth platforms that can accommodate and facilitate the erection of multiple businesses of substantial size.

All businesses have a limitation on the number of new products, businesses and acquisitions they can assimilate, in terms of the number of executives that can focus on these challenges. It is often as easy to acquire and integrate a 2x business as it is a 1x business, but there is a limitation in terms of the number of businesses that can be acquired. There is a limited "open-to-do," before financial dimensions are even considered.

For these reasons it is important to think in the multiple time frames and in the right scale. Think long, think larger, and win today and tomorrow.

FUNCTIONAL MYOPIA

From the moment we are born, our parents focus time, attention and love on us. We are the center of their lives, and they make us feel like we are the most important thing is the world. After years of this sort of experience, it becomes easy for us to believe that each of us is the "Center of the Universe."

Our educational experience reinforces this perspective. Medical students are told that medicine is the savior of civilization. Law school students are taught that everything revolves around the law. Engineers come to believe that they are destined to solve mankind's problems.

Business schools also reinforce this point of view, and, in fact, take it to another level. Manufacturing majors are explicitly or implicitly taught that manufacturing is the "hub" of a business, and that marketing, finance human resources, and other functions are "spokes." Meanwhile, across the hall finance majors are taught that finance is the "hub" and manufacturing, marketing, HR, etc. are "spokes." For marketing majors, marketing becomes the hub, and every other function is a spoke.

Early experiences in business perpetuate this perspective. Finance people work in a finance department, interact the most with other financial people professionally, and often, socially. At the same time marketing people work in marketing departments, manufacturing people in their own department, and so on.

As people progress in their careers and become more involved in strategic decisions, they bring this history and perspective with them. Manufacturing people are more likely to see business and corporate strategy from a manufacturing point-of-view, while marketing people see it primarily through a marketing lens, and finance folks think of it from a financial perspective. All of them have only a partial perspective, and overrate the importance of their view relative to other considerations. *This is the functional myopia problem.*

Functional expertise is absolutely critical in developing high-yield business and corporate strategies, but the strategy is the hub, and all of the functions are the spokes, to continue the analogy. Similarly, while people tend to think of strategies in terms of "what is in it for me" and how they will fare personally, business is a team sport, and individual egos and politics need to be channeled and sublimated to the collective effort and the collective good. Corporate politics is to business and corporate strategy what cancer is to people.

CORPORATE MYOPIA

The roots and history of a business strongly influence how people in it learn to view environmental and competitive developments, trends, and opportunities. Just as people are products of their environment and experience, businesses have the same characteristic in a collective sense. *This is the corporate myopia problem.* Consider:

- Sara Lee was a successful food manufacturer that expanded into underwear, lingerie, and apparel. The skills and perspectives required for success in lingerie and apparel businesses differ from the success requirements in the food business. When the CEO of Coach wanted to open his own retail stores to increase earnings and enhance the Coach brand, corporate executives did not want to incur the risks associated with signing store leases. Consequently, Sara Lee spun Coach out into a publicly-held company, and during the first three years, the new Company compounded earnings per share at 62 percent per year while earning an average return on assets of 33%. Meanwhile, Sara Lee grew its earnings at 9% per year and earned 8.5% return on average assets. The risks that Sara Lee was unwilling to assume are the same risks that every retailer routinely accepts. Sara Lee had a different corporate perspective.

Of course the fact that Sara Lee spun Coach out is not necessary bad. In fact, it may have been the right thing to do. On the other hand, Coach is unquestionably one of the great success stories of recent years.

The point here is to recognize the corporate myopia issue and consider carefully how to deal with it. Having outsiders' perspectives on important issues can be helpful if their insights are accurate and are taken seriously. Having highly successful executives with meaningful experience outside the company and industry is probably the most effective. It is dangerous not to have differing perspectives and so it is important to architect the culture so that there is a mix of people with different life experiences.

Inclusion and Collaboration

Historically, it was most common for CEO's to limit the number and type of people that were involved in developing business and corporate strategies. In single-unit businesses, perhaps only the COO would be involved, or maybe he would be joined by the CFO and one or more members of a planning staff, if, in fact, the latter existed. The same types of people generally comprise the strategic group in multi-division enterprises, with their counterparts at the operating division level involved in developing business strategies for their respective divisions.

In order to deal most intelligently with the complexities and dynamics of the current environment, it is important to think about including more, rather than fewer, people, more functions, and a more diverse set of perspectives that emanate from levels in the organization, age and socioeconomic background, and other characteristics that may produce fresh insights. These people and functions need not be included in the entire process, but rather those parts where they can make important contributions. This may include a preview of the entire strategy and "big picture." Inclusiveness and collaboration often increases the sophistication, appropriateness, and effectiveness of the final result, and contributes to "buy-in," because the executives have been involved in framing the strategy.

Being Aggressive and Conservative

Anticipated economic, environmental, and competitive conditions largely determine the posture that is most appropriate on an aggressive/conservative continuum. The more difficult the scenario, the more conservative the strategy, generally speaking.

However, given any forecasted scenarios, the same issues still arise . . . how aggressive or conservative should we be? Of course, it is always a matter of degree, and there is the issue of financial prudence which is paramount.

But, experience indicates that in most instances aggressive postures produce better results than conservative ones, even when aggressive targets are not met. The fact is that companies that use "stretched performance" management techniques do better for shareholders than companies that are managed conservatively.

High-yield strategies are comprised of various growth and strategic initiatives . . . some are aggressive while others are conservative, or at least not so aggressive. The key issue is balance; that is, whether on balance the initiatives constitute a reasonable amount and level of risk given the forecasted scenario, *and in the event that less desirable scenarios actually occur.* This is one of the most important strategic judgments that a CEO and Board makes, and rarely is it quantifiable to the degree that everyone would like.

It is also important to distinguish between actual and perceived aggressiveness and conservatism. This involves an assessment of the CEO and senior management. Obviously, some people in business are more aggressive than others, and two people looking at the same initiatives may have a different view of how risky they are. Business and corporate strategies may be more or less aggressive than they are positioned, depending on the perspectives of the CEO, the management team, the Board, and the dynamics between them. Making these distinctions requires insight and diplomacy.

MAINTAINING AN ANTICIPATORY AND FLEXIBLE POSTURE

Strategies almost never work out the exact way that they are planned. Careful consideration should be given to what the consequences would be if key assumptions change. This involves formulating strategies under multiple scenarios.

It is important to consider, and weight carefully, what happens when things are worse than planned, as well as when they are better than anticipated. The position that the enterprise would be in under these unanticipated, but possible, situations should be acceptable, at least in the sense that the organization can recover. Particularly critical is anticipatory financing that makes it possible to continue to operate even if "worst likely case" conditions become reality. "Betting the business" is not acceptable, except perhaps, in extreme conditions.

A CONCLUDING NOTE

These, then, are the major viewpoints and perspectives that shape our approach to business and corporate strategy. We will utilize these insights as we move to Part II of this book, comprised of Chapters 3–11, which presents a template for developing a long-term business strategy for a business comprised of one operating division. Then, in Part III we will use the same principles to develop long-term corporate strategies for multi-division enterprises.

PART II

DEVELOPING LONG-TERM BUSINESS STRATEGIES

The eight chapters (Chapters 3–11) that comprise Part II are concerned with developing long-term business strategies for a single unit enterprise. These types of businesses typically have one operating division, rather than several. Examples would include Panera Bread, Pacific Sunwear of California, and Tempur-Pedic International. Most start-up businesses would also fall into this category.

The same template can be used to develop long-term business strategies for individual operating divisions of multi-division businesses. Some illustrations would include the Buick division of General Motors, or the Pottery Barn division of Williams Sonoma; or the Dockers division of Levi Strauss.

Finally, this template can also be used to develop long-term business strategies for specific, individual products. These can include brands offered by manufacturers as well as wholesalers.

Formulating long-term business strategies is not a one-time act, but rather a continuing on-going process of anticipating, adapting, and reacting to technological, environmental, market, and competitive conditions. This continuous process consists of the following components:

- **A Strategic Audit.** The audit identifies the technological, economic, environmental, and competitive environment that is expected to exist in the future.
- **Business Mission, Vision, and Values.** Describes what the business is, or is trying to become, the key standards of performance, and the guiding values and principles.
- **Business Objectives.** Specifies the targeted rate of earnings-per-share growth, profitability, and other major drivers.
- **Business Strategy.** Identifies which target market segments the company will serve, and how it will gain and maintain competitive advantage.
- **Business Strategic Gaps and Discretionary Financial Resources.** Measures the differences between the levels of performance specified in the

objectives and the probable outcomes from a continuation of current operations, and the magnitude of financial resources that are available to close whatever gaps exist.

- **Business Growth Initiatives.** Describe the specific initiatives that the company will pursue to close strategic gaps and achieve business objectives.
- **Business Strategic Initiatives.** Identify the precise initiatives that the company will pursue to enhance gross margins and improve operating expense leverage through economies of scale, scope, and focus.
- **Business Organizational Design and Development Initiatives.** Specifies the organizational structure that will be employed, development programs for key executives, and incentive compensation programs.
- **Pro-Forma Financial Statements, Financial Structure and Financial Strategy.** Presents income statements, balance sheets, cash flow statements; changes in the debt/equity structure of the balance sheet; and dividend and stock repurchase policies that are anticipated as a result of the long-term strategy. (Operating divisions of multi-division enterprises will not have the debt/equity, dividend and stock repurchase components.)

The discussion of these components will proceed in the order in which they are presented. In actual use, the process is generally iterative, with frequent revisions as executives more through the components.

In some instances, it is more useful to start from a different point in the process. Start-up businesses may start at the beginning, or, more likely, with a potential strategy. On-going businesses may approach the components from the perspective of what, if any, changes are appropriate. The relative emphasis or focus on a component may vary from year to year depending on the circumstances and challenges that exist.

CHAPTER 3

STRATEGIC AUDIT

*"An optimist sees an opportunity in every calamity;
a pessimist sees a calamity in every opportunity."*

Sir Winston Churchill

The starting point for the formulation of a business strategy is usually the strategic audit, (Figure 3.1), which involves analyses and decisions with respect to:

- Industry conditions and trends.
- Market share developments and trends.
- Comparative competence analysis.
- Benchmarking.
- Best practices.
- Environmental trends.
- Supply chain developments and trends.
- Distribution market conditions and trends.
- Consumer/customer/user market developments and trends.
- Most likely moves of competitors.

Developing a common point of view about the future is critically important. Many organizations do not have a common view that is shared by senior executives. This is the stage in the strategy formulation process to air these differences and arrive at consensus viewpoints, because the latter have a powerful impact on the long-term strategy. Following the consensus, differences can and should be voiced continuously, but unless they rise to the level of modifying or revising the current common point of view, they should not become the basis for strategy.

Figure 3.1 Conduct a business strategic audit

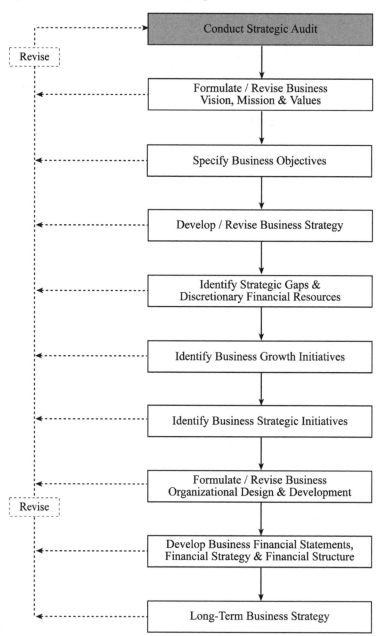

INDUSTRY CONDITIONS AND TRENDS

Figure 3.2 presents a template for an industry analysis. If the company is considering entering the industry for the first time, this analysis should be exhaustive, and should include a forecast of anticipated trends in appropriate and critical areas.

26

Figure 3.2 Major components of an industry analysis*

I. Market analysis
- A. Size of market in dollars & units
- B. Projected growth of market in dollars & units
- C. Major market segments
  1. Size in dollars & units
  2. Projected growth in dollars & units
- D. Market shares of the leading companies in total & by major market segments
- E. Trends in these market shares

II. Customer analysis
- A. Number of customers & projected growth
- B. Important customer segments & trends
- C. Switching costs

III. Supply conditions
- A. Raw materials: number of suppliers, cost, availability, substitute availability
- B. Labor: availability, costs, importance of unions
- C. Technology requirements & availability
- D. Location availability & costs

IV. Demand conditions
- A. Cyclical & seasonal character of demand
- B. Availability of close substitutes
- C. Price-value characteristics of substitutes
- D. Price-elasticity of industry demand
- E. Availability of compliments
- F. Price-value characteristics of compliments

V. Market structure
- A. Number of sellers & buyers
- B. Product differentiation
- C. Significant barriers to entry
- D. Investment requirements
- E. Cost structures
- F. Vertical integration
- G. Diversification
- H. Capacity utilization
- I. Significant economies of scale requirements
- J. Potential entrants access to distribution channels
- K. Potential entrants access to raw materials
- L. Potential entrants access to technology
- M. Potential entrants access to favorable locations
- N. Strategic advantages of incumbents

VI. Industry economics
- A. Profit margins
- B. Asset turnover ratios
- C. Capital requirements for entry
- D. Capital requirements to compete & grow
- E. Technology requirements for entry
- F. Technology requirements to compete & grow
- G. Return on assets & return on invested capital
- H. Cash flow return on assets & invested capital
- I. Composite EPS growth rates last year, last 3 years, last 5 years
- J. Composite PE multiples last year, last 3 years, last 5 years

VII. Public policy issues
- A. Taxes & subsidies
- B. International trade rules
- C. Regulation issues
- D. Price controls
- E. Antitrust issues

VIII. Human resource issues
- A. Unique or unusual human resource requirements
- B. Availability & cost of key human resource requirements
- C. Unique or unusual organizational design issues & requirements

IX. Key requirements for success
- A.
- B.
- C.

---

* This figure compiled with input from David Besanko, David Dranove, Mark Shanley & Scott Shaeffer *Economies of Strategy, 3rd Ed.* (New York: John Wiley & Sons, 2004), pp. 349-351; and Garth Saloner, Andrea Shepard & John Podolny, *Strategic Management.* (New York: John Wiley & Sons, Inc. 2001), pp. 125

If the company has been in the industry, this analysis can be an update; or confined to "what has changed since the last evaluation." In this situation, the most intense attention should be paid to anticipated trends or developments in areas that are extraordinarily critical to the company's success going forward.

The major dimensions that should be included in most industry analyses include:

- Size of the market in dollars and units.
- Projected growth of the market in dollars and units.
- Market shares of the leading companies and recent trends in these shares.
- Availability and cost of resources.
- Price-elasticity of demand.
- Industry profitability and trends.
- Barriers to entry.

One of the most critical factors to consider is whether new competitors will enter the industry. This is more likely to occur when the barriers to entry are low. Generally, there are six major sources of barriers to entry:

- **Economies of scale.** The more difficult and/or time consuming it is to achieve economies of scale; the less likely it is that new companies will enter.
- **Product differentiation.** If products are differentiated in ways that customers find really meaningful, the less likely it is that new companies will enter. If products are commoditized, new competition is more likely, especially if there are not significant economies of scale to deal with.
- **Capital requirements.** The higher the capital requirements, the less likely new companies will enter the industry. Similarly, the longer the time period required to recoup the investment required for entry and profitability, the less likely it is that competitors will enter.
- **Cost disadvantages independent of size.** The greater the cost disadvantage that a new company entering the industry would have, the less likely they will enter.
- **Access to distribution channels.** Restricted access to distribution channels, as in the case of a new packaged goods company trying to attain shelf space in supermarkets, can make it less likely for new competitors to enter the industry.
- **Government policy.** Government requirements and policies regarding entry, operating requirements, or other conditions can make it less likely that new companies will enter the industry.[5]

Looking at this from the reverse perspective, it is usually desirable to attempt to erect barriers to entry or strengthen the barriers that exist. Product differentiation is, in fact, at the heart of the business strategy, and strategic initiatives designed to achieve additional economies of scale should almost always be part of a high-yield strategy.

CURRENT MARKET ANALYSIS

This section of the analysis should present multi-year market share trends for each product and/or service in the company's portfolio. It should also identify the major factors contributing to the company's success or failure for each product. An analysis of the actions necessary to improve future market shares should also be included along with the costs and capital expenditure requirements needed to make these improvements.

Some companies have a policy that requires that a product must be either first or second in market share. If products do not have this position, they are given some timetable to attain it, or be sold. While this target may be too high for some companies, or inappropriate for whatever reasons, it may be a good idea to have some market share position that is expected over some reasonable time period. Achieving top 5, or top 10 status, or being in the upper quartile, are examples of alternative market share targets that companies may find useful.

COMPARATIVE COMPETENCE ANALYSIS

This section identifies the strengths, weaknesses, and problems of the company and its major competitors. This includes detailed and systematic comparative analyses in terms of:

- **Human resources.** An evaluation of the breadth, depth, and "bandwidth" of management, managers, and employees in all functions, and at least the top two or three levels of the organization.
- **Financial capacity.** An evaluation of cost structures and so-called "under-pricing capabilities." An analysis of capital structures including ability to finance capital intensive strategies. Also, an analysis of financial planning and control procedures and financial capacities to expand.
- **Research, development and engineering.** Comparative analyses of the nature and depth of R&D capabilities, including ability and willingness to spend, perspective on innovation, brainpower, and other major strengths and weaknesses.

- **Product innovation.** Comparative analyses of product innovations over the past few years. Most likely innovation agendas for each competitor.
- **Manufacturing and/or Sourcing.** If applicable, comparisons of the nature of manufacturing processes, the costs, the investment requirements, the facilities, the skills, the adaptability to future conditions, and the vulnerabilities. If sourcing, comparisons of the number of sources, costs, quality, speed, etc.
- **Marketing.** Comparative analyses of the present product line and capability of developing new products and markets; pricing strategies and tactics, including under-pricing capabilities; advertising and sales promotion abilities; skill in doing business with distribution channels; expertise in marketing research, testing, and market information systems.[6]
- **Organizational capabilities.** Including the ability to attract, motivate and retain competent and committed people; competence in obtaining high performance from associates; ability to work across organizational boundaries to achieve efficiency and leverage; ability to generate ideas with impact; success in embedding leaders throughout the organization; ability to innovate in critical processes.[7]
- **Summary list of major strengths, weaknesses and vulnerabilities.** A separate compilation for the company and each major competitor.

Significant differences between the company and its major competitors become potential distinctive competences that may be used in formulating strategies, particularly if they contribute to the satisfaction of customer needs, wants, problems, preferences, and expectations. With respect to the company's relative strengths, the challenge is how these can be exploited more fully and effectively. With respect to weaknesses, the issue is whether these need to be corrected, and, if so, whether they should be corrected internally, and/or through acquiring and developing resources and capabilities, and/or through outsourcing.

Benchmarking

As used here, benchmarking involves detailed financial comparisons of the company and each major competitor on every major line item in the income statement and balance sheet. From the income statement the key items are measures of sales productivity, gross profit and/or gross margin, operating expenses, and operating income margins. From the balance sheet the key comparisons are inventory turnover, day's sales outstanding, and fixed asset turnover. Summary measures, specifically after-tax profit margins, asset turnover, and after-tax return on assets are also included.

Growth comparisons are also helpful. These include multi-year comparisons of the growth in sales, operating income, net profit before taxes, net profit after taxes, and earnings-per-share. One, two, three, four, and five year comparisons are generally most useful, but other time frames may also be appropriate.

Based on this analysis, the company can determine where it compares favorably, and where it does not. Favorable metrics may become the basis for strategic programs; that is, how can the business best exploit its financial strengths. Items where the company does not compare favorably, may be opportunities for improvement.

BEST PRACTICES

Best practices, as used here, uses a different reference for comparison purposes. Here the comparison is not competitors, but rather who is the "best in the world" in this area, regardless of industry. This is an important distinction because too many companies confine their thinking to other companies in their own industry, which, over time tends to lead to an incestuous sameness and lack of creativity. In contrast, significant innovations in almost every area of business often come from companies outside the industry.

For example, General Electric is widely regarded as the world leader in executive education. So the question is "what could we learn from their approach that would be useful and helpful to us?" Wal-Mart is probably the world leader in logistics, so the issue becomes, "what could we learn from their approach to logistics that would be helpful to us?"

Best practices analysis involves asking this question for each of the income statement and balance sheet items listed above, as well as every organizational capability: "Who is the best in the world in this? How do they do it? How could we apply this to our business?" This is a key vehicle for developing break-though innovation, particularly process innovation. No country, industry, company, or person has a monopoly on innovation, creativity, or insight. In an era of accelerating global competition characterized by blinding change and nano-second response time, continuous best practices analysis is critical.

ENVIRONMENTAL ANALYSIS

This component of the strategic audit forecasts the "most likely" economic, technological, political, legal, regulatory, and life style conditions and trends *that are relevant to the company*. It is also useful to include "worst likely" conditions and trends that have a reasonable probability of occurring, say greater than 20 or 30 percent. Some illustrative types of analyses might include:

- The forecasts for economic growth, consumption expenditures and inflation in the countries in which the company operates.
- The technological developments or trends that could affect the industry.
- Changes in regulations, taxes, or other incentives that might influence the strategy.
- Current and changing life-styles and how they could impact the business.
- The relevant demographic trends that will affect the size of the market and/or the business.

This analysis is complicated and tricky. Even Bill Gates missed, at least initially, the impact of the internet on Microsoft. It seems that the closer you are to something, the less likely you are to see it. In addition to contempt, familiarity often breeds blindness. So this section deserves extraordinary scrutiny, and the input of outsiders is often a good idea.

Overall, the key issues that should be inserted into the strategy formulation process are:

- The significant trends and future events.
- The key threats and opportunities.
- The areas of uncertainty that have an impact on strategy.[8]

Many staff people confuse length of exposition with quality of thought. While these issues can be complicated, they can almost always be summarized into less than one page in terms of their strategic implications.

SUPPLY CHAIN ANALYSIS

This section describes current conditions and forecasts future conditions for all members of the company's supply chain. It should include estimates of the availability and prices of real estate, raw materials, plant and equipment, labor, and all other supplier groups and critical resources.

Particular attention should be focused on supplier groups and other resources that:

- Are dominated by a few companies and are more concentrated than the industry is.
- Have unique, or meaningfully differentiated products.
- Have products or services that would entail significant "switching costs".

- Appear to have the capability and interest in integrating forward into the business you are in.
- Your company and industry is not an important customer.[9]

These conditions contribute to the type of environment in which disruptive behavior becomes more likely.

DISTRIBUTION MARKET ANALYSIS

Here the focus is on the current status and the future size, structure, and economics of the company's channels of distribution, if any. This may involve brokers, wholesalers, retailers, industrial distributors, and a wide variety of other types of businesses.

If the company uses these types of channels of distribution, particular attention should be paid to those channel members when:

- They purchase in large volumes.
- Your products are standard or undifferentiated.
- Your product(s) that they purchase form a component of the buyer's products, and it represents a significant fraction of the cost.
- The buyer earns little or no profit.
- Your product is unimportant to the quality of the buyers' products or services.
- Your product or service does not save the buyer money, or improve return-on-investment.
- The buyer has the capability and interest of integrating backward to make your product.[10]

These circumstances often increase the power of the channel member relative to the company, and may signal future difficulties.

The changing structure of distribution may present problems as well as opportunities. For example, one of the major trends is the consolidation of retail in the United States, in certain sectors. During the last twenty years the discount department store industry has consolidated into Wal-Mart, Target, Costco, and a few other players. Similarly, the department store sector has consolidated into Federated, Dillards, and a few regional players. Over time, the retailers that remain will reduce the number of companies they do business with in a given merchandise category as they define it; bargain down, or dictate prices and other terms of sale; require more and better sales training; and institute other types of requirements as a condition for doing business. Accordingly, many companies that utilize these retail outlets will be shut out of distribution or suffer downward pressure on their margins. As a result, they will need to develop a new channel strategy . . . including, in some instances, opening their own stores and/or e-commerce sites.

CUSTOMER MARKET ANALYSIS

The first major component of this analysis should include research findings relative to customer satisfaction with the company's products and services; ratings of the company and major competitors on each factor that is important in the purchase decision (e.g.; service, quality, price/value, availability, speed of delivery, etc); and other variables that may be important in the decision to use the company's products or services. This type of information should be obtained every two or three years, if not annually, through the appropriate research methodologies including focus groups, visual observation of actual usage, and quantitative surveys. Many companies tend to get sloppy and lose focus with respect to exceeding their customer's expectations thereby creating an opening for competitors. This exercise should be designed to identify the problems, or nascent issues, so that corrective action can be taken before the situation deteriorates.

The other section in this analysis forecasts the future size of all of the company's present and potential consumption markets . . . consumers and/or business users . . . and attempts to identify the future trends, needs, wants, problems, preferences, and buying behavior of these markets. This analysis is extraordinarily important, and can require very sophisticated analyses and perceptive thinking. Often the consequences of mistakes can be very painful. Consider just one recent example:

- Between 1998 and early 2004, Nokia was the industry leader in mobile phones. But suddenly their market share fell from 38 to 30 percent world wide and from 51 to 33 percent in Europe. The company did not recognize that phones had become more than just a digital device. Mobile phones had become a fashion accessory, and Nokia had not reacted, and has still not recovered.[11]

COMPETITIVE STRATEGY ANALYSIS

Using the preceding components of the strategic audit, this section attempts to identify the most likely moves that major competitors will make, when they will make them, and the impact that they will have on the company. The major factors to consider in making these forecasts include:[12]

- What are competitors' objectives and strategies?
- How committed are they to the business?
- What is their cost structure?
- Do they have a cost advantage or disadvantage?
- What is their image and positioning strategy?
- What are the strengths and weaknesses of each competitor?
- What leverage points could competitors exploit to enter the market, or become more serious competitors?
  - How could they best exploit our strategic weaknesses?
  - Are there customer problems and/or unmet needs that they could satisfy better than anyone else and have a competitive advantage?

These forecasts and judgments provide input into the strategy for the future. Once the future strategy is formulated or revised, it may be useful to speculate as to how and when competitors will react, and try to architect elements of the strategy that will preclude or limit the effectives of their responses.

ANTICIPATING THE FUTURE

As Walter Wriston, the former chairman of what is now Citigroup, once said: "the future always arrives a little before you are ready to give up the past." Anticipating the future is extraordinarily difficult. Regardless, it is mandatory that senior executives think creatively and insightfully about the future, and the implications for the company. This should involve a carefully orchestrated mixture of sophisticated analyses and imaginative thinking. What could the company make happen? What are the discontinuities that could be exploited? What are the breakthrough ideas that would make a real difference?[13] This is the type of thinking that can help create strategic advantage.

CHAPTER 4

MISSION, VISION AND VALUES

"If you don't have a dream, how can you have a dream come true?"

Leslie H. Wexner
Founder and Chairman
Limited Brands

As Figure 4.1 indicates, the second step in developing a long-term business strategy in a single division business is to articulate a mission, vision and values. For existing businesses, the challenge is to reconsider whether the existing mission, vision and values are appropriate for the future, for sometimes they are not, and failure to adapt and adjust can be painful.

Mission, vision and values define, in general terms, what the business is, or is trying to become, and the general rules that define how it will operate. For these reasons, this is a critical, defining step in the business strategy formulation process.

DEVELOPING A MISSION AND VISION

Some businesses separate mission and vision into two different statements. Our experience is that this causes confusion about which is which, and focuses attention on that issue rather than the fundamental issues involved. Therefore, we prefer one statement.

A MISSION/VISION STATEMENT

As used here, a mission *is a long-term vision of what the company is, or is trying to become*. The most useful mission statements have two critical components:

- What business are we in, or do we want to be in?
- What are the standards of performance?

Figure 4.1 Formulate/revise business vision, mission & values

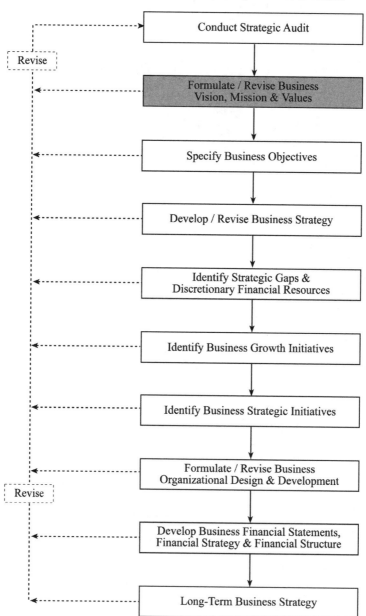

The mission statement outlines what the company is trying to achieve at the present time, as well as what it is trying to become in the future. It provides the major bridge from the present to the future of the organization.[14]

Shortly after Leslie Wexner invented Limited Stores, he and his senior executives defined the mission of the business as follows:

> "To be the fastest growing, most profitable women's apparel specialty retailer in America."

This illustrates the components of a useful mission statement. Mr. Wexner defined his business as women's apparel, not men's or children's apparel. He further defined the business as a specialty store, not a department store, or a discount department store. The standards of performance were very specific and bold: "to be the fastest growing and most profitable." Every person in the business knew what business they were in, where they were going, and how the score was going to be kept. This was a challenging and motivating mission that guided the business to a 43 percent compound annual growth rate in earnings-per-share and an average return on equity of 45 percent over the next decade of its existence.

MISSION COMPONENTS

What business are we in?   Determining the first component of a mission . . . the business the company is in, or is trying to be in . . . is complicated and requires serious thought and reflection. Things are always changing, and the issue always is whether the mission is still appropriate for the conditions that prevail, or are expected to prevail. "Should we still be in this business," is, unfortunately, a question that is sometimes not asked when it should be.

In the classic case, Levitt argued that railroads did not stop growing because the need for passenger and freight transportation declined. That grew. Rather, according to Professor Levitt, they let others take customers away from them because they assumed themselves to be in the railroad business rather than the transportation business. They defined their business incorrectly, according to Levitt.[15]

Jim Collins' study of the characteristics of companies that have gone from good to great, as contrasted with those that did not, provides important insight into defining the business properly. Collins discovered the importance of what he terms the "hedgehog concept" for companies that have achieved greatness. Hedgehog refers to the common space resulting from the intersection of three circles:

- What are you deeply passionate about?
- What can you be best in the world at?
- How do you really make money; i.e., what drives the economic engine?

The results of Collins' study is that *if* you cannot be the best in the world at your core business, then your core business cannot form the basis of your hedgehog concept, and you are unlikely to go from wherever you are to great.

Collins also found that you do not need to be in a great industry to produce sustained great results. No matter how bad the industry, every company that went from good to great figured out how to produce superior economic returns.[16]

What are the standards of performance?   The standards of performance component of the mission is equally important. Limited would probably never have achieved the success that it has enjoyed if the mission was not so bold and aggressive. Companies tend to achieve more if they have challenging, heroic, missions that may approach "cult-like" status. Mission statements should be motivational and stretch the performance expectations of all people and functions in the organization. They should be imaginative, creative, and fun. They should make the pursuit more than just a job . . . a noble, worthwhile adventure that is worth more to every individual that the effort that is involved.[17] Great missions are very important in creating charismatic organizations.

FORMULATING A MISSION

Developing an insightful mission for a business involves a consideration of stakeholder expectations, environmental trends and issues, and the company's distinctive, or core, competences.

Stakeholder Expectations.   The stakeholders of a business are its owners; its customers; its managers and employees; supply chain members; non-owner sources of capital, including brokers and underwriters, creditors and lenders; and the society in which it operates. These stakeholders are generally most interested in those characteristics of the business that affect their own interests. For example, owners are interested in increasing shareholder value through stock appreciation and, perhaps, dividends. Executives, managers, and other employees are interested in compensation, advancement, continuity, recognition, challenge and learning. Supply chain members have varying interests, but are primarily concerned with the company's growth, stability, continuity, and profitability, at least to the extent that it facilitates the former. Customers are interested in products and/or services that satisfy their needs, wants, problems, preferences, and expectations better than alternatives that are available.

The expectations of all of these stakeholders may not be consistent and reinforcing. Rather, there may be significant inconsistencies that require judgments regarding trade-offs and the right balance between competing interests.

The challenge, then, is to combine and integrate the interests and expectations of all of these stakeholders into a mission that is compelling to each of them. Since these interests and expectations can, and frequently do, change over time, existing mission statements in on-going businesses need to be reviewed periodically for their appropriateness.

Environmental Trends and Expectations. The mission should also consider the present and future environment of the enterprise. As was discussed in the previous chapter, this is part of the Strategic Audit, and involves a consideration of:

- The economic environment, including forecasted growth, unemployment, wage and income trends, and so on.
- Technological developments and trends, particularly those that will or may impact the industry and/or company.
- Political, legal and regulatory trends that will impact the industry or company, particularly those that impact the company's products, markets, and methods of doing business.
- Cultural and life style trends, particularly those that will impact the company's labor and consumption markets.

In framing or revising the business mission it is also important to decide how the company will interact with its environment. What type of corporate citizen is it, or does it wish to become? For example:

- What kind of progress should the company make in energy efficiency, waste reduction, water conservation, pollution reduction, greenhouse gas reduction, and so on?
- Does the company's supply chain engage in healthy environmental practices? What role should the business play in helping these members do a better job in the future?
- Can the company and its supply chain be "greener?" Do customers have environmental needs that the company can help solve either through better processes, or better products?

Many observers believe that human activity now exceeds sustainability on a global scale. This has created major social and environmental challenges for the planet including climate change, pollution, resource depletion, poverty and inequality. Companies can help change the way customers think about these issues by creating products and services that are consistent with environmental stability.

Dupont has developed a metric called "shareholder value added per pound of production." They use SVA as an indicator of the long-term environmental stability of different growth strategies, and have set stretch goals to increase SVA over the next decade.[18] While Dupont is a large, multi-division business, even the smallest of businesses can use a similar philosophy to help guide its actions and frame its mission.

In its 2005 annual report, General Electric has attached an 89 page "Citizenship Report." This document details GE's policies, activities and status in areas such as environment health and safety; community; globalization; customers, products and services; suppliers; employees; and several other areas. Again, while GE is a large company, every business regardless of size can profit from seeing whether any of GE's ideas in this area might benefit their company.

Clearly, decisions regarding how a business is going to relate to, interact with, and affect the various dimensions of its environment are important considerations in framing or revising a business mission. Just a few short years ago these complex environmental issues were often thought of by some companies as "irrelevant," or "not our problem," or "nice to do if you have a chance." Going forward, this is not the case. Thoughtful and responsible companies will incorporate appropriate environmental issues in their mission and be leaders in solving, or at least ameliorating, the problems they are interacting with.

Core Competences.   Core, or distinctive, competences refer to those things that a company does well . . . preferably better than its competitors. Some companies, for example, are particularly good in marketing, others in manufacturing, or finance, or some other functional area of the business. A company can also have core competences in various processes, like innovation, or speed-to-market, or management development.

The identification of distinctive competences is part of the Strategic Audit that was described in the previous chapter. The process involves comparing the company to each of its competitors in terms of strengths and weaknesses, and also "benchmarked" against competitors. If done objectively, this exercise can create a short list of the company's core competences.

Most businesses think of themselves in terms of the products or services that they provide, and the consumption markets they provide them to. This perspective provides some possible links to the future, but overlooks others. If the company also thinks of itself in terms of a portfolio of competencies, then the question becomes: "where are the other opportunities to use these competencies to be successful?" This additional and different perspective may open up completely new types of opportunities.[19]

One of the most common examples would be businesses that have core competence in managing their distribution channels. In those cases, it may be possible to develop and market a much broader assortment of products or services through that same distribution channel, and achieve operating leverage because of the channel core competence. In these instances, the "what business are we in" component of the mission might become much broader than previously thought.

Thinking of a business in terms of its core competences is very important in developing or revising a business mission.

EXAMPLES OF BUSINESS MISSIONS

The business missions of some businesses in the United States are as follows:

- **Dell.** "To be the most successful computer company in the world by delivering the best customer experience in markets we serve."
- **Southwest Airlines.** "Dedication to the highest quality of Customer Service delivered with a sense of warmth, friendliness, individual pride, and Company Spirit."
- **Kelly Services.** "To be the world's best staffing services company and to be recognized as the best."
- **Progressive Group of Insurance Companies.** "To reduce the human trauma and economic costs associated with automobile accidents."
- **Steelcase.** "To provide a better work experience."
- **Tiffany.** "To be recognized as the world's most respected and successful designer, manufacturer and marketer of the finest jewelry, timepieces, selected accessories and tabletop products."
- **Ryland Homes.** "To build homes of the highest quality and value, while providing the highest level of satisfaction to our customers, employees and shareholders."
- **Home Depot.** "We are in the home improvement business and our goal is to provide the highest level of service, the broadest selection of products, and the most competitive prices."

ADAPTING BUSINESS MISSIONS TO CHANGING CONDITIONS

Insightful companies change their mission when market, environmental, and/or competitive conditions change, or are expected to change. Often the change results from changes in the market the business is trying to serve. For example:

- Since going public in 1986, Harley-Davidson has increased its earnings at more than 30 percent annually. The company reinvented the industry by selling a lifestyle, while its competitors were perceived as simply selling motorcycles. Harley became an extraordinarily strong brand with a cult-like following.[20]
- Originally Cisco's mission was to dominate the market for "networking gear" . . . primarily internet routers and switches sold to large corporate customers. When the internet bubble burst in 2000 and Cisco's 50 percent growth rate dropped dramatically, the company expanded their mission to include the telecommunications industry. [21]

Sometimes a slow-growth market causes a company to change its mission For example:

- Hershey controls 43 percent of the U.S. candy market, but their revenue growth has declined to less than three percent in recent years. The total snack market, however, is growing twice as fast as the candy market. To increase their growth, Hershey changed their corporate mission from a U.S. candy company into a global candy and snack maker.[22]

Formulating, or rethinking, a business mission, then, is a very important task that can be complicated and "slippery." It is critical to make certain that the mission is appropriate for the market, environment, and competitive conditions the company faces, and will face in the future.

CULTURE AND VALUES

The commonly held values and beliefs of people in an organization both constrain and enable the actions that can be taken, and also partially determine how effectively and efficiently they will be executed. Associates regard a decision that they perceive to be consistent with common values and beliefs as appropriate and worthy of support. Conversely, people will resist a course of action that they perceive violates the culture of the firm. Culture trumps strategy.

CRITICAL VALUES AND BELIEFS

One set of values needs to deal with how the company and its associates are expected to "behave" relative to their relationships and interactions with:

- Shareholders.
- Suppliers.
- Customers.
- Associates.
- Government.
- Community.
- Environment.

In each of these relationships, it is important to specify what the company "gives" to the other party and what it holds itself responsible and accountable for.

Conversely, it is critical to articulate what the company expects from that party, and what that party's responsibilities and deliverables are.

The other value set should be crafted to facilitate and encourage the type of behavior that is required for the company to achieve its business strategy and execute its growth and strategic initiatives in a way that achieves the objectives of the business. For example, a culture that supports continuous change, learning, and constant improvement are essential. Similarly, a culture that supports resource sharing and communication can be helpful, as can a culture that fosters inter-functional cooperation. Other values should focus on the expected relationships between the company and its associates; interpersonal relationships among associates; activities and behaviors that are encouraged, and those that are discouraged and not tolerated. Most useful are common values that focus on the importance of the customer, and those that deal with improving the company's competitive advantage.[23]

EXAMPLES OF BELIEF AND VALUE STATEMENTS

Tom's of Maine . . . an innovative small company focusing on toothpaste, mouthwashes, and other products made with natural ingredients . . . has long been a thought leader in developing insightful belief and value systems that guide the company's strategy. Tom's states its beliefs as follows:

- We believe that both human beings and nature have inherent worth and deserve our respect.
- We believe in products that are safe, effective, and made of natural ingredients.
- We believe that our company and our products are unique and worthwhile, and that we can sustain these genuine qualities with an ongoing commitment to innovation and creativity.
- We believe that we have a responsibility to cultivate the best relationships possible with our co-workers, customers, owners, agents, suppliers, and our community.
- We believe in providing employees with a safe and fulfilling work environment, and an opportunity to grow and learn.
- We believe that our company can be financially successful while behaving in a socially responsible and environmentally sensitive manner.[24]

Levi Strauss describes its core values as:

- **Empathy.** Walking in other people's shoes.
- **Originality.** Being authentic and innovative.

- **Integrity.** Doing the right thing.
- **Courage.** Standing up for what we believe.

Denny's, the 24 hour family restaurant, believes that their core values bind them together as a company through a code of shared beliefs:

- **Giving our best.** We step up, reach out, pitch in, and find ways to go above and beyond to extend the hospitality and service that are fundamental to the business.
- **Appreciating others.** We recognize the value of different approaches, thinking, perspectives, and people.
- **A Can-Do attitude.** We are resilient when faced with obstacles; constantly looking for ways to say "yes" and proud of being part of the marathon team in family dining.

Hewitt Associates, a provider of human resources outsourcing and consulting services, describes their core values:

- **People.** We threat one another, our clients, participants, business partners and suppliers with respect and dignity. We build positive relationships through open communication, sharing, and valuing diverse perspectives.
- **Excellence.** We all share the responsibility to deliver to clients solutions that demonstrate quality, reliability, and innovation in our work. We achieve excellence in what we do through personal initiative and continuous development of skills and knowledge, with strong support from the company.
- **Collaboration/Teamwork.** Teamwork unites our individual talents to serve our clients and their people exceptionally well. Working together we can leverage individual ideas and contributions into a greater result benefiting clients, other associates, our company, our business partners, and our service providers.
- **Integrity.** Ethical behavior, honesty, and integrity are fundamental characteristics of our conduct in all aspects of our work.

Whole Foods, the highly successful operator of stores selling organic foods, refers to their core values as the *soul of their company*. Their core values are:

- Selling the highest quality natural and organic products available.
- Satisfying and delighting their customers.
- Supporting team members happiness and excellence.

- Creating wealth through profits and growth.
- Caring about their communities and environment.

DESIGNING AN ENABLING AND UPLIFTING CULTURE

In his landmark study of companies that have gone from good to great, Jim Collins concluded that enduring great companies do not exist simply to deliver returns to shareholders. In a truly great company, according to Collins, profits and cash flow become like blood and water to a healthy body . . . they are essential for life, but they are not the very point of life.

Rather, Collins' research indicates that enduring great companies preserve their core values and purpose while their business strategies and operating practices endlessly adapt to a changing world. Great companies preserve the core ideology as an anchor point while stimulating change, improvement, innovation, and renewal in everything else.[25]

In architecting the values of a business, it is important to go beyond providing the foundation for strategy to another dimension that is equally critical . . . unifying and inspiring the efforts of everyone involved. An insightful value system will encourage everyone is the organization to:

- Be better than they ever thought they could be.
- Get better every day.
- Help make everyone around them better.
- Give back to their associates, to the community, and to the other institutions that have facilitated their lives.

This is the type of value system that great executives create from whatever they inherited, and this is, perhaps, the most valuable legacy that they can leave.

THE MISSION, VISION AND VALUES STATEMENT

The output of this phase in the formulation of a long-term business strategy should be a concise statement of the mission and vision of the organization, and the values that will guide it. This becomes the foundation for the strategy formulation process.

CHAPTER 5

BUSINESS OBJECTIVES

"Having lost sight of our objectives, we redoubled our efforts."

Anonymous

While a mission and values shape the general direction and character of a business, greater precision is needed for strategic and operational decisions. This is the role of objectives, the third step in the process of developing a long-term strategy for a single-division business like Panera Bread or Under Armour, Inc.

Figure 5.1 shows the relationship between objectives and the other components of the strategy formulation process. Objectives are a critical step in this process because they establish the quantitative levels and dimensions of performance that the strategy must produce while being consistent with the culture and values of the business.

The types of objectives that are appropriate depend, in the first instance, on whether a company is publicly or privately held. For privately-held companies the objectives may be:

- To satisfy a certain life style.
- To maximize profits.
- To enjoy some life style and then maximize profits.
- To accomplish certain financial and non-financial results and activities that will lead to the most successful public offering.

For publicly-held companies, the overarching objective is almost always to maximize shareholder value at some reasonable level of risk.

Figure 5.1 Specify business objectives

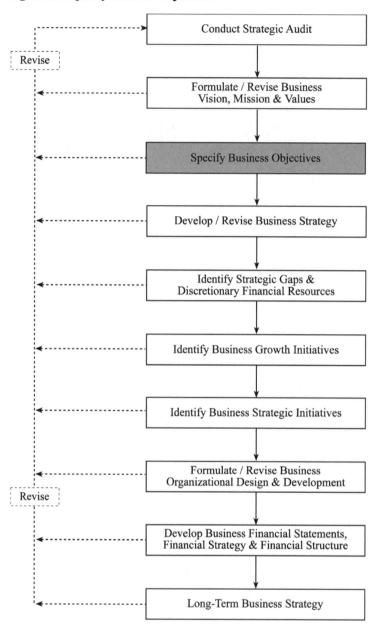

The focus here is on maximizing shareholder value. This commonly involves five major types of objectives:

- Earnings-per-share growth.
- Profitability.
- Competitive strength.
- Internal efficiency.
- Flexibility.

EARNINGS-PER-SHARE GROWTH RATE OBJECTIVES

In today's environment, this objective is the major driver of the business strategy. It establishes the level and quality of performance that the strategy must deliver. Stated differently, business strategies need to be designed to achieve the earnings-per-share (EPS) growth objective for the organization for the time period in question.

What rate of EPS growth should a company target? Obviously, faster is better than slower, but only to a point. The EPS growth rate target is one of the most important decisions that a CEO and the executive team, along with the Board of Directors, make. Andy Grove, the former CEO and Chairman of Intel, explains the fundamental issue from his point of view:

> "There is a growth rate at which everybody fails and the whole situation results in a chaos. I feel that it is my most important function to identify the maximum growth rate at which the wholesale failure phenomenon begins."[26]

During Grove's tenure as CEO, Intel achieved a compound annual growth rate in EPS of around 30 percent.

Earnings Growth Guidelines.   There are a variety of guidelines that can be used to set a target EPS growth rate. One is the profit growth rate of the industry. A second metric is the profit growth rate of the leading company or companies in the industry. Generally, it is desirable to exceed the profit growth rate of the industry, and be among the top quartile of companies, preferably first or second.

In situations where these growth rates are unreasonable, the question becomes "why?" If the issues are short-term that is one thing. If, however, the company is unable, over a 3–5 year time period, to make reasonable progress toward an earnings growth rate that is at least industry average, it may be appropriate to retain an investment banker and explore strategic options.

Another guideline or perspective is whether the business wants to be known as a growth company. The EPS growth requirement for this varies by industry and over time, but a general guide would be a growth rate in excess of 15–20 percent per year.

Figure 5.2 identifies the fastest growing companies in the United States during the ten year period, 1996–2006. Companies on this list change from year to year, and membership is strongly influenced by economic and environmental forces like oil prices, interest rates, and so on. Nevertheless, Figure 5.2 provides a frame of reference for what the fastest growing companies were able to achieve.

Figure 5.2 The fastest growing, most profitable companies in the United States-2006*

Company	10 Year Average Annual Growth Rate in Earnings Per Share	After-Tax Return on Assets 2006	Net Sales 2006	Net Profit After Taxes 2006	Total Investor Return 10 Year Average Annual Rate
1. Commercial Metals	54.4%	16.2%	$7,555.9	$356.3	31.9%
2. Texas Instruments	51.9%	31.2%	$14,630.0	$4,341.0	14.2%
3. XTO Energy	48.6%	14.4%	$4,576.0	$1,860.0	9.1%
4. BJ Services	31.6%	20.8%	$4,637.9	$804.6	16.6%
5. Bed Bath & Beyond	29.7%	16.9%	$5,809.6	$572.8	20.2%
6. Starbucks	26.3%	12.7%	$7,786.9	$564.3	25.8%
7. Kohl's	25.6%	12.3%	$15,544.2	$1,108.7	21.4%
8. Expeditors International	24.9%	12.9%	$4,626.0	$235.1	30.8%
9. CDW	23.6%	13.6%	$6,785.5	$266.1	17.2%
10. Nucor	23.2%	22.3%	$14,751.0	$1,757.7	17.5%

* Top ten publicly-held companies with a ten-year average annual increase in earnings per share of at least 23 percent, and an average after-tax return on assets of at least 12.3 percent. Data source: *Fortune*, April 30, 2007.

EPS Growth Rates and Market Capitalization.

A company's market capitalization represents the market's estimate of the discounted cash flow of the business over a multi-year time period. Therefore, the market's view of a company's 3–5 year EPS growth rate is a rough proxy of its stock price and market capitalization. The conventional wisdom has been that a stock deserves a price/earnings multiple about equal to its consensus 3–5 year EPS growth rate. In other words, if the market believes that a company can grow its earnings at a 15 percent compound annual rate, it deserves a 15x price/earnings multiple(PE), a 20 percent EPS deserves a 20x multiple, and so on. In addition, the market appreciates stability. So, a company with a 15 percent EPS growth rate and low earnings volatility will have a higher PE than one with the same 15 percent growth rate but a higher perceived earnings volatility. While this is a gross oversimplification, the general principle holds that the faster the market believes a company can grow its earnings, the higher its PE multiple, and hence the higher its stock price and market capitalization.

In recent years, PEG ratios have exceeded the normal one-to-one relationship between earnings growth and PE multiples. Today, the average is around 1.8x. The market has been assigning higher PE multiples, and other factors, principally earnings predictability and stability, or beta, also influence PEG ratios. Nevertheless, the general principle holds that the higher the earnings growth rate, the higher the PE multiple, and hence the higher the share price and market capitalization.

Selecting a Target EPS Growth Rate.   To maximize shareholder value, it is important to have an aggressive EPS growth rate target. Aggressive usually means in the top half of the industry, preferably in the upper quartile, and ideally the first or second fastest rate.

Selecting a target EPS growth rate that strikes an insightful compromise between being too slow on the one hand or too fast on the other, is always difficult. Of course, it is important to consider the financial capacity of the organization, the amount and type of risk that is involved, and the ability of the organization to achieve the rate that is targeted, among other things. Assessing how fast the people and organization can grow is particularly difficult. Whatever rate is chosen, it should be achievable, sustainable, and believable.

It is difficult for a Board of Directors to evaluate the earnings growth target, except as it compares to the industry average, industry leaders, and companies in other industries that may be interesting for one reason or another. Most board members are too far removed from the day-to-day operations of a business to have the sensitivity that this organizational assessment requires. Therefore, it is usually wise for a Board to support the CEO's EPS target, unless it is obviously too high or too low.

The penalty for missing earnings targets is generally severe in terms of reduction in share price. For this reason, it is usually best to "under promise and over deliver." Accordingly, the "publicly stated" EPS growth objective, or "street guidance," should usually be lower than the one that is used for strategy formulation purposes.

PROFITABILITY OBJECTIVES

The profitability objectives of most companies are expressed in terms of return-on-investment, or some variation or refinement. These measures include return on assets, return on equity, cash flow return on assets, cash flow return on equity, return on capital employed, to mention just a few. (These, and other financial ratios and metrics are defined and described in Appendix A.)

A Return on Investment Model.   Figure 5.3 is a schematic illustration of a basic return-on-investment model that is used here. The top half of the diagram charts the profit and loss statement, the bottom half depicts the asset structure of the balance sheet.

As the model indicates, a company's return-on-investment is the mathematical product of three key ratios . . . the profit margin, asset turnover, and the leverage ratio. It follows that a business can increase its profitability by improving its profit margin, by increasing its asset turnover, and/or by leveraging its operation more highly.

Figure 5.3 A generic return-on-investment model

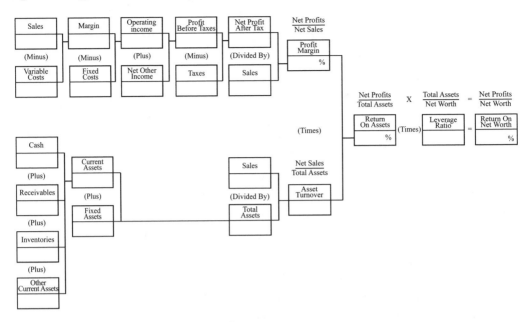

The reason that this model is preferred over others is that it is managerially operational in the sense that it highlights the three paths to improved profitability. Moreover, decades of historical data are available for these metrics. Other measures are more common in different industries, and some companies prefer other metrics. Obviously, there is nothing wrong with alternative measures. At the same time, we prefer return on net worth and return on assets.

Why Return-on-Investment Is Important.   Return-on-investment affects the net profit of the business, hence the EPS, and therefore the stock price and market capitalization. Second, the ROI affects the rate at which the company can grow without changing its capital structure. The higher the ROI, the faster a company can grow its EPS without increasing its debt level. And, as we have just observed, the faster the EPS growth rate, the higher the PE multiple, and the higher the stock price and market capitalization of the company. So, a higher ROI tends to have a positive impact on shareholder value. In fact, studies by major consulting companies have shown that return-on-investment is the most important determinant of the rate at which a company can increase its market capitalization.[27]

Selecting a Return-on-Investment Target.   What level of profitability should a company try to achieve? It depends, in part, on the industry, since the rate of return varies considerably across industry sectors. (See Figure 5.4)

Figure 5.4 Financial performance of major industries in the United States-2006*

Rank	Company	2006 Profits as % of Assets
24	Aerospace & Defense	5.9
38	Airlines	3.0
10	Apparel	8.5
40	Automotive Retailing, Services	2.9
30	Beverages	4.4
17	Chemicals	6.6
46	Commercial Banks	1.4
16	Computers, Office Equipment	7.4
47	Diversified Financials	1.4
18	Electronics, Electrical Equipment	6.5
39	Energy	2.9
31	Engineering, Construction	4.1
29	Entertainment	4.5
25	Financial Data Services	5.8
22	Food & Drug Stores	6.0
20	Food Consumer Prodcuts	6.3
50	Food Production	-1.4
4	Food Services	12.5
15	General Merchandisers	7.5
32	Health Care: Medical Facilities	3.8
23	Health Care: Insurance, Managed Care	6.0
9	Health Care: Pharmacy, Other Services	8.8
21	Homebuilders	6.0
36	Hotels, Casinos	3.5
8	Household & Personal Products	9.0
12	Industrial & Farm Equipment	7.8
43	Information Technology Services	2.6
49	Insurance: Life, Health (Stock)	0.8
35	Insurance: P&C (Stock)	3.6
28	Internet Services & Retailing	5.4
6	Medical Products & Equipment	11.0
3	Metals	12.6
11	Mining, Crude-Oil Production	8.2
51	Motor Vehicles & Parts	-1.9
5	Network, Other Communication Equipment	11.2
1	Oil & Gas Equipment Services	14.0
45	Packaging, Containers	2.3
2	Petroleum Refining	13.2
7	Pharmaceuticals	9.9
44	Pipelines	2.5
26	Publishing, Printing	5.8
27	Railroads	5.5
48	Securities	0.9
37	Semiconductors, Other	3.3
13	Specialty Retailers	7.8
42	Telecommunications	2.7
41	Utilities: Gas & Electric	2.8
14	Wholesalers: Diversified	7.7
33	Wholesalers: Electronic Office Equipment	3.7
19	Wholesalers: Food & Grocery	6.3
34	Wholesalers: Health Care	3.7
	The 500 Median	4.6

*Source: *Fortune*, April 30, 2007

Within the industry, a company should be, or strive to become, in the upper quartile, preferably the first or second most profitable business as measured by return on assets or the measure of profitability that is most commonly accepted in the industry. In those situations where an organization is achieving below-average profitability, achieving these levels may require several years of improvement. In these cases, the question is whether the organization is making reasonable progress toward an acceptable rate. If such progress is not being made then the issue is whether the current leadership should continue and/or whether an investment banker should be hired to recommend strategic options, including a sale.

ECONOMIC VALUE ADDED OBJECTIVES

Many experts would argue that economic value added (EVA) is the best measure of business performance. However, since earnings-per-share and return-on-investment metrics are universally accepted, we are proposing EVA *in addition to*, rather than instead of, the EPS and ROI metrics.

EVA is a measure of *economic profit,* as opposed to *accounting profit,* that reduces operating profit by the cost of all of the capital that a company employs, including equity capital. Capital, of course, is used to purchase current assets . . . inventory, accounts receivable, etc. . . . and fixed assets . . . principally plant and equipment . . . to generate sales and hopefully profits. EVA thus charges the business and its executives for the cost of the assets that they employ.

After deciding on the precise definitions of each of the components, EVA is used to value a company, a product or product grouping, a geographical area of business, a store or group of stores, and other segments and aggregations of a business. EVA and net present value (NPV) give identical answers in valuing companies. NPV is the most appropriate measure of the value of an enterprise according to most financial experts and economists.

EVA produces a dollar number. Growth rate objectives can obviously be expressed as some percentage increase in EVA, and profitability objectives can be stated in dollars. This same procedure and process can be applied to other segments and aggregations of a business. Executive bonus and stock option programs can also be tied to EVA.

EVA has been adopted by a variety of companies including Coca-Cola, Eli Lilly, Herman Miller, Target, and Whole Foods.[28] It will probably enjoy more widespread usage in the future, and could become the dominate metric for stating growth and profitability objectives. At the present time, however, earnings-per-share and return-on-investment are the most common, and, for that reason, EVA has been assigned a supplementary role.

COMPETITIVE STRENGTH OBJECTIVES

These types of objectives are sometimes used in addition to growth and profitability objectives. Competitive strength objectives might include growth objectives stated in terms of targeted annual rates of increase in sales, operating income, and market share. Also common are stability objectives expressed in terms of maximum fluctuations in sales and earnings, and, in manufacturing organizations, capacity utilization.

INTERNAL EFFICIENCY OBJECTIVES

To increase the chances of achieving target levels of longer-term profitability, it may be useful to set certain internal efficiency objectives in the short run. Target turnover ratios may be particularly helpful. The key turnover ratio is return on sales or profit margin, while supporting ones are turnover of working capital, net worth, inventory, and accounts receivable.

Additional objectives might focus on the quality of fixed assets. For example, a manufacturer might specify the target age of plant and equipment; an airline might target the age of aircraft; while a retailer should be concerned with the age of its store fleet, and the proportion of that fleet that has the most current, or most productive, store design.

FLEXIBILITY OBJECTIVES

In some instances it may be appropriate to buy "insurance" against unforeseeable events by maintaining certain types of flexibilities. For example, it may be prudent to specify some maximum percentage of sales and/or profits that can be derived from a single customer, or customer segment, or product, or product group. Similarly, it may be appropriate to specify maximum proportions of sales and/or profits from certain technological processes, or patents, or licenses.

In terms of financial flexibility, liquidity measures can be useful. The most common indices would include target ranges for the current ratio, the acid-test ratio, and the debt-to-equity ratio.

EPS GROWTH RATES VS. PROFITABILITY: THE TRADEOFFS

Of the five types of objectives that have been presented, EPS growth rates and profitability are generally the most important. The relative importance of these two objectives varies over time, but at the present time earnings growth is clearly the most important. This is the case despite the fact that studies have indicated that the most important determinant of market capitalization is profitability.[29]

What about the tradeoffs in a specific situation? Does the greatest potential for increased shareholder value lie in faster growth or increased profitability?

For some companies, convincing the market that they can increase growth by just one additional percentage point can be worth six, seven, or even ten points of margin improvement. Adding a point of sustainable growth may be harder to achieve than improving margin, but the largest profits usually result from faster growth, due primarily to the effects of compounding. For most companies, investing in growth generates more shareholder value than cost cutting does.[30] Having said that, it is obviously important for a company to understand the numerical relationship between EPS growth and profitability in its specific situation when designing a strategy for the future.[31]

EXAMPLES OF BUSINESS OBJECTIVES

Public announcements of business objectives are generally more conservative than those that are used internally because the penalty for missing targets is usually severe. Some examples of public statements are:

- **Harley Davidson.** The iconic manufacturer of motorcycles. Sales growth of 7–9 percent per year, and an earnings growth rate in the mid-teens.
- **Select Comfort.** A vertically integrated manufacturer, marketer and retailer of adjustable firmness mattresses. Net sales growth of 15 percent or higher, and earnings growth of 20 percent or higher.
- **Big Lots.** The largest close-out retailer in the United States with sales in 2006 of $4.7 billion. Target annual earnings-per-share growth rate of 20 percent. Achieve an operating profit rate of 5.5 percent within three years. Generate cumulative cash flow of $550–600 million over the next three years.
- **Whole Foods.** The largest operator of supermarkets focusing on natural and organic foods. To increase sales from $5.6 billion in 2006 to $12 billion by 2010.
- **J Crew.** A brand of classic apparel with stores and an e-commerce site. Comparable store sales growth in the mid single digit range. Net square footage expansion in the 7–9 percent range. Direct sales growth in the high single digits and diluted EPS growth in excess of 20 percent per year.

SETTING STRETCH OBJECTIVES

We have discussed the importance of setting a bold, imaginative, uplifting vision and mission, and developing a culture and values that support it. Properly designed, the mission, vision, culture and values should unify people in the organization and motivate and inspire them to a level of achievement that exceeds their expectations.

Well architected objectives have the same characteristics. They should stretch the performance of the business and the people in it to the rational edge of attainability and sustainability.

Incremental, marginal, improvements in performance are boring and uninspiring, and attract and retain the kind of people that are content in that type of environment. They do not maximize behavior, performance, or shareholder value.

Stretched objectives will produce better results as long as they are not stretched to the point of being perceived as unbelievable or unattainable. Stretched objectives will help attract and retain people who want to be part of a winning team . . . a team that wins in an exemplary way. Stretched objectives are more likely to produce greater shareholder value.

Set earnings- per- share, profitability and other objectives at levels that will stretch the performance of the business, but are also attainable and sustainable and involve a tolerable level of risk. These objectives, covering a three, five or some other time period, when combined with the mission, vision and values, establish the direction and goals that the business strategy must achieve and satisfy.

CHAPTER 6
BUSINESS STRATEGY

"For too many companies life consists of working very hard to make small differences in performance produce small differences in profitability. The really significant alterations in corporate fortunes, however, depend upon those relatively few major and basic decisions that determine the chances of success—decisions that enable the company to fight corporate wars with its best weapons, not those of competitors, and enable it to choose the time and place where competitive strength really counts."[32]

Bruce Henderson
Founder and Former CEO
Boston Consulting Group

The next step in developing a long-term strategy for a single-unit business, or an operating division within a multi-division enterprise, is to formulate or revise the basic business strategy. (Figure 6.1) There are major differences between corporate strategy and business strategy. *Corporate* strategy defines the scope of the business in terms of the industries and markets in which it competes, including the allocation of resources between different businesses, diversification, divestitures, and other related issues. *Business* strategy is concerned with how to compete within a particular industry or market. To achieve high-yield results within a particular industry or market, it is important to achieve a competitive advantage, preferably one that is sustainable for a reasonable period of time.

While different, business and corporate strategy are related. First, and most obviously, for executives working in a single-unit organization, business strategy and corporate strategy are the same. Second, in multi-division businesses, each operating division, or units within it, needs to have their own robust business strategy. Third, multi-division businesses with certain kinds of business portfolios can produce competitive advantages for some or all of its operating divisions. Finally, the competitive advantages that a given business has, can be an important determinant of the type and range of businesses and markets that an enterprise can expand into.[33]

Figure 6.1 Developing/revising a business strategy

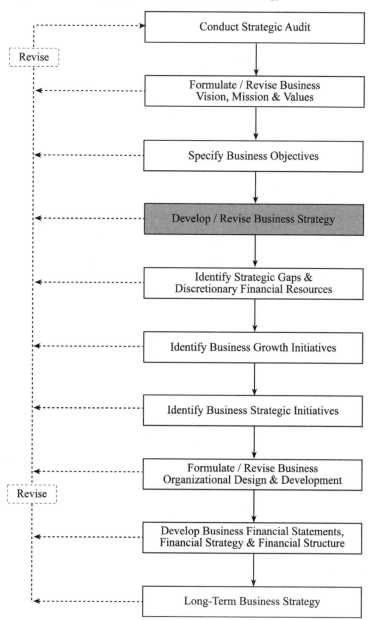

Approaches to business strategy have evolved over the years from relatively simple points of view to more comprehensive and complex perspectives.[34] Figure 6.2 presents our approach. The process begins with the selections of the target market segment and the identification of the needs, wants, problems and expectations of customers in that segment that need to be solved. The next step is to design the value proposition that will satisfy these needs, wants and problems in a way that is prefer-

Figure 6.2 Major components of business strategy

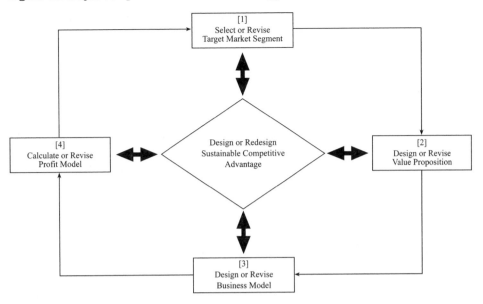

able to the offers of other companies. Third, a business model is developed that will deliver the value proposition in a differentiated and advantaged way relative to competitors. Fourth, a basic profit model is constructed to make certain that the business strategy satisfies the financial requirements of the business. The final challenge is to craft the strategy in a way that results in a competitive advantage for the business relative to competition, hopefully for an extended period of time.

These five components provide the framework for designing an initial business strategy. If a strategy already exists, as is usually the case, these same components should be reviewed to make certain they are appropriate for the conditions that are expected to exist in the future. Each component of the business model will now be discussed in greater detail.

SELECTING A TARGET MARKET SEGMENT

Who is the customer? What customer needs, wants, problems, preferences and/or expectations is the business attempting to satisfy in a way that is preferable to competition?

The starting point in developing a profitable business strategy is to select a target market segment. The idea here is to focus on some part, or segment, of a market rather than the entire market because, properly executed, the segmentation approach will be more effective in satisfying customers' wants, needs, and problems, and simultaneously more profitable to the business.

There are many ways to segment markets; some common methods are summarized in Figure 6.3. For consumer markets, some of the most common approaches are to segment by geography, or demography, or behavioral characteristics, or benefit preferences, or usage patterns, like heavy users or light users. For business-to-business markets, it is common to segment by geography, or industry, or customer size, or type of application.

The segmentation thought process should be very rigorous because it forms the foundation of the business strategy. Figure 6.4 presents an illustrative multi-dimensional segmentation for apparel. Using a variety of techniques including focus groups, physical observations of consumer usage (ethnography), and national consumer surveys, it has been determined that a useful way to segment the market for women's apparel is by price and by style. Using sophisticated statistical techniques, consumer preferences for fashion and style are segmented into seven market segments and plotted on the style-price map with the size of each segment noted. Consumer perceptions of the major brands are then plotted on the same map. This type of analysis can be very useful in selecting a target market segment, identifying the relevant competitors for that segment and analyzing their value propositions, and then designing the value proposition for the business in question. For an existing brand, this type of analysis can provide valuable input into whether the existing value proposition should be changed, and if so, in what ways. While Figure 6.4 is focused on consumer markets, the same concepts and techniques can be used in segmenting business-to-business markets.

Figure 6.3 Illustrative ways of segmenting markets

Consumer Markets - Segmentation Options	Business-to-Business Markets - Segmentation Options

I. Geographic Segments
    A. Continents
    B. Regions
    C. Countries
    D. Regions of Countries
    E. Urban; Rural
    F. Zip Codes
	I. Geographic Segments
	    A. Continents
	    B. Regions
	    C. Countries
	    D. Regions of Countries

II. Demographic Segments
    A. Age
    B. Stage in life cycle
    C. Income
    D. Occupation
    E. Education
	II. Industry Segmentation
	    A. SIC codes
	
	III. Customer Size Segmentation
	
	IV. Application Segmentation

III. Individual Behavioral Segments
    A. Attitudes
    B. Personality
    C. Lifestyles / psychographics
    D. Brand loyalty	

IV. Benefit Segments A. Benefit preferences	
V. Usage Segments A. Heavy, medium, light & non-users	

Figure 6.4 Illustrative multi-dimensional segmentation

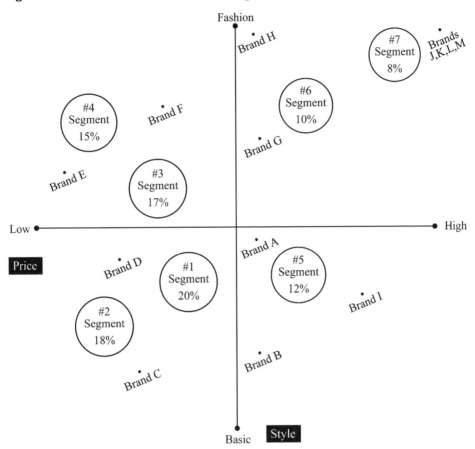

While the techniques used in Figure 6.4 are interesting and insightful, they are not necessarily the best way to segment markets. In fact, there is no one best way to segment markets; it depends on the situation, and the most useful techniques often involve a blend of creativity and technical sophistication. The challenge, of course, is to focus on that segment, or those segments, that will allow the business to make the most money over time. This may be the largest segment(s) in terms of sales potential, or it may be a smaller segment that the company can capture a larger market share of for whatever reason. In some instances it may be an underserved market, or it may be a market of whatever size that has limited competition . . . Sometimes it involves segmenting a market differently in order to gain a competitive advantage. To illustrate, consider the following:

- Virgin Mobile USA became one of the largest wireless providers in the U.S. market by targeting the youth market. While more than 60 percent of the U.S. population had a cell phone, only about 35 percent of 15–24 year olds did.[35]

65

- When Sony launched the Cyber-shot, it was not trying to appeal to the photography enthusiast. Instead they tapped into the mass-market of amateur picture takers who wanted a digital camera that was easy to use, simple to understand, and fun. Cyber-shot became the leader in the digital camera market with a 20% plus market share, ahead of Canon, the leader in cameras.[36]
- Enterprise is the largest car rental company in America. While Hertz dominates the on-airport rental market, Enterprise rules the off-airport market by doing most of its business in downtown and suburban locations. In addition to consumers, Enterprise targets U.S. auto insurance companies who account for about 33% of its sales.[37]

Sometimes the most lucrative strategy is not to find a segment within an existing market space, but to create a new market that is uniquely suited to the company's own strengths, or strengths the company can create in a way that is differentiated and advantaged over other companies. This approach can serve as a foundation for reinventing companies, and be part of the basis for new businesses. The iPod and iPhone from Steve Jobs and Apple are examples of the former, while FedEx, Starbucks, Whole Foods, and Google, and are examples of the latter.

The fundamental issues that should be analyzed before selecting or revising a target market segment are:

- What is the current size of the market?
- What is the projected growth rate of the market?
- What is the competitive intensity of the market? How many competitors are there, what are their market shares, etc?
- What is the profitability of companies in the market? How strong are they financially, and in critical areas of the business like research and development?
- Are some current customers dissatisfied? Why?
- Are their any unmet customer needs that present an opportunity?
- Can the market be segmented to provide the company with a point of difference and a competitive advantage over existing and potential competitors?

Favorable responses to these questions, and others that may be appropriate in specific situations, should usually be a perquisite for selecting a target market segment.

For existing businesses, the challenge is to determine whether the existing market segment is the most appropriate for the future. It is very important to review this issue because things change. The size of the segment can change. The benefits that customers in that segment are looking for can change. The number and intensity of competition can change. The value propositions that competitors are offering can change. Often these changes are minor and/or subtle, and are easy to overlook, or disregard as unimportant. A rigorous review of the appropriateness of target markets is very important.

CREATING A VALUE PROPOSITION

Given the selection of a target market segment, the next step is to create a value proposition, or "offer," that satisfies the needs, wants, problems, preferences, and expectations (NWPPE) of customers in that segment in a way that is differentiated from competition and enables the company to achieve a competitive advantage that is sustainable over a reasonable time period. The prerequisite for success here is that the value proposition must satisfy NWPPE as defined by the customer, or, stated differently, from the customer's perspective. Not from the company's perspectives; from the customer's point of view. There are other success requirements, but this is the fundamental prerequisite for success. Unfortunately, most companies do not have a clear definition of their value proposition.[38]

Figure 6.5 presents the components of a value proposition. These components are generic in the sense that additions, deletions, and variations may be more appropriate in specific situations that a company faces. These components of the value proposition articulate the company's offer, or solution to the customers' NWPPE. It is critical that customers think that the company excels in those components that are most important to them, and be at least acceptable in the other components.[39] Again; these are customers' judgments, not those of executives in the business.

Figure 6.5 A generic value proposition

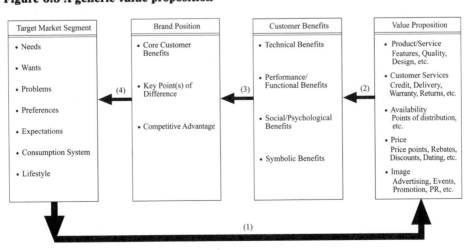

Product or Service.   Creating the product or service is the most important step in creating an effective value proposition. Product dimensions can include technical characteristics, functions performed, performance, features, design, quality, materials, fit, style, color, flavor, etc. Getting the product "right" is a difficult, challenging and ongoing issue.

Guess, for example, has long been an iconic brand of jeans. Under pressure from its channel members to lower price points to compete with discount stores, average prices fell from $68 to $29. Sales fell and earnings turned into losses. Guess senior executives, the Marciano brothers, responded by taking their brand more upscale, shifting their denim sources from the United States to the finer weaves of Italy and Japan. Consumers understood the quality and design and were willing to pay more. Prices were increased to more than $100 per pair.[40]

Another example. The low-cost, low-style approach that enabled Dell to achieve outstanding growth and profitability during the 1990's no longer seems to be working as well as it once did. Branding and product design have become more important. Dell still markets mainly on price and performance, and its machines risk being superseded by competitors with more style.[41] Dell is responding with new products that it feels have a higher design content.

Customer Services.   Creating great customer service can be an important way of enhancing the customer's experience by making it more enjoyable or memorable, and thereby creating a stronger bond between the company and the customer. It can also be a powerful way of differentiating a company from competitors. Appropriate services vary depending on the product and the customer, but may include credit, delivery, warranties, liberal exchange and return policies and a wide variety of "perks."

For example Southwest Airlines sends out letters, and sometimes, flight vouchers, to customers caught in major storms, air traffic jams, or other travel inconveniences. Four Seasons has a "guest historian" charged with tracking guest preferences, and is attempting to identify in advance customers who have stayed at the hotel as infrequently as five times and hand them their room keys as they step out of their car. FedEx was the first to offer overnight delivery, guarantee 10:30 a.m. deliveries, and let customers track the status of their packages.[42]

Price.   The price component of the value proposition includes decisions relative to the actual price as well as price discounts, price rebates, gift-with-purchase, purchase-with-purchase, buy-one-get-one-free, terms-of-sale, invoice dating and so on. Low prices can be a major determinant of value to the customer and a central component of the business strategy, as is demonstrated by Dell, Wal-Mart, and many others. Conversely, high prices can be used along with quality and other components of the value proposition to create value in some customer's minds, as illustrated by Ralph Lauren's Polo in men's and women's apparel, and home furnishings, or Cartier watches and jewelry.

Availability.   This component of the value proposition involves decisions regarding the number of points of distribution, the types of distribution points, and the physical and esthetic characteristics of where the product or service is purchased. Products or services that the customer want to purchase conveniently generally have the largest number of points of distribution, while exclusive products tend to have limited availability . . . For example, a product that targets a large middle-market segment like GE appliances has wide availability, while a higher-quality brand targeting an up-scale market, like Sub Zero and Wolf, have limited availability through different types of retail outlets that enhance the value of their brands.

Image.   The final step in creating the value proposition is to create the proper image for the product or service. The previous components of the value proposition . . . product/service, customer service, pricing, and availability . . . create part of the image, but this often needs to be enhanced with the proper advertising, sales promotion, point-of-purchase materials, public relations, events marketing, guerilla marketing, word-of-mouth and "buzz marketing," internet marketing and/or other techniques. These efforts need to be integrated into a communication package that presents the product or service as the best possible solution to the customers' needs, wants, problems, preferences, and expectations. Consider the unique approach that Apple developed for its iPod, an image that, over time, has become instantly recognizable as the brand.

Integrating the Components.   To be effective, all of the components of the value proposition need to be consistent with each other and integrated together so that they present a unified, consistent, reinforcing solution to the customers' needs, wants, problems, preferences, and expectations that is viewed by the customer as better than, and different from, competitors. The effectiveness of this integration increases the power of the value proposition exponentially.

For example, Charles Schwab launched his company with a single idea that was contrarian at the time . . . that there must be a business in selling stock to the middle class. He established trading commissions 50 percent lower than competitors, and launched a TV ad campaign that promoted ownership of stock, suggesting that anybody could get rich in the stock market. Schwab was able to attract a new market segment, and became their advisor and advocate. He was the first to bundle mutual funds together, one of the first to force the funds, not his clients, to absorb trading fees, and the first discounter to expand availability through a branch network.[43]

Or, consider Amazon. Jeff Bezos, while researching potential new business opportunities for a hedge fund in 1994, noticed that the Web was growing 2,300% a year! The Web, of course, makes availability ubiquitous to everyone who has access to it . . . the largest distribution mechanism yet invented. A few months later, Bezos started an on-line book store that made it faster, easier, and most personal than buying in traditional mass-merchandized stores like Borders and Barns and Noble. From books he expanded into a wide assortment of products ranging from toys and clothing to electronics and hardware. Avoiding the costs for stores and staffing, he capitalized on the lower cost of operating on the internet, and is able to offer niche products that stores can not afford to stock. Moreover, he expanded the market segment from consumers to include companies ranging in size from very small ones to giants like Target, to sell items on Amazon.com.[44] Some question the profitability and long-term viability of Amazon, and that view may prevail. Meanwhile, Bezos' net worth is now in excess of $4 billion.

Focusing the Value Proposition.   The effectiveness and profitability of value propositions can be enhanced by transforming products or services into brands. This involves many things, but at this point the concern is identifying customer benefits and brand positioning (Figure 6.5).

(1) Customer Benefits.   The value proposition should be translated into benefits that are meaningful to, and resonate with, customers in the target market segment. The types of benefits that are most important include *technical, performance/ functional, social/psychological, and symbolic*.

Under Armour, for example, designs and markets sports apparel that provides compression, and wicks perspiration off the skin rather than absorbing it. (wicking and compression are technical benefits.) The apparel regulates temperature, and keeps users cool, dry and light.(functional benefits) Exercise can improve health, wellness and longevity (functional and social/psychological benefits) Being a slim, healthy person is seen as socially desirable by some people (social/psychological and symbolic benefits) Under Armour's distinctive exterior label communicates these social/psychological benefits.

Patagonia apparel and footwear is constructed with environmental sensitivity, and uses processes and materials that are both renewable and sustainable. This part of their value proposition provides technical and functional benefits, but, equally important, helps consumers feel that they are being environmentally responsible, and signals to others that they, in fact, are . . . thereby providing social/ psychological and symbolic benefits.

Oracle is an example from the technology sector. Oracle is the world's leading supplier of software for information management, and the world's second largest independent software company. Their products can be found in virtually every industry, and in 98 of the top 100 Fortune 500 companies. In addition to the technical and functional benefits, customers are confident that the applications and systems will work today and in the future, and that Oracle will be in business to help them when they need assistance. No one is going to be criticized or fired for buying an Oracle system. Oracle provides powerful social/psychological and symbolic benefits.

In the retail sector, Abercrombie and Fitch is focused on the 18–22 year old consumer offering apparel and related products exemplifying East Coast traditions and an Ivy League heritage. Its distinctive and recognizable style of apparel is sold at prices producing extraordinary gross margins through its exciting stores which feature unique merchandise presentation techniques; young hosts (salespeople) that personify the A&F lifestyle; and a store experience with low lighting and hip music that is more like a club than a store. Here the technical and functional benefits are combined with social/psychological and symbolic benefits of being "cool" and belonging to a lifestyle that is appealing, even if it is not attainable beyond a few pieces or wardrobe of clothes.

There are many other examples of companies that are using multiple types of customer benefits successfully, including Absolute vodka, Jet Blue, Ben & Jerry's, Callaway Golf; Manolo Blahnik, Boston Beer, Canyon Ranch, Cheesecake Factory, and Target, to name a few.

Value propositions can often be strengthened by using the entire benefit spectrum. Social/psychological and symbolic benefits are very useful in helping transform products into brands instead of becoming commodities. They can help create emotional engagement and involvement with customers, are extraordinarily useful in differentiating the brand from competition, and can be very difficult to duplicate.

(2) Brand Positioning.   The brand position should serve as the strategic mandate and guideline for all communications with the customer. It should specify the target audience, if it differs from the target market segment. Most importantly, it should articulate the core points of difference and the competitive advantage(s) of the brand relative to competitors. It should focus on the one or two customer benefits that are most important and meaningful to the target market segment, and most differentiating from competition.

Developing the brand position is the responsibility of the chief executive with possible input from the chief marketing officer. It is not the role of the advertising agency. The value of a product or service, and whether it will be considered a brand or a commodity, is strongly influenced by whether it is perceived by customers to be different from, and better than competitors, in ways that are most important and relevant to them. The brand position should capture the most important and one or two components of the value proposition that resonate with customers, and the company must deliver what is promised. This is one of the most critical decisions a CEO makes, and it should not be delegated down in the organization, or outsourced, although input from these parties may be appropriate.

As an example, consider Polo Ralph Lauren. Celebrating their 40th birthday, RL is one of the world's premier brands with a sales volume in 2006 of $5.5 billion. The brand position is sophistication and luxury, superior quality and design, and enduring style. This single, heritage-driven, positioning has enabled the company to expand from its beginnings in men's ties into apparel for men, women, and children, accessories, furniture and home furnishings, eyewear, and precious jewelry and luxury watches throughout the United States, Asia, and Europe.

The Cheesecake Factory has the highest sales per outlet of any restaurant in their competitive space . . . more than $10 million. Cheesecake's positioning is exceptional value with generous food portions at moderate prices. To deliver this positioning, substantially all menu items (except deserts) are prepared on the restaurant premises using high quality, fresh ingredients based on proprietary recipes. Desert items are manufactured at their bakery production facilities, and are considered by many to be extraordinary, particularly the nearly endless variety of cheesecakes.

Target's sales reached $59.5 billion in 2006, and over the last ten years it has generated a total annualized return to shareholders of nearly 22 percent, substantially above the S&P 500, and most retail competitors. Target's brand positioning is to deliver a merchandise assortment that is distinctive, exclusive and unexpected in its design and value in clean bright stores. Their advertising tag line is "Expect More. Pay Less." They deliver.

Revising/Changing Value Propositions. For established businesses with existing value propositions, it is imperative to review them continuously and revise them as needed. This should involve rethinking each component of the proposition for its appropriateness and effectiveness in view of changing environmental and competitive conditions. It should also include an evaluation of the integration of the components with the idea of looking for better and more effective ways of solving the customers' needs, wants, problems, preferences, and expectations in a way that is better than, and different from, competitors. Most importantly, it should involve a review of the appropriateness and effectiveness of customer benefits, the brand position, and how the position is communicated.

Harley-Davidson, for example, developed a revised value proposition that turned a motorcycle company with a mediocre product into a unique, differentiated lifestyle company. They market several new bikes a year. They introduce hundreds of new motorcycle accessories each year so the owners can customize their bikes. They design and sell a large array of branded fashion clothing and accessories, and license other companies to produce additional products. These products are sold through Harley's own dealer network plus other authorized retailers. The Harley Owners Group (H.O.G.) is the largest motorcycle enthusiast club in the world. The group hosts large rallies throughout the world attended by millions of fans. Harley operates Rider's Edge, a school that introduces more than 20,000 new customers to motorcycling and the company's products each year. The Company also has an Authorized Rentals program which enable people to experience the motorcycles and the lifestyle. The company has created a strong and unique lifestyle around its products resulting in a consumer following that is almost cult-like. Harley is one of the fastest growing, most profitable companies in America.

CRAFTING THE BUSINESS MODEL

The next step is to construct a business model that delivers the value proposition to customers in the target market segment in a way that is competitively advantaged and satisfies the company's profitability requirements. Figure 6.6 presents a generic business model.

Functional Area Strategies. Functional area strategies spell out the mission and objectives of each functional area of the business in delivering the value proposition, particularly the core customer benefits. The functional areas involved vary by industry and company, but may involve research and development, procurement, manufacturing, marketing, sales and distribution, as well as accounting, legal and human resource activities.

Figure 6.6 A generic business model

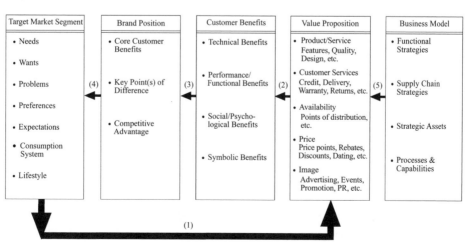

73

If a business is to develop and maintain a superior value proposition, it must have, or develop, the functional capabilities to deliver that proposition. Those functional areas that are most critical in delivering the value proposition are, or should be, the most important to the business. These are *core functions, and the business should develop extraordinary competence in these functions so that they become core competences*. All other functional areas should think of themselves, and justify their existence, in terms of how they contribute to, or add value to, the value proposition from the perspective of the customer.

The pivotal issue is which functions should be performed internally and which should be outsourced. The requires a comprehensive functional sourcing strategy which identifies which functions the company needs to own and protect, and which can best be performed by what kind of partners, and how to structure a productive relationship. Functions that are critical to delivering the value proposition, differentiating the offer, and/or creating competitive advantage should usually not be outsourced unless there are extenuating circumstances.[45]

Supply Chain Strategies.[46]   In attempting to deliver a superior value proposition, a business competes within a supply chain as well as an independent enterprise. That is, business A and its supply chain competes against businesses B, C, D, etc. and their supply chains.

Supply chain management is the integration of key business processes from customers through original suppliers that provide products, services, and information. The integration of selected business processes across selected companies in the supply chain can provide the opportunity to deliver a better value proposition than competitors.

The first step is to identify the major types of businesses and key companies that are involved in the supply chain from customers through original suppliers, as well as all other functions and activities that must be performed to get the product or service to market. The second step is to identify which businesses are key in delivering the value proposition to the target market segment in a differentiated and advantaged way. These are *core businesses*. The third step is to determine how these core businesses should be linked to each other and the company. The key processes for integrating and managing these core businesses are *customers relationship management* and *supplier relationship management*.

While many companies have done a great job streamlining their internal processes, the processes that involve interactions with other companies have not received equal attention. Designing insightful supply chain processes, and continuously improving them, is a great opportunity to increase efficiency, productivity and profitability, as well as improving speed and flexibility.[47] Supply chain strategy is a critical component of the business model.

Strategic Assets.   Another part of crafting the business model is to determine which assets are necessary to deliver the value proposition to customers in the target market segment in a differentiated and advantaged way. This involves both current and fixed assets. The most critical current assets are receivables and inventory, and the issue is what role should each of these play in delivering the value proposition. Credit, warranties, discounts, dating, rebates, returns, and so on, must be managed primarily from the perspective of how they contribute to the value proposition, and, secondly, the financial consequences of such policies. Many companies reverse this order.

How can fixed assets . . . like manufacturing facilities, warehouses, and distribution centers . . . be used to deliver the value proposition in an advantaged way? Should they be owned or leased? Where should they be located? How could they be used to facilitate a competitive advantage in functions and/or features, or quality, or speed-to-market? Generally factories located in the Far East provide products at lower costs, but U.S. based factories may enable a company to go to market faster. Which is most important? Is there a blend that would be most profitable?

Processes and Capabilities.   The final component of the business model is to identify and/or create those processes and capabilities that are necessary to deliver the value proposition that delivers the benefits that satisfies the needs, wants, problems, preferences, and expectations of the target market segment in a differentiated and advantaged way. The processes that are most critical are called *core processes, and these processes should become core competences.* This involves transforming these core processes into strategic capabilities which requires strategic investments in a support infrastructure that links together and transcends functions.

The strategic capabilities that are generally most important are innovation, learning, quality improvement, speed-to-market, efficiency and productivity. These capabilities cut across departments and functions, and therefore need to be designed, directed and supported by senior executives and the CEO.[48] The effectiveness of these capabilities is an extraordinarily important determinant of the success of a business strategy, and can also be a powerful barrier to entry by potential competitors.[49] These capabilities can also provide a foundation for launching new growth initiatives.

United Technologies, for example, is a relatively unknown company with sales in excess of $30 billion. Their business consists of basic manufacturing operations that are susceptible to quality, efficiency, and technological improvements. The ability to continually achieve incremental gains in these areas is the company's greatest strength. This focus and skill set has allowed the organization to take commodity products, such as elevators and air conditioners, and turn them into high-margin businesses.[50]

Bed, Bath and Beyond is an interesting retail example of selecting a target market segment, developing a value proposition, and then building a business model to deliver the offer. Since 1992, when the company had 34 stores, BBB has expanded into a national chain with more than 600 stores. They created this business by recognizing a market void resulting from the inability and/or unwillingness of discount department stores and department stores to satisfy the needs of the middle to upper-middle consumer market. Today, BBB is the nation's largest operator of stores selling predominantly better quality domestic merchandise and home furnishings at everyday low prices. Their merchandise lines include bed linens, bath accessories, kitchen textiles, cookware, dinnerware, glassware, and basic house wares. The company continually tests new merchandise categories and adjusts the categories of merchandise carried in its stores based on sales results. They add new departments and expand or reduce the size of other departments based on sales patterns. Local store personnel are primarily responsible for monitoring inventory levels and reordering merchandise.tailored to local sales trends and market conditions. Merchandising at the local store level, rather than centrally, encourages market-specific entrepreneurship and allows them to maintain better in-stock-availability. In order to offer every day low prices, they developed and maintain a very low cost structure. As a result of this strategy, BBB is one of the fastest-growing, most-profitable companies in America.

BUILDING THE PROFIT MODEL

The next step in designing/revising a business strategy is to translate the decisions made regarding the value proposition and the business model into a basic return-on-investment model. (Figure 6.7) The purpose here is not to construct a full-blown pro-forma profit and loss statement and balance sheet, but rather to estimate whether the decisions that are being made have a reasonable probability of achieving a level and rate of profitability that are acceptable.

What level of sales can be reasonably expected? What gross margin and gross profit are most likely? What will be the operating expense rate and the sales volume level that is anticipated? What will be the net profit margin before and after taxes?

From a balance sheet perspective, what level of asset investment is required to generate and support the level of sales that is expected? In terms of current assets, what rate of inventory turnover can be expected? How many days-sales-outstanding should there be?

How much cash and other current assets will be required? Figuring out fixed asset requirement, how much needs to be invested in such things as computers, warehouses, distribution centers, manufacturing facilities, stores, and so on? Should these be owned or leased? Does the resultant asset turnover rate look acceptable?

Figure 6.7 A generic profit model

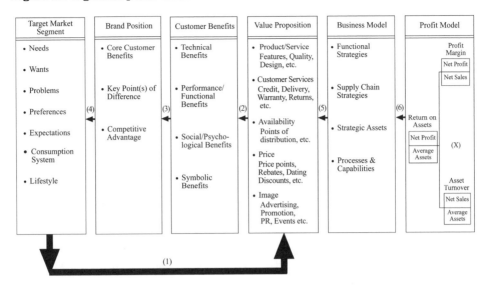

Combining the profit margin and the asset turnover, is the return-on-asset level acceptable? Does it meet the profitability objective? Does it exceed the cost of capital? If not, what changes need to be made? Can the strategy be adjusted or adapted, or are fundamental changes needed? Should the strategy be postponed or abandoned?

Going through this "front-of-the-envelope" exercise is very useful because it provides a hurdle that must be cleared before spending additional time, money and other resources.

Select Comfort is an example of a company that has selected a target market segment, developed a compelling value proposition, built an effective business model, and done it in a way that results in an exciting profit model. SCSS's target market is middle and upper-market consumers suffering from back pain and/or having a sleeping partner that has different preferences in terms of mattress firmness. The product is a sophisticated, high-quality air mattress encased in comfort-enhancing materials with a firmness adjusting mechanism that permits dual adjustability whenever the consumers desire it. If the man prefers a very firm mattress, and the woman a much softer one, both can enjoy their preferences simultaneously. The company's availability strategy includes company-owned direct response, catalogue, internet, and more than 400 stores, which contain only demonstration beds, no back-up inventory. The company increases availability by also offering the product to other selected up-scale retailers. Consumers place their order through one of these distribution channels, and pay for the bed using cash or third-party credit. The company receives payment for the order before it begins production. Orders are transmitted daily to one of the companies manufacturing plants, where just-in-time inventory methods are used to minimize inventory investment. Orders are shipped to the customer using the company-owned hub and spoke distribution system and installed in the customer's home by company delivery personnel. This results in an after-tax profit margin of around 7 percent, an asset turnover of 3x, and a resulting after-tax return-on-assets of around 20 percent. SCSS has created a business and engineered a profit model that makes it a top-tier company in terms of profitability. And, it solves real consumer problems in a unique and differentiated way.

ARCHITECTING COMPETITIVE ADVANTAGE

Another consideration in formulating an effective business strategy is whether the value proposition that satisfies the needs, wants, problems, preferences and expectations of customers in the target market segment will do so in a way that not only enables the company to differentiate itself from competition, but also creates a competitive advantage over competitors, at least for some reasonable period of time. To accomplish this, the value proposition must appeal to the NWPPE of customers in the target market so well, and so strong, that competitors can retaliate only over an extended time period and/or at a prohibitive cost.

Types of Competitive Advantages. Combining target market selection and value proposition with the cost structure of the business relative to competition yields two basic approaches to achieving a competitive advantage:[51]

- *Cost leadership.* Products can be produced and marketed at a lower cost per unit than competitor's products. With this advantage, it is possible to under-price competitors and sell more than they do; or match competitors' prices and attain higher operating margins than they can.
- *Value proposition leadership.* Products are capable of commanding a price premium relative to competitors because of certain benefits they are perceived to have. With this advantage, it is possible to match competitor's prices and sell more than they do, or charge a price premium and attain higher operating margins than they can.

Companies that have been consistently successful over a long period tend to be those that have pursued value proposition leadership rather than cost leadership. They tend to be those companies that have pursued differentiation through quality, branding and innovation. Relatively few of these successes are companies that have competed primarily on the basis of cost leadership.[52]

This historic pattern may be changing. Another study found that the difference between the high-growth companies and their less successful competitors was *value innovation* . . . the simultaneous pursuit of radically superior value for customers and lower costs.[53] In other words; the most successful companies excelled at value proposition leadership and cost leadership.

Engineering a Competitive Advantage. The objective is to select a target market segment, develop a value proposition that is viewed by customers in the segment as superior to the propositions offered by competitors, and then craft a business model that delivers the proposition with a capital and cost structure that is superior to, or at least at parity with, competitors. There are many ways of creating a competitive advantage; Figure 6.8 presents an illustrative list of options. This list can be used to select the right combination of options that will create an advantaged position in the specific situation that a business faces.

Sustaining a Competitive Advantage. In constructing a competitive advantage, it is desirable to do it in a way that is sustainable over a long period of time. This is the "holy grail" of business strategy; a goal that is rarely reached, but worthy of pursuit nonetheless. Figure 6.9 presents some illustrative techniques that are useful in extending the life of competitive advantage techniques.

Figure 6.8 Illustrative ways of achieving competitive advantage*

Achieving a superior benefit value proposition by:	Achieving a superior cost value proposition by:
1. Better features/functionality	1. Low-cost location
2. Better quality	2. Low-cost raw materials
3. Superior design	3. Low-cost labor
4. Product customization	4. Access to more and/or cheaper capital
5. More favorable credit terms	5. Preferred access to supplies
6. Faster delivery	6. Better productivity management
7. Better/longer warranty	7. More efficient process technology
8. More liberal exchange/return policies	8. Better time management
9. Lower price	9. Economies of scale
10. Better discounts	10. Economies of scope
11. More liberal rebates	11. Larger installed base
12. Better / longer dating	12. Superior ability to manage critical processes
13. More advantageous/convenient financing	13. Superior information management
14. Referred services related to the sale	14. Patents
15. Better customer services	15. Proprietary technology
16. Transaction convenience	16. Cross-subsidization of global markets
17. Better shopping/purchasing environment/atmosphere	17. Controlled distribution
18. Stronger brand image	
19. Superior post-purchase experience	
20. Patents	
21. Superior technology	* Some of these options were adopted from Philippe Lassere, *Global*
22. Controlled distribution network	*Strategic Management.* (NY: Palgrove MacMillan, 2003), p. 47; and G.S.
23. More frequent product cycles	Yip, *Total Global Strategy: Managing for Worldwide Competitive*
24. Faster product development	*Advantage.* (Englewood Cliffs, NJ: Prentice Hall, 1995)
25. Superior market intelligence	

Figure 6.9 Illustrative techniques for sustaining competitive advantage*

1. Very strong brand name

2. Customers have formidable switching costs in time, money, or both

3. Having multiple brands in a product category

4. Creating multiple retail formats in a product category

5. Forms of vertical integration that prevent competitors from using key distribution channels

6. Charging a price significantly low to discourage new competitors

7. Reducing price to a point that drives competitors out of the market

8. Patents and copyrights

9. Controlled preferred access to key or scarce resources or processes

10. Large volume requirements to achieve economies of scale

11. More frequent product cycles

12. Faster and/or better product development

13. Superior understanding of the customer

14. Better understanding of, and adjustment to, customer market trends

15. Speed-to-market

* Some of these techniques were adapted from David Besanko, David Dranove, Mark Shanley and Scott Schaefer, *Economies of Strategy*. 3rd Edition (NY: John Wiley & Sons, Inc., 2001), pp 310-318 & p. 449; and Garth Saloner, Andrea Shepard and Joel Podolny, *Strategic Management*. (NY: John Wiley & Sons, Inc., 2001), pp 232-238

In a specific business situation, techniques that have all of the following characteristics, are most likely to generate a sustained competitive advantage . . . *valuable, rare, and costly to imitate*. The technique must be valuable in exploiting competitive opportunities, or neutralizing environmental threats. If a technique is valuable, but not rare, exploiting it will only generate competitive parity, but failure to exploit it may put a company at a competitive disadvantage. If a technique is valuable and rare, but not costly to imitate, adopting it will generate only a temporary competitive advantage. So, techniques that are valuable, rare and costly to imitate are most likely to create sustainable competitive advantage.[54]

Two of the most significant competitive advantages that Harley-Davidson has is its owned distribution network and its strong, lifestyle image that approximates a cult. These would appear to be sustainable over a reasonable time period. Apple, through its iTunes, sleek iPod and iPhone, and hip image has created a competitive advantage that is probably sustainable unless and until a displacing new technology by a new brand that becomes even hipper than Apple emerges. Improbable as this may seem, it was not too many years ago that Sony dominated this space with its Walkman. McDonalds has invented a new coffee that allegedly is better tasting than Starbucks, but even if the product is technically superior, the differentiated experience and image that Starbucks has created may insulate them from serious market share erosion, at least for awhile.

Reinventing Competitive Advantage.   These examples of competitive advantages that have a high probability of being sustainable are rare, so **the** prudent planning assumption is: "whatever competitive advantage you have, some competitor will eventually take it from you." As discussed above, even Dell's primary competitive advantage—direct distribution to the consumer and selling at lower prices—has been minimized by competitors like HP who have found their own efficiencies so that they can compete on price. Moreover, it is probably wise to assume that the erosion of advantage will occur sooner rather than later. Consequently, it is critically important to continually reinvent competitive advantage, which means having the "next techniques" identified, tested, and ready to go when the need arises.

PRODUCT/MARKET SCOPE

The final component of the business strategy addresses the range of products and/or services the business will provide, and the markets that it will offer them to. While the mission statement addresses the business the company or operating division is in, or is going to be in, the product/market scope details the specific products, specific services, and for each product and service, the specific target market segments and geographic markets, including international markets, that the company is, or will be concerned with. For new businesses, the question is pivotal, and, for existing businesses, whether changes should be made, and, if so, what changes, are equally consequential.

To illustrate, consider NVR. This company sells and constructs single family detached homes, town homes, and condominium buildings under three brand names: Ryan Homes, NV Homes and Fox Ridge Homes. Unlike its major competitors, NVR is not a land developer. Instead they acquire finished building lots at market prices under fixed price purchase agreements. This lot acquisition strategy reduces the financial requirements and risk associated with direct land ownership, and allows NVR to focus on its primary strength: the efficient construction and sale of quality homes. NVR also provides a number of mortgage-related services to its customers, and then sells all of the mortgage loans it closes into a secondary market thereby reducing both capital requirements and risk of default. NVR focuses on increasing market share in existing markets thereby leveraging existing management talent and business relationships. This business strategy has helped NVR become one of the fastest-growing, most-profitable companies in America during the ten years preceding the bursting of the housing bubble in 2007, and, its land acquisition and mortgage loan sell-off strategies enabled it to weather the downturn better than many other companies.

AutoZone provides a different kind of example of a compelling business strategy and product/market scope. AutoZone's primary target market is the "do-it-yourself" automotive customer, a nearly $40 billion market that is growing in excess of 4 percent annually. AutoZone observed that this market opportunity was being poorly served by small independent specialty stores, automotive stores, discount department stores, Sears, Penney's, and others. They put together a broad assortment of products for the target do-it-yourself customer and created a store and business structure that resulted in an operating expense structure many points below competitors, and allowed them to offer lower prices which stimulated sales, which was turned into additional economies of scale. The company has over 3600 retail stores in the U.S. staffed with trained employees, many of whom have achieved the Automotive Service Excellence certification. They have introduced a number of proprietary brands to differentiate themselves and improve gross margins. They are currently expanding into Mexico and currently have more than 100 stores in that country.

THE BUSINESS STRATEGY AGENDA

So far, a business strategy consists of a vision, mission, and values; objectives, particularly EPS growth and profitability objectives, and then the approach to implementing the mission and achieving the objectives . . . selecting the target market segment, developing the value proposition, crafting the business model, architecting the profit model, developing a competitive advantage that is sustainable over a reasonable time horizon, and specifying the product/market scope for the business.

These components provide the framework for developing a strategy for a new business. For existing single-unit businesses, and operating divisions of multi-division companies, each of these components need to be re-evaluated continuously to make certain that they are appropriate for the environmental and competitive conditions that are expected to exist in the future.

The relentless re-evaluation of the business strategies of existing businesses is something that is not done as frequently as needed, or as thoughtfully and intensely as it should be. Rather, it is too often assumed that the current strategy is appropriate for the future when, in fact, the environmental and/or competitive conditions that made the strategy appropriate have changed in meaningful ways. Eventually results deteriorate, and often continue to erode until ever-so-gradually the need for strategic change is recognized. Smart executives anticipate these changing conditions, react before competitors, and reap the rewards.

CHAPTER 7

BUSINESS STRATEGIC GAPS & DISCRETIONARY FINANCIAL RESOURCES

"The two most important rules in business are:

'Don't lose your health'
'Do not run out of cash'"

David T. Kollat

As Figure 7.1 indicates, the next step in developing or revising a business strategy for a single-unit business, or an operating division within a multi-division enterprise, is to identify and measure strategic gaps and discretionary financial resources. Strategic gaps identify the challenges . . . primarily sales and profit shortfalls . . . that must be satisfied in achieving business objectives, while the discretionary financial resources measure the approximate amount of money that will be available to close the gaps and achieve the objectives.

STRATEGIC GAPS

Strategic gaps measure the difference between levels of performance specified in the enterprise objectives (see Chapter 5), and the levels attainable through the continuation and improvement of current operations. Since there are generally multiple objectives, there are usually multiple gaps.

SALES GAPS

Figure 7.2 depicts a strategic sales gap. Figure 7.2(A) illustrates an original sales gap for a hypothetical company. The objective is to achieve a 15 percent compound

Figure 7.1 Identifying business strategic gaps & discretionary financial resources

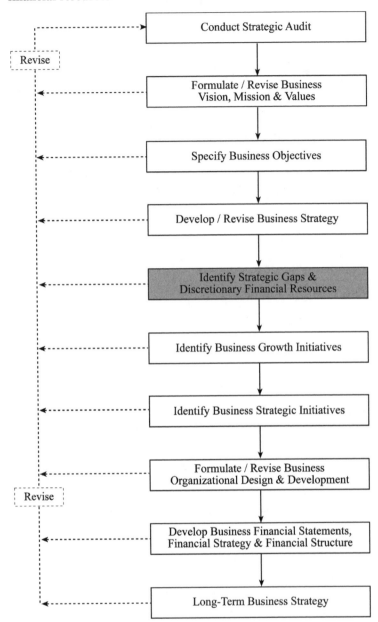

annual growth rate in sales over a five year period. For our company, this means increasing sales from $100 million to $200 million. The original forecast predicts the company's future sales performance based on a continuation of current strategies and tactics, at about 7.5 percent per year. The difference between the sales objective and the original forecast is the original sales gap, which by the end of the fifth year amounts to $57 million in volume.

Figure 7.2 Strategic Gaps

| | (A) Original Sales Gap | | | | | | (B) Revised Sales Gap | | | | | |
| | Year | | | | | | | Year | | | | |
	Base	1	2	3	4	5	Base	1	2	3	4	5
Sales Objective	$100	115	132	152	175	200	$100	115	132	152	175	200
Original Forecast	100	107	115	124	133	143						
Original Sales Gap	$0	8	17	28	42	57						
Revised Forecast							100	109	119	130	141	154
Revised Sales Gap							$0	6	13	22	34	46

Sales Gap Summary

| | Year | | | | | |
	Base	1	2	3	4	5
Execution Gap	$0	2	4	6	8	11
Strategic Gap	0	6	13	22	34	46
Total Sales Gap	0	8	17	28	42	57

Figure 7.2(B) depicts the revised sales gap. A new forecast projects the level of performance that the company can attain if it makes progress in correcting its weaknesses, capitalizing as appropriate on its strengths, and taking other corrective action growing out of its "benchmarking" and "best practices" analyses conducted during the strategic audit phase of the strategy process. (see Chapter 3). The difference between the original and the revised forecast is termed the *execution gap,* or the amount of the total sales gap that will be closed by improving productivity, effectiveness, and efficiency. These issues will be discussed in Chapter 9. The difference between the revised forecast and objective is the *strategic gap* that needs to be closed by growth options, which discussed in the next chapter. For our illustrative company, the strategic gap grows to $46 million by the end of the fifth year. Stated differently, senior executives know that they need to develop or acquire a business that will contribute $46 million in volume by the end of year five. They also know that they need to execute productivity, effectiveness and efficiency initiatives that will boost sales in year 5 by $11million.

In some instances there will not be an original gap. This may suggest the need for an upward revision in objectives. Unless a business is stretching, associates are more likely to lose their vitality and edge, and shareholders' are less likely to be rewarded to the degree that they should be. On the other hand, gaps may be too large, and management may decide to revise objectives downward.

ADDITIONAL GAPS

Since most companies have several objectives, multiple gaps exist. The same process outlined in Figure 7.2 should be repeated for each objective. As Chapter 5 discussed, this would usually include, at a minimum, earnings-per-share objectives and gaps, as well as objectives and gaps for the major profitability metrics used in the business . . . operating income, pre-tax income, after-tax income, after-tax profit margins, asset turnover, after-tax return on equity, cash flow, cash flow return on assets, and so on. Additional objectives can be "gapped" in the same manner. As appropriate, each gap can be subdivided into its execution and strategic components.

SCOPING

It is also useful to scope the business out over an extended time horizon beyond the current one. This extended time horizon is referred to as T3. T3 will vary depending on the industry and business, but 10 or more years may be useful. Scoping should usually be confined to sales and EPS objectives, although others may also be useful in some situations. By measuring sales and earnings gaps out over T3 and dividing them into their execution and strategic components, the CEO and his senior executives can gain a much more comprehensive and rich understanding of the strategic challenges the company faces. This, in turn, will add an additional perspective to the immediate challenges. It may also allow the business to achieve higher long-term EPS growth rates than would otherwise be possible.

DISCRETIONARY FINANCIAL RESOURCES

The next step is to determine the financial resources available to the business for closing strategic gaps. The resources available for growth and expansion can be estimated by use of the revised forecast described above. The primary determinants are the net cash flow and the equity base available for acquisition activity, if the latter is a consideration.

From this financial pool the amount required to close the execution gap is subtracted. This includes all expenses required for all initiatives involved. The remainder is the initial amount available for developing and implementing growth initiatives. Next, the capital expenditure requirements for both execution and strategic initiatives should be determined. This amount may need to be revised if the new initiatives involve acquisitions, because the acquired company may have cash and/or unused debt capacity.

Execution and strategic gaps are examined in relation to the available financial resources. If the pool of financial resources is not adequate, and/or if the cost and investment involved in the initiatives threaten the financial stability of the business, the objectives may again be revised downward. If the resources are available, the process moves to the next phase.

For businesses that are part of a larger organization, the process is different. In these cases, the issues are whether the business is making the required operating income contribution to the parent, the return-on-investment of the operating division, the profitability of all of the initiatives in absolute terms and relative to the profitability of initiatives from other divisions, the amount of capital the parent has, how much capital the parent wants to invest in the business in question, and a variety of other factors. Answers to these types of issues will determine whether the process moves forward or other directions are taken, including lowering certain objectives.

THE STRATEGIC GAP AND FINANCIAL RESOURCES AGENDA

The "output" from this phase in the process is quantitative measures of the gaps that the company faces in achieving its objectives over the planning period . . . primarily operating income, earnings-per-share, and profitability goals. The second output is a quantitative measure of how much money the company has, or can obtain, to close these gaps.

With this information, executives are prepared to proceed to identify, evaluate, and select growth and strategic initiatives to close these gaps and achieve the business objectives.

Chapter 8

Business Growth Initiatives

"The real discipline comes in saying no to the wrong opportunities."

Peter Drucker

The next step in developing a long-term business strategy for a single-unit business or an operating division within a multi-unit enterprise is to identify, evaluate and ultimately select growth initiatives that will close the strategic gaps within the limitations imposed by the discretionary financial resources and thereby enable the business to achieve its objectives. (Figure 8.1) This chapter presents techniques for identifying growth options, and then describes a template for evaluating the growth options that have been generated.

Identifying Business Growth Options

Figure 8.2 presents a framework that can be used to generate a list of growth options.[55] The objective at this point is to identify growth options, not to evaluate or select them. Better results are obtained when the process is separated into at least these three phases.

Strategies 1–4 are generally less risky than strategies 5–8, which in turn, are usually less risky than strategies 9 and 10. Several studies indicate that as a company expands from its "core" the risk increases and the chances of success decrease.[56] For these reasons, it may be wise to exhaust thinking in the first four strategic growth options, and option 11, before exploring the others.

Figure 8.1 Identifying business growth initiatives

```
┌──────────────────────────────────┐
│      Conduct Strategic Audit     │◄┄┄┄┄┐
└──────────────────────────────────┘     ┆
                 │                         ┆
  ┌ ─ ─ ┐        ▼                         ┆
  ┆Revise┆ ┌──────────────────────────┐   ┆
  └ ─ ─ ┘ │  Formulate / Revise Business │◄┄┄┄┤
  ◄┄┄┄┄┄┄ │   Vision, Mission & Values    │   ┆
          └──────────────────────────┘   ┆
                 │                         ┆
                 ▼                         ┆
  ◄┄┄┄┄┄┄ ┌──────────────────────────┐   ┆
          │  Specify Business Objectives │◄┄┄┄┤
          └──────────────────────────┘   ┆
```

Conduct Strategic Audit

Revise

Formulate / Revise Business Vision, Mission & Values

Specify Business Objectives

Develop / Revise Business Strategy

Identify Strategic Gaps & Discretionary Financial Resources

Identify Business Growth Initiatives

Identify Business Strategic Initiatives

Formulate / Revise Business Organizational Design & Development

Revise

Develop Business Financial Statements, Financial Strategy & Financial Structure

Long-Term Business Strategy

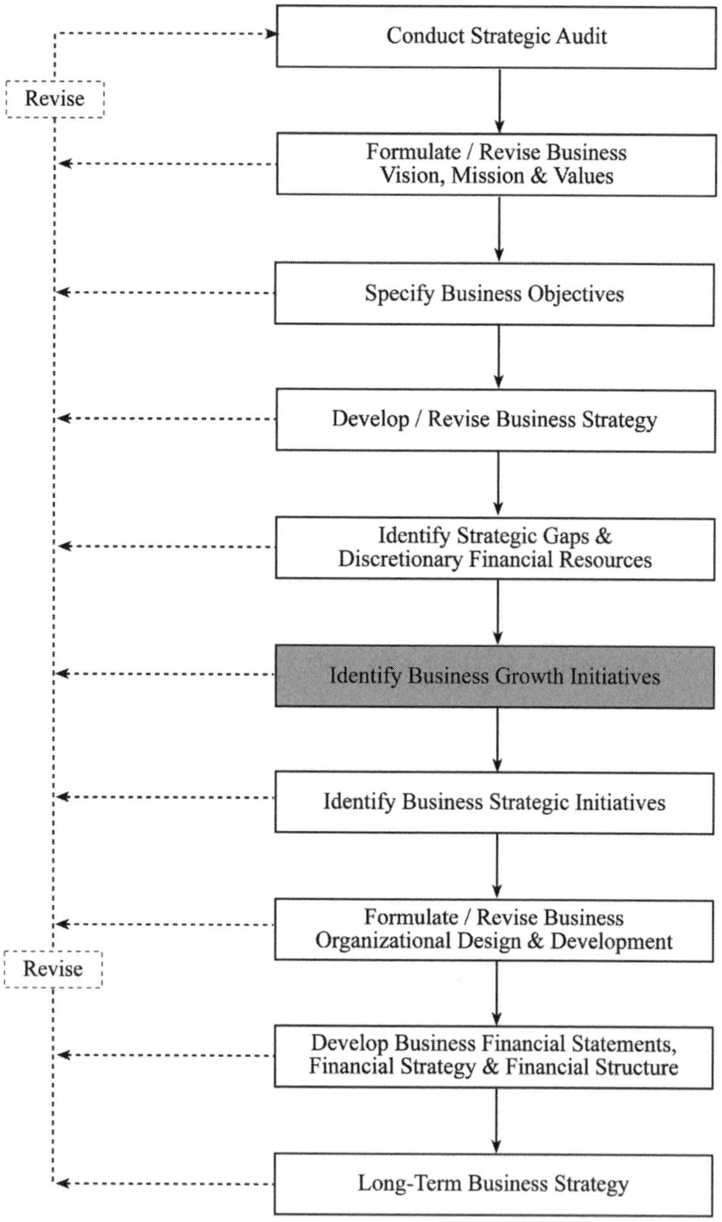

MARKET PENETRATION STRATEGIES

This strategy attempts to improve the company's position with its present products in its current markets. This can be achieved by improving the efficiency and/or effectiveness of any functional area of the business, and/or the supply chain. Some of these techniques have been discussed and included in closing what was termed the *execution gap* in Chapter 7. Some other techniques and examples that can be used are:

Figure 8.2 Growth initiative options

Products / Markets	Present Products	Improvements in Present Products	New Products with Related Technology		New Products with Unrelated Technology
			Assortment Manipulation	Expansion of the Variety in the Product Line	
Consumer and/or Business Markets · Same Markets	(1) Market penetration strategies	(3) Reformulation strategies	(5) Replacement strategies	(7) Product-line extension strategies	(9) Horizontal diversification strategies
New Markets	(2) Market development strategies	(4) Market extension strategies	(6) Market segmentation/ product differentiation strategies	(8) Concentric diversification strategies	(10) Conglomerate diversification strategies
Supply Chain	(11) Forward and/or backward integration strategies				

- Bill Ruprecht, the CEO of upscale auction house Sotheby's, has been pursuing a number of strategies to try to re-energize the company following the high-profile collusion scandal that plagued the company for several years. Among other things, he has refocused the company toward high end items, and eliminated the low end. Sotheby's no longer targets run-of-the mill stamps or coins or everyday furnishings. It will still auction a set of china, for example, but only as part of a larger collection. The average lot sale has increased by 50 percent and net earnings have grown by 39 percent.[57]

- Peter van Stolk started his business in 1987 by selling freshly squeezed juice on street corners. In 2000 he moved his company to Seattle and changed the name to Jones Soda. Their flavored drinks, such as Blue Bubblegum, Green Apple, and Bada Bing! were a big hit with skateboarders, surfers and tattoo artist in the late 1990's. But in 1998 the company lost $1.5 million on sales of $4.7 million, and these loses continued through 2002. Jones was spending 40 per cent of sales on advertising and distributor incentives. Then three of his largest distributors went bankrupt and competitors quickly took the empty shelf space. Fortunately, the company changed its supply chain and now sells 22 per cent of its beverages directly to retailers, including Starbucks, Target, Panera Bread and Barnes & Noble. Today Jones is profitable, and growth has accelerated, despite the fact that Starbucks eventually decided to eliminate sodas from their display counter so they could have more room to display sandwiches.[58]

- In 1994 Robert Kraft purchased the New England Patriots, a team that had won less than half of its games since it's founding in 1959. He paid $172 million, a substantial sum, particularly for a team of that caliber. Kraft launched a bold campaign that promised to bring a championship to New England. In 1999 he promoted Bill Belichich to head coach despite the fact he had never been one. With a strict "non superstars" policy in place, the two men built a team filled with unsung players like Tom Brady, a sixth round draft choice and wide receiver Tony Brown, an eighth rough pick. Belichick compiled a database of stats for every position in the NFL going back 25 years, and then put together procedural manuals covering all phases of the season. In 2001 the team won their first Super Bowl and Kraft build a new stadium that was much more profitable than the old one because of its suites and club seats. The Pats were Super Bowl champs again in 2003 and 2004. Kraft turned the Patriots into one of sports' richest franchises.[59]

MARKET DEVELOPMENT STRATEGIES

Another way to generate growth options is to think of new types of customers that can use the company's present products. This can include different segments of customers or consumers, and/or geographic markets in which the company does not compete currently. Some examples are:

- Nokia is one of the most innovative companies in the world, according to its peers. The company's growth strategies include expansion into the emerging countries, including India and China. In order to understand how to make low cost phones for markets with an above-average proportion of illiterate people, Nokia engaged in a combination of basic ethnographic and long-term user research. As a result, they designed phones that were more durable and moisture-resistant and allow users to navigate contact lists made up of images.[60]
- As the market for office superstores that fueled Staples' rapid growth is maturing, the company is looking elsewhere to continue its earnings momentum. One strategy is to deliver office supplies from their warehouses directly to businesses, including mid-sized companies and large corporations.[61]
- The first thing Arte Moreno did in May 2003 when he bought the World Series-winning, money-losing Angels was to try to enlarge the fan

base. He lowered ticket prices, slashed the price of beer and concessions, and offered better customer service in order to stimulate fan activity and generate enough revenue to offset lower margins. With a larger market segment, he believes he can increase operating revenue from concessions, parking, stadium advertising and luxury box sales, and then eventually capture a larger share of the advertising market in Los Angeles.[62]

REFORMULATION/REPOSITIONING STRATEGIES

Another technique for generating growth options is to focus on improving present products so that a business can increase sales of those products to current customers. This is one of the most widely used strategies because of the lower risk and higher return-on-investment that is commonly involved in this approach. Some examples include:

- For years after its founding in 1965 Subway was a dependable, yet bland chain of sandwich shops. In 2000, Subway was approached by Jared Fogle, a customer who had managed to lose nearly 250 pounds by eating exclusively at Subway restaurants. Eventually Subway decided to focus its marketing on seven of its subs as having six grams or less of fat . . . and tasted good too.[63]

- Cirque de Soliel is the acrobatic troupe that has built a $600 million business combining daredevil stunts with leading edge technology and a devoted public that will pay up to $195 to see one of its shows. The troupe has five touring productions and five more in residence in Las Vegas and Orlando. The founder, Guy Laliberte, continually develops fresh new shows, each better than the last. Their partner and financier, MGM Mirage, spends substantial sums of money to keep the shows coming in order to keep their theaters and casinos filled.[64]

MARKET EXTENSION STRATEGIES

Another way to generate growth option ideas is to focus on ways to reach new classes of customers by modifying the company's present products. Some examples of this technique are:

- Dunkin' Donuts has a large presence in the northeast and mid-Atlantic regions, but the rest of the U.S. is almost untouched. As a result the company has launched an aggressive expansion with plans to triple the number of locations to 15,000 over the next decade. In addition, they are expanding the menu focusing on the immense coffee market with their version of an Americanized expresso and Turbo Ice-iced coffee with a shot of espresso.[65]

- Old Spice has inched by Right Guard to become the leading deodorant and anti-perspirant for men, with 20% of the $1billion market. When Proctor & Gamble purchased the brand in 1990, it was mostly known for its graying customer base. P&G refocused the brand on performance, launching Old Spice High Endurance deodorant in 1994. It was targeted to men 18 to 34, but struggled because men remembered dad's Old Spice. To reach a younger demographic, they handed out samples to fifth-grade health classes and distributed additional samples to junior high schools. In 2000, P&G launched Old Spice Red Zone, offering more protection, but priced 25 per cent higher. Grassroots marketing at skateboarding and high-school football events and using video game tie-ins instead of TV ads made Red Zone the top-selling teen brand. P&G also launched Old Spice body sprays and washes and has licensed sales of razors and shaving cream.[66]

- Viacom's MTV continually expands its operations outside the United States. MTV Networks operates 72 international channels which reach over 321 million homes across Europe, Asia, Canada, Australia and Latin America. One of the more difficult markets to tap is India where MTV launched in 1991. India's youth does not appreciate American rock or rap music, or many TV shows like the Osbournes. As a result, MTV created programming hosted by and targeted toward India's youth and their interest in cricket and fashion.[67]

REPLACEMENT STRATEGIES

This technique for generating growth options focuses on replacing current products with new products having better ingredients or formulations. Gillette, for example, consistently and continuously replaces its razor blades every few years with ones that are presumably better, and, parenthetically, more expensive. Similarly, computer manufacturers like Dell, Hewlett Packard, and others continually replace their products with ones that are faster, or have more memory, or are lighter, or better in some other way. Other examples include:

- Back in the 1950's, 80 per cent of the luxury cars sold in the US were Cadillac's. Over time, that market share eroded embarrassingly due to the efforts of BMW, Mercedes, Lexus, and others, *and* GM's own design and marketing mistakes. Younger consumers associate Cadillac with

"Florida retirees". Beginning in 2000 GM began a multi-year, multi-billion dollar program to resurrect the fading brand. Cadillac dropped the stodgy design tradition with stealth-fighter angles and aggressive looking grills. Moreover, GM engineered its new Cadillacs to drive more like sports cars than cruisers, and marketed them with rock'n'roll advertising aimed at younger buyers. A new, highly efficient $540 million plant in Lansing, Michigan was built to produce high-performance cars with quality and reliability.[68]

- The Public Broadcasting Service's average nightly prime-time ratings are down substantially, to about 1.8 million households at any given time. PBS's loyal audience is aging, and the explosion of cable channels is taking its toll. PBS stations have a dilemma: "How to best draw in new viewers while maintaining the quality programming that has been public TV's million." The Chicao affiliate hired a former rock DJ and Fox personality to host its public affairs program, *Chicago Tonight*. The *News Hour with Jim Lehrer* is trying shorter reports and launching an advertising campaign to counter *The O'Reilly Factor*. Public TV has a strong audience in the under-five year old set with programs like *Barney* and *Arthur*, and with the over-50 year old segment, so the key is to reach the large audience in between. PBS's attempts to lure younger viewers could alienate its older audience and dilute its education and service mission. On the other hand, if public support declines with viewership, PBS could slowly starve.[69]

MARKET SEGMENTATION/PRODUCT DIFFERENTIATION STRATEGIES

This method of generating growth options focuses on attracting new customers by expanding the assortments of existing product lines. Some examples:

- In 2003, Proctor and Gamble introduced new "sexy" flavors of its Crest toothpaste. The objective was to reach the Hispanic market and appeal to their spicier palate. The "Crest Whitening Expressions" line features gourmet toothpaste flavors including cinnamon, citrus and herbal mint. To market the new product, P&G obtained the endorsement of celebrity chef Emeril Lagassee and his "kick it up a notch" cooking style. P&G hopes the new product will boost its 29% share of the $1.3 billion toothpaste market closer to the leader, Colgate, and their 34%.[70]
- Autodesk Ltd., a 23 year old software design company has survived by consistently finding new ways to refresh and adapt its core product,

AutoCAD. Autodesk makes the software that companies use to design buildings, bridges, and other structures. It has long dominated architecture and engineering software. Several years ago the company started designing programs for specific industries such as manufacturing, infrastructure, and entertainment. One new software product, for example, allows engineers to mock up 3-D designs, and then automatically draws the images into two dimensions. This allows several people to work on the same design at one time. These new programs for the new industries now account for a nearly 50 percent of sales.[71]

- Once an iconic brand for youth worldwide, Levi Strauss attempted to halt its painful sales decline by going down-market. The company developed a line of discount jeans. The new "Signature Line" for men, women and teens sold for under $25 per pair at Wal-Mart, Target and similar discounters. The price is half as much as the classic Red Tab line of 501 and 505s. Levi's used lower quality denim and materials to keep costs low, limited styles and colors, and stayed away from advertising. But, the risks are substantial including creating a poor quality product that looks and feels too cheap, boring customers with a lack of variety, and turning off full-price 501 and 505 customers.[72]

PRODUCT LINE EXTENSION STRATEGIES

Another way to generate growth options is to use related technology to broaden the line of products offered to present customers. Cereal companies add breakfast bars and nutrition bars; Sony offers TV's, stereos, radios, and a long line of consumer electronics. Other examples include:

- Tamara Mellon borrowed $225,000 from her father and went into business with Jimmy Choo, a Malaysian shoemaker. Sales of Jimmy Choo shoes exploded in the late 1990s when stiletto heels were extraordinarily popular and the brand was featured on the popular TV show *Sex and the City*. Mellon expanded aggressively increasing sales by 50 percent a year by opening retail boutiques and extending the product line into handbags. Now the company is worth nearly $200 million.[73]
- H&R Block is the nation's largest tax preparer with a 20 percent market share of commercially prepared returns filed with the IRS. However, their core tax business has been losing customers to computer based tax preparation software like TurboTax, and the tax preparation business is highly seasonal with all the problems that seasonality presents. In 1999, the new CEO launched a $100 million marketing campaign to promote

Block as a one-stop financial business offering mortgages, IRA's, and various investment products. The strategy is not working as planned. The financial-advisors unit has already lost $330 million, partly because the average Block customer has an adjusted gross income of only $42,000. While the mortgage business initially showed promise, it has suffered sharp declines as the Fed increases interest rates. To make matters worse, the company has lost more than one million of its tax customers, apparently because they are tired of waiting two to three hours to be served.[74]

CONCENTRIC DIVERSIFICATION STRATEGIES

This approach to generating growth options thinks about attracting new classes of customers by adding new products that have technological and/or marketing synergies with the existing product line. Some examples:

- Coach has become an extraordinarily successfully company with its line of up-scale purses, bags, and small leather goods. Now it is extending the brand into secondary categories, including jewelry and watches.[75]
- Nucor has long been considered the best operator in the steel business, famous for innovative employee compensation and relations, and new technologies. Historically, the company has grown organically, but recently it has made a series of acquisition that broaden its product line into areas such as steel floors and roof decks, which help its migration to higher-margin products.[76]

HORIZONTAL DIVERSIFICATION STRATEGIES

This technique for generating growth options focuses on broadening the line of products offered to present customers through technology unrelated to the company's present products. Some examples include:

- Faced with intensifying competition from Wal-Mart, Costco, and others, Best Buy acquired Geek Squad, a Minneapolis start-up specializing in repairing and installing PC's. The CEO, Brad Anderson, knew that digital devices and home networks were growing in complexity, and that the technical services market had huge potential. Moreover, he thought that his major competitors would not get into this complex area, so it would provide a sustainable competitive advantage for his core business.[77]

- EBay has spent more that $6 billion to begin evolving from a pure Internet auction house into an e-commerce businesses that sells Web tools to small businesses. Some of the key acquisitions have been internet-phone operator Skype, online payments service PayPal, ticket reseller StubHub, and a series of classified sites including a minority interest in Craigslist and Kurant, whose technology is used to set up online store-fronts separate from eBay.[78]
- Founded in 1949, the Otto Group developed a catalogue business selling clothing to Germans following WW II. With the emergence of the internet, Otto used it to service and enhance their traditional mail-order business. Otto allows customers to order on the net but get a bill in the mail and pay by bank transfer. That encourages online shopping by Germans without credit cards. The site lets women create images of themselves, they try on clothing combinations virtually, thereby increasing sales and reducing costly returns. Otto's multichannel strategy has helped it grow despite the prolonged spending slump in Germany.[79]

Conglomerate Diversification Strategies

This method of generating growth options focuses on attracting new classes of customers by diversifying into products that have no relationship to the company's current technology, products, or markets. Generally, this is the most risky type of strategy and should therefore be pursued with extreme caution. Some examples include:

- Berkshire Hathaway is one of the most admired companies in America. From one perspective, the company is a large, highly diversified, multi-division business. However, from another point of view, it is a very small company run by Warren Buffet and his long-time fellow billionaire, Charles Munger. Since Berkshire purchased National Indemnity in 1967, property casualty insurance has been the company's core business and the propellant of its growth. The insurance "float" has provided enormous funds that Buffet and Munger have used to acquire the securities and businesses that now comprise the portfolio. Berkshire is theoretically paid for holding other people's money, which is why Buffet considers float "better than free." Buffet and Munger have used these float funds to acquire business that raise the intrinsic value of Berkshire stock. Berkshire looks for companies with strong market position, significant momentum and terrific managers. Today BH owns 68 very distinct businesses . . . including candy, desert/treat, jewelry, and furniture retailers, recreational vehicle, modular home, carpet, and apparel manufacturers . . . and continues to grow. In addition to these businesses, the company also makes sizable investments in common stock to acquire minority positions in companies like American Express, Coca-Cola, P&G and Wells Fargo, with total holdings in these stocks of around $50 billion. BH also holds money in bonds, cash, and foreign currency.[80]

- Since going public in 1982, Starbucks has grown from 165 coffee shops to more than 13,000. They continually add new products and services to attract new customers to the store as well as encourage existing customers to visit more frequently. For example, the company has tested Chantico, an extraordinarily rich chocolate drink to draw more afternoon customers. Sandwiches, sold at 2200 of the company's stores attract a lunch crowd. Beyond food, Starbucks sells compilation CD's by artists like Tony Bennett, Ray Charles, Norah Jones, Joss Stone, and others.[81]

INTEGRATION STRATEGIES

This approach to generating growth options focuses on increasing sales, profitability, efficiency, and/or control by moving backward in the system to produce within the company those components which were previously purchased; or forward into additional fabrication, assembly, or distribution functions. In other words, it involves redefining the supply chain and/or supply chain relationships. Some examples:

- In 2004, FedEx acquired Kinko's, giving it an additional 1200 retail locations and a successful retail business, with its own revenue and profit stream.[82]
- Historically, Home Depot has relied on independent plumbers, electricians and handymen to install many of the products purchased in their stores. Recently the company has decided to placed more emphasis on the installation business because it makes customers more likely to buy a big-ticket item; it builds repeat business; and it further aligns the company to contractors, who account for about 30 percent of store sales. Moreover, the professional contractor market is twice the size of the do-it-yourself business, and is characterized in many geographic areas by fragmented and relatively unsophisticated competition.[83]

EVALUATING GROWTH OPTIONS

Having generated a number of growth options that presumably will close strategic gaps and allow the company to achieve its objectives for the planning period, the next step is to evaluate each of these options against a set of evaluative criteria. These criteria will vary from one industry to another, and from company to company depending on the situation that each business is in. Each company should develop its own set of criteria that are appropriate for its situation. Some common criteria are summarized below.

COMPETITIVE ADVANTAGE

One of the most important evaluative criteria is whether the business will have a competitive advantage in pursuing a specific growth option. This analysis should examine the following issues:

- Identify the success requirements for the growth option.
- Specify the existing core competences of the current business, and other companies that are competing in these markets at the present time, and those businesses that are likely to enter this market in the future.
- The business is most likely to have a competitive advantage in those situations where:
  - The success requirements correspond to the company's core competences.
  - Other companies do not have these competences; and
  - Other businesses are not able to attain these competences except at a significant investment and/or over an extended period of time.

The most desirable situation is, of course, when the business would have a competitive advantage, and competitors do not; or the business would have competitive advantages superior to competitors. In those situations where the business does not have a competitive advantage, the option becomes less desirable; and if the company would be unable to develop competitive advantages, the option becomes even less desirable, and perhaps questionable.

STRATEGIC VULNERABILITY

Growth options should also be evaluated on the basis of the longevity of the company's competitive advantage as well as other factors that could be destabilizing like the likelihood of additional competitors, technological obsolesce/vulnerability, demand erosion, and so on.

GROWTH PLATFORM

For many companies, the strategic gaps are large and growing, and it is difficult, if not impossible, to close them through individual growth option initiatives. Consequently, it is important to evaluate each option through a *new platform perspective*. This involves evaluating each growth option in terms of the products, services, or businesses that can be created from it. This enables a company to accelerate time to market and generate additional revenue that can be substantial and meaningful.[84]

SYNERGY

Each growth option should be evaluated in terms of its synergy, or the fit between the option and what the business is already doing. There are several types of synergy. One is *sales synergy*. This can occur when a growth option uses existing distribution channels; and/or a common sales force; and/or existing warehousing; and/or common advertising or sales promotion.

A second type is *operating synergy*. This can result, for example, when the growth option results in higher utilization of facilities and personnel, spreading of overhead, and purchasing economies.

Investment synergy is another important consideration. This can result if the growth option would involve joint use of plant, common raw-materials inventories, carryover of research and development, and/or common tooling and machinery.

Management synergy can be another important consideration in evaluating growth options. If the growth option presents strategic, administrative and/or operating characteristics similar to those management is encountering, or has encountered in the past, it would be in a better position to provide effective leadership.

Growth options are likely to have different synergy characteristics, and it is important to consider them in evaluating the appropriateness and desirability of each alternative.

SCALE AND PRO-FORMA'S

Each growth option needs to be analyzed in terms of its financial scale including sales, gross margin, operating expenses, and investment requirements . . . both working capital and fixed assets . . . and operating income and net profit.

There are two important dimensions of scale that need to be analyzed at this point. One is the "roll-out" potential of the growth option in terms of its sales and profit characteristics when it is fully implemented. The second is most likely pro-forma profit and loss statements by year from date of launch.

This analysis can be used to rank-order the growth options in terms of their sales and profit potential by year following implementation. Obviously, those options that have the highest sales and profit potential, probably deserve preferential consideration. Those options that do not make a meaningful contribution to sales and profit may be eliminated or postponed.

The same two types of analyses should be repeated for the growth platforms represented by each growth option. That is, the roll-out potential of each growth option should be computed, as well as the estimated pro-forma profit and loss statements by year from date of implementation. Those growth options with the highest platform sales and profit potential usually deserve the most attention. Moreover, this analysis may change the desirability of a specific growth option because it may provide the foundation for a more significant total sales and profit opportunity as a result of its superior platform.

PROFITABILITY

Using the pro-forma profit and loss statements mentioned above, incremental pro-forma balance sheets should be constructed for each growth option that has appropriate scale, competitive advantage, synergy, platform potential, and other characteristics that make it appealing. Using these two financial statements, appropriate profitability metrics can be computed like incremental profit as a percent of incremental asset requirements, discounted cash flow, economic value added, and/or whatever other measures the business finds useful. These profitability measures can be used to compare and evaluate growth options and their growth platforms.

SUFFICIENCY AND BALANCE

The process described above can be used to generate a list of most desirable growth options and platforms. The sum of the sales and profits that would result from the implementation of these initiatives should be sufficient to achieve the company's objectives, particularly EPS growth rate targets and return-on investment levels. If they do not, the process of identifying and evaluating growth options and platforms should be continued until they produce a portfolio of growth initiatives that will achieve the objectives, or the objectives should be lowered.

Once the portfolio of growth initiatives has been selected, it should be further evaluated for balance and risk. Is there a reasonable balance of short and long-term initiatives? What type of pressures and incremental work loads will the portfolio place on each function and level in the organization? Is this palatable? Does the management talent exist to implement this portfolio of initiatives, and, if not, what specifically is needed? Are the total capital requirements digestible? Will these initiatives place any of the core business in jeopardy? Is the organization really capable of achieving the suite of options? Is the amount of risk reasonable, and does the risk/reward ratio make sense? These are the types of issues that need to be resolved before proceeding.

THE GROWTH INITIATIVE AGENDA

Using the concepts and processes describe above, the organization should now have a list of growth options and platforms that, if successfully implemented and executed, will allow the business to achieve its objectives, particularly its EPS and return-on-investment targets.

Chapter 9

Business Strategic Initiatives

"It's an ongoing thing, you're constantly learning, and I'm trying to get it to a place where I'll be a little more satisfied. You're never going to learn it all, but I'm trying to get a little closer to some of my original aspirations as a musician. If I get to the point where I can't hold up my end of the bargain and satisfy my audience, then definitely I'll quit. Then I'll just go home and practice in my own room."

Sonny Rollins
Legendary Jazz Saxophonist
Age: 77

The next step in developing a business strategy for a single-unit business, or an operating division in a multi-division enterprise, is to develop strategic initiatives for the planning period. (Figure 9.1). These initiatives focus on strengthening the strategic condition of the enterprise, and increasing its ability to anticipate and react to future opportunities and other developments on the one hand, while simultaneously improving the productivity, profitability, effectiveness, and efficiency of the business in the current time frame.

People in organizations tend to follow established patterns of behavior. But environmental, competitive, and other conditions change, and some of the established patterns become less than optimum. Successful businesses need a rigorous, intensive, relentless, and continuing program of improvement. Every person, and every function and process in the business should be expected to improve every day. This attitude needs to be a core part of the culture.of a company.

This continuous drive for improvement should be viewed not as evil or ruthless, but as a matter of pride and principle. It should be institutionalized, and everyone should be included. Even Michael Jordon went to basketball practice, and, it is said, worked harder than everyone else. After spending his entire life in music and achieving iconic status, at age 77 Sonny Rollins spends every day just trying to get better.

Figure 9.1 Identifying business strategic initiatives

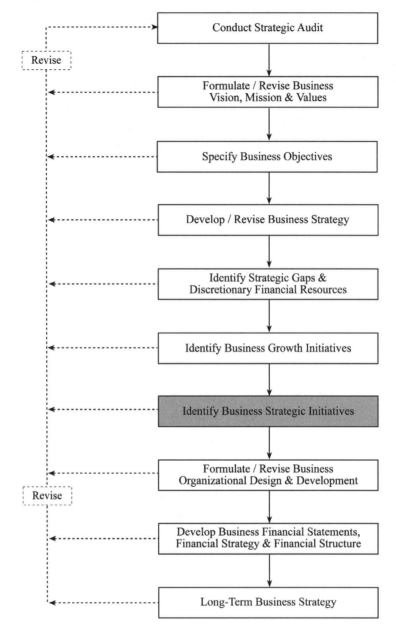

The specific strategic initiatives that a company should have obviously depend on the specific situation that it faces. However, as a framework for identifying specific initiatives, the following framework is generally useful:

- Improving gross margin.
- Increasing operating expense leverage.
- Improving balance sheet productivity.

- Strengthening competitive advantage.
- Developing infrastructure and capabilities.

GROSS MARGIN ENHANCEMENT

This category of strategic initiatives focuses on increasing the product margin, gross margin, and gross profit of the business. By improvement, here we are speaking about increasing the margin rate, as opposed to margin dollars, which are equally or more important but have been discussed in the preceding chapter.

One avenue is to focus on initiatives to increase prices. This might involve unit price increases, and/or programs designed to increase the units per transaction, and/or programs to change the units in the transaction. It could also include increasing the size of the unit sold, or conversely, decreasing the contents per unit sold. Several operating divisions of General Mills, for example, recently reduced the size of their cereal boxes in response to raw material price increases.

A second avenue to gross margin enhancement is to reduce the cost of goods sold. This might include initiatives designed to change the mix of manufactured to out-sourced sourcing, and/or reduce the number of manufacturing or sourcing points in order to increase the volume at the remaining ones, and/or changing the bill of materials content, and/or changing the manufacturing process, and/or pressing vendors for lower component costs, and/or a long list of supply chain economies in procurement, warehousing, and distribution.

The third avenue to improving gross margins is initiatives designed to change the mix of products sold by placing more emphasis on those with relatively higher margins. For example, in recent years Kellogg's has shifted resources to higher margin products like Special K, Kashi and Nutri Grain bars, as opposed to focusing on the low margin brands like Frosted Flakes. Similarly, Wolverine World Wide has engineered substantial gross margin improvement in recent years by placing strategic resources behind higher margin shoes, particularly its Merrell brand of athletic footwear.

IMPROVING OPERATING EXPENSE LEVERAGE

A second category of strategic initiatives should focus on reducing operating expenses as a percent of sales. For most businesses, there are economies of scale, scope, and focus. Economies of scale exist if a company's unit costs decrease as the level of output increases. Economies of scope exist if a business is able to achieve savings as it broadens the variety of goods and services it produces or handles.

Economies of focus is the opposite of scope, resulting from the contraction of goods and services; e.g., a warehouse handling only one product should be more efficient than one handling many products if the volume is the same or similar. Economies of scale and scope can occur at any point in the supply chain from acquisition of the most basic raw materials through processing, and then through distribution channels to the ultimate customer. It is rare for economies not to exist.[85]

In most instances there are economies of scale and scope, but for a variety of reasons managers and executives are unable or unwilling to recognize them. Instead, sales and unit volume continue to increase, but operating costs remain constant as a percent of sales or sometimes even increase. Economies of scale and scope exist in economics textbooks, but often not in real business situations unless *management makes it happen.*

Economies of scale and scope often have to be forced, in fact extracted, from a business because human beings, left to their own devices, are unable and/or unwilling to do what it takes to achieve them. One useful way to do this is through a collaborative effort with senior management that establishes a target rate of cost leverage for the business. For example, it might be that total costs can only increase at 50 percent of the rate of the sales increase. Or, it could be 30, or 20, or 70 percent, or some other number. The point is to pick a reasonable number and, in effect, say: "that is all the money there is." This, in effect, mandates cost leverage.

The ideal expense rate leverage is one that, when combined with margin enhancement, allows a business to increase net profit after taxes at a rate substantially faster than sales increases, while simultaneously funding growth and strategic initiatives. While this is difficult, and will be challenged by nearly everyone as unrealistic, the fact is that it needs to happen, and well-managed companies make it happen.

Having identified the ideal expense leverage, the next challenge is to analyze each individual cost of goods sold line item, and each individual operating expense line item, and decide how each should behave relative to volume increases, keeping in mind the growth and strategic initiatives for the time period in question. Some items are, of course, fixed, and should not increase as sales grow. Other items will increase, but not as fast as sales grow. Still other items may have operating expense rate increases because they are necessary to achieve growth and strategic initiatives.

This type of analysis may result in the conclusion that a business can not achieve the ideal expense leverage. The reaction to this should be: "go back and rethink the whole process." People can be extraordinarily stubborn about this issue. Only after repeated and exhaustive attempts should the target leverage be lowered.

In terms of personnel costs, in addition to the obvious tactic of reducing the number of people, or changing the type of people, additional expense leverage can be achieved by changing their work. This includes "things to stop doing," or "doing things with different frequencies." For managers it is often useful to have *activity and time budgets* that can be edited and monitored to increase efficiency.

Achieving operating expense leverage can be also be achieved by designing completely new ways of performing various functions. The quest for these types of operational improvements should be intense and continuous, and nothing should be exempted from this scrutiny. Some methods that can be used to achieve these types of economies include:[86]

- Benchmarking competitors to find out who does it best, and how they do it.
- "Best in class" thinking to find out who does it best regardless of the industry they are in, and how they do it.
- Identify *a* or *the* constraining assumption, step, process, etc. Then figure out how to get rid of it, or make it present less of the time.
- Think about the behavior and processes that would be used in a crisis situation. Then ask: "why can't these be used everyday?" Or, modified to be used every day?
- Rethink the dimensions of every function, process and line item in the budget. For each ask: "Are the results that are produced really necessary?" "Can they be produced less frequently?" "Can someone else perform them better and/or more efficiently?"

There are a variety of other techniques that can be used to achieve expense leverage. For example:[87]

- Is it possible to change the timing of any costs that are incurred?
- Continually asking: "Do we really need to do this?"
- Is there any new technology that would improve productivity for the functions and processes that we use?
- Can any internal control processes be automated?
- Can we replace things, reduce things, redesign things, and/or redistribute things to increase productivity?

Businesses, like people, develop cholesterol, and every year more accumulates. The proof is that whenever a business confronts a life-threatening, or even a serious, crisis, management is able to take 10 to 20 percent or more out of the expense structure. So, the expense leverage is always there. There needs to be a continuous program of strategic initiatives designed to achieve operating expense leverage.

INCREASING BALANCE SHEET PRODUCTIVITY

The third category of strategic initiatives focus on increasing the productivity of current and fixed asset investments, as well as improving the relationship between current assets and liabilities, so that the asset turnover of the business improves. (sales/average assets) This results when asset investment generates more sales, or, conversely, when it takes less assets to generate a given level of sales. Historically, executives have focused primarily on managing the profit and loss statement, and have paid much less attention to the balance sheet. Improved balance sheet management is a powerful avenue to increased profitability and cash flow.

Improved inventory management is generally the most significant avenue to increased asset turnover. Over time there seems to be an almost natural tendency for inventories to become "bloated" as a business strives for ever-increasing sales, and/or less-than-optimum inventory selection results in ever-diminishing inventory productivity. On-going programs to reduce or eliminate inventory by deleting slow sellers, editing out the slowest sellers, collapsing categories, classifications, and SKU's , and so on will usually produce positive results. These programs are difficult to initiate, and even more difficult to sustain, because executives resist inventory rationalization initiatives. Nevertheless, well-run companies have initiatives in place that enable the business to equal or exceed industry standards for inventory turnover, and thereby substantially improve cash flow.

The second most powerful avenue to increased asset turnover is generally better accounts receivable management. Like inventories, receivables also tend to "bulge" unnecessarily as a business expands, and/or when it faces difficult sales challenges. No one wants to lose a customer, and/or lose an order, so various customer accommodations are made that cause receivables to become larger than they should be. Initiatives designed to achieve a "day's sales outstanding" level that is in line with industry standards is an important way of improving cash flow.

A third avenue is to examine "non-performing" or "under-performing" assets. These often hide in the "all other category" of assets, and sometimes account for 30 or more percent of the total asset investment of the business. These should be subjected to intense scrutiny. Are these really necessary? If they are not generating any sales or assets, why do we have them?

Fixed asset investments are another category that can often be rationalized to improve asset turnover. Should all of these assets be owned? What about sale and lease-backs? What about out-sourcing? Manufacturing facilities, warehouses, distribution centers, machinery and equipment all need to be examined periodically to see if alternative financial transactions might improve return-on-investment and/or cash flow.

Some additional potential opportunities to increase balance sheet productivity;[88]

- Can the number of hours assets are used be increased?
- Is it possible to pool the use of some assets with non-competing firms?
- Can payment to some vendors be delayed profitably? Can you get discounts greater than the cost of capital for early payment?
- Is it profitable to accelerate cash receipts from your customers?
- Is it possible and profitable to accelerate the customer's ordering cycle?
- Can you profitably automate the payments from customers? What about electronic payment options, do they make sense?

An insightful list of strategic initiatives will almost always include a number of action programs designed to improve balance sheet productivity.

STRENGTHENING COMPETITIVE ADVANTAGE

These strategic initiatives focus on improving the value proposition and/or the business model in order to improve the company's ability to satisfy the targeted needs, wants problems, preferences and/or expectations of customers in the target market segment better than competitors.

The value proposition consists of the product/service, customer service, price, availability, and image. (See Figure 6.6) Initiatives might focus on changes or improvements in any or all elements of the offer to the customer. Of these, the most powerful weapon is often changes in the product . . . be it features, functions, quality, design, and so on . . . and the product cycle. This has been a favorite strategy of chip manufacturers like Intel, or computer manufacturers, or cell phone and smart phone marketers.

Having a faster product cycle than competitors, and a robust pipeline of product changes and improvements that are relevant and meaningful to the customer can often be a sustainable competitive advantage. There should almost always be strategic initiatives addressing this area.

The other area to focus on is improving the business model that produces the value proposition. This includes all of the functional areas of the business, the supply chain, strategic assets, and business processes and capabilities. Here the emphasis should be on those things that are *core* in satisfying the targeted customers' needs, wants, problems, preferences and expectations better than competition. Continually strengthening core competences is critical to maintaining competitive advantage.

Consider Victoria's Secret, for example. They have the capability to identify "white space" in the women's lingerie market. They also have the ability to anticipate women's fashion lingerie preferences. They can source large quantities of technically complicated products, like bras. They are very adept at speed sourcing products at costs that enable them to provide acceptable quality at power price points. They have highly productive and esthetically pleasing store designs and have used supermodels, fashion shows, and fashion events to create a strong image that differentiates them from competitors.

The key, or core, components of the business model should be continuously strengthened through strategic initiatives designed to address the issues that are involved in specific situations. This also may involve protecting or insulating these components from competitive emulations. And it may also involve building and/or strengthening those parts of the business model that will weaken competitor's competitive advantages.

DEVELOPING INFRASTRUCTURE AND CAPABILITIES

The last area to think about in developing strategic initiatives, are the capabilities and infrastructure of the business. As used here, capabilities refer to all of the resources of the business model . . . functions, supply chain, assets, and processes. What capabilities do we need now, that we currently do not have? What capabilities will we need in the future, that we currently do not have? Do we have the correct infrastructure?

These capabilities are beyond strengthening the company's competitive advantage, an area that has already been addressed. Rather it can include strengthening existing resources, or adding new resources. It may involve upgrading to alternative resources. It may include strengthening and/or adding resources that weaken or eliminate competitor's key resources, particularly those that are important to their competitive advantage. And, it might involve adding or upgrading resources that will allow the business to compete in new markets that are of interest, or may become of interest.[89]

Special attention should be focused on strategic initiatives that build and strengthen resources and capabilities that can be used across multiple businesses, and ideally create competitive advantages in more than one type of business. Examples for manufacturing companies would include product and process innovation, just-in-time procurement, lean manufacturing, six-sigma, brand management systems, and distribution and IT systems. For retailers it would include real estate acquisition processes, store design skills, sourcing, inventory management, store management, and so one. Obviously, those capabilities that create competitive advantages that can be leveraged across multiple businesses in the future are often the most valuable.

THE STRATEGIC INITIATIVES AGENDA

The output of this stage in the business strategy process should be a list of strategic initiatives that the business will implement during the time horizon of the plan. These initiatives should focus on gross margin enhancement, leveraging operating expenses, improving balance sheet productivity, enhancing competitive advantage, and, if needed, developing new capabilities and infrastructure.

The list of strategic initiatives should then be prioritized in terms of their importance to the strategy and their financial contributions to the business and scheduled accordingly. In most instances, the list will be too long and will need to be edited down so that the business is focused on the few initiatives that are most critical and have the largest impact. Deleted initiatives can be reinstated after the ones with the largest potential have been successfully implemented.

CHAPTER 10

BUSINESS ORGANIZATIONAL DESIGN AND DEVELOPMENT

"Recognize the skills and traits you don't possess, and hire people who have them."

Warren G. Bennis
Professor and Founding
Chairman of The Leadership
Institute at the University of
Southern California

This phase in the process of developing a business strategy for a single-unit business, or an operating division of a multi-division enterprises focuses on the organizational changes that are required to execute the strategy. (Figure 10.1). There is wide disparity in the way organizations deal with these issues. On one end of the continuum are companies who simply have a human resource function that is focused exclusively on salary administration and legal issues related to people, and may report directly to some officer other than the CEO. At the other end of the spectrum are companies that use organizational design and development not only to develop and implement corporate strategies, growth initiatives, and strategic initiatives, but also as a way of achieving a competitive advantage. The latter perspective is the one prescribed here.

To be most effective, organizational design and development decisions should be made in a way that at least enables, and hopefully enhances, a company's ability to achieve its strategic agenda. In addition to the normal things that have been used in the past, the key is to add mechanisms and processes that enable and promote innovation, adaptability, testing, and learning. Our approach consists of the following dimensions:

- Culture and value alignment.
- Organizational design.

Figure 10.1 Formulating/revising business organizational design & development issues

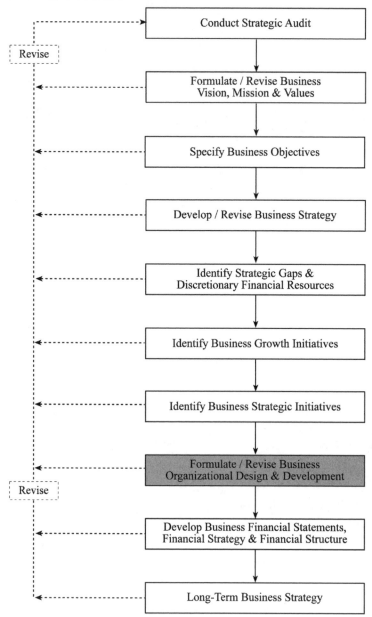

- Lateral linking mechanisms.
- Incentive compensation schemes.
- Executive assessment and development.
- Organizational development.
- Governance systems.
- Leadership styles.

Culture and Value Alignment

The first issue is to make certain that the vision, mission, objectives, strategy, and growth and strategic initiatives are consistent with the culture and values of the business. Culture trumps strategy. If the strategic agenda is consistent with the culture and values, then it is safe to proceed. If they are not consistent, then either they need to be aligned by changing one or the other, or, perhaps both. If it is the values and culture that need to be changed, there obviously needs to be a plan and program to make the needed adjustments. The most common mistakes here are to either ignore the alignment requirement, or to underestimate the effort and time that it takes to achieve reasonable compatibility. Culture and value change, when successful, is usually a continuous program spanning several years.

Companies that are technologically- oriented do not become customer-oriented easily, and certainly not within a few months. Businesses lacking a culture of discipline, do not develop one quickly. A fact-based approach to decision making can not be installed successfully with a few speeches. Seniority-based thinking makes collaborative management very difficult.

A company that has been growing relatively slowly for years can usually not move quickly into a fast-growth mode. Rather it takes an agonizing period of coaching and changes in attitudes, information systems, meeting schedules and agenda, coordinating mechanisms and a variety of other things to accelerate growth successfully and profitably.

The values and culture of the business need to be aligned with the corporate agenda . . . vision, mission, objectives, strategy, and growth and strategic initiatives.

Organizational Design

Structure should follow strategy. That is, the organizational structure should at least assist, and hopefully enhance, the achievement of objectives, strategies, and initiatives.[90] It is obvious that if the objectives, strategies, and/or initiatives are changing relative to the past, a serious review of organizational structure is in order. But, even if these changes are only slight modifications from the past, a review should be conducted to make certain that an alternative structure would not be more effective.

Figure 10.2 presents four organizational structures that are most common among businesses consisting of a single operating unit. Figure 10.2(A) presents a typical functional organizational structure for a single operating unit business that is operating in only one major geographical market, like the United States. If the single operating unit consists of multiple brands, a common alternative is to organize by brand, with a central services area providing financial, legal, accounting and related services, and a separate manufacturing division, or divisions, as appropriate.

Figure 10.2(A) Illustrative functional organizational structure*

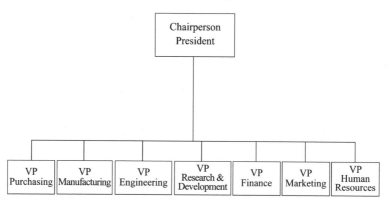

* Adapted from Phillipe Lassere, *Global Strategic Management.* (New York: Palgrave MacMillan, 2003), pp. 72-91.

In this situation, organizing by brand is often preferred because it enhances communication, and, most importantly, accountability.

If the business operates in multiple geographic markets, like the United States, Europe, and Asia, there are three basic choices, notated as Figure 10.2(B), (C), and (D). Here the options are to organize globally by brand, or to organize brands by global area, or a "matrix" that attempts to combine the two approaches. The advantages of one approach are the disadvantages of the other, and vice-versa, so there is no perfect solution. The matrix approach attempts to reconcile these pros and cons, but often results in making matters worse, because executives have two bosses which create another layer of problems including lack of speed and responsiveness, and compromises that produce the "worst of both worlds.[91]

For global single-unit companies, the major challenge is how to gain global coordination and efficiencies on the one hand, and local responsiveness, particularly in sales, marketing, and human resources, on the other hand. The structure that is the best compromise in a specific situation is the one to use, bearing in mind that the best compromise today may change in the future.

LATERAL LINKING MECHANISMS

Another focus should be on designing/reviewing the integration, coordination and communication mechanisms that are used to connect functions, geographies, and brands. Permanent or temporary committees or task forces are generally the most useful. The use of these mechanisms for operational problems and issues should be reviewed to make certain that their continued use and method of operation are appropriate given

Figure 10.2(B) Illustrative global functional organizational structure*

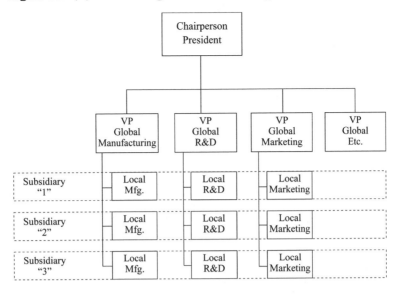

STRUCTURE:
- Global centralization of decision making & control of all major functional activities
- Country subsidiaries are local legal entities; their autonomous decisions are confined to implementation of policies, local legal compliance & local personnel management issues

ADVANTAGES:
- Most appropriate where there is a company need for global coordination & integration, efficiencies, economies of scale, & rapid transmission of best practices

DISADVANTAGES:
- Lack of adaptation to local conditions. Can discourage local initiatives

* Adapted from Phillipe Lassere, *Global Strategic Management.* (New York: Palgrave MacMillan, 2003), pp. 72-91.

the new strategic agenda. Or, stated conversely, does the strategy agenda make it necessary to change these mechanisms, and if so, what is the planned change?

Beyond the operational issues, the question is can horizontal linking mechanisms be helpful in achieving the strategic agenda . . . specifically, the strategy and the growth and strategic initiatives? For example:

- Can lateral linking mechanisms (LLM) increase the effectiveness and efficiency of implementing competitive advantage requirements that involve more than one function, brand, or geography?

121

Figure 10.2(C) Illustrative global geographical organizational structure*

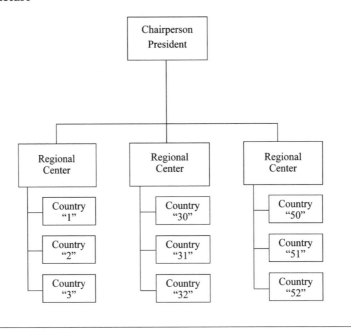

STRUCTURE:
- Global decentralization of decision making, coordination & control at the level of subsidiaries (countries)
- No authority links between the subsidiaries & the functional directors at the corporate center
- Functional heads within subsidiaries (countries) report to the CEO of that subsidiary (country)

ADVANTAGES:
- Adaptability to local conditions
- Flexibility

DISADVANTAGES:
- Lack of efficiencies, economies of scale, and rapid transmission of best practices
- Difficult to serve global customers

* Adapted from Phillipe Lassere, *Global Strategic Management.* (New York: Palgrave MacMillan, 2003), pp. 72-91.

- Should LLM's be created to execute gross margin enhancement and operating expense leverage initiatives that affect more than one function, brand, or geography?
- Would LLM's be useful in getting better results from balance sheet productivity initiatives that cut across functions, geographies, or brands?
- How should product innovation be organized? Who should be involved and how should the group operate and be managed?

Figure 10.2(D) Illustrative global single matrix organizational structure*

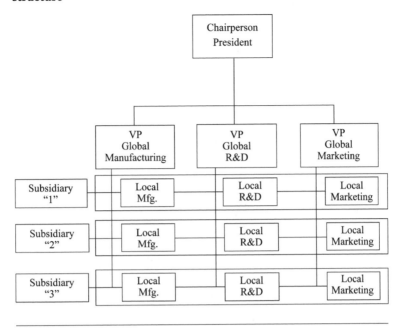

STRUCTURE:
- Both functions & subsidiaries (countries) have equal decision making, coordination, & control responsibilities
- Function heads in subsidiaries (countries) have two bosses...the subsidiary CEO & the global functional head

ADVANTAGES:
- Theoretically, global economies of scale & local adaptability

DISADVANTAGES:
- Two bosses may create power struggles, compromises, and/or delayed action or inaction. These potential developments can can offset the advantages unless they are managed effectively

* Adapted from Phillipe Lassere, *Global Strategic Management*. (New York: Palgrave MacMillan, 2003), pp. 72-91.

This type of thinking and rethinking should be applied to all components of the business strategy and every growth and strategic initiative. The creative and effective use of LLM's are often as important, or more important than organizational structure, and typically do not get the focus and attention they deserve.

INCENTIVE COMPENSATION

The incentive components of the compensation structure . . . bonuses and equity grants . . . should be reviewed to determine whether they promote the type of

123

behavior required to achieve the strategic agenda . . . objectives, strategies, growth initiatives, and strategic initiatives. The major elements of the incentive compensation structure might include some combination of the following:

- Company (operating division) performance.
- Individual performance.
- Cooperation incentives.
- Incentives to contribute to various initiatives.

The issues are which of these should be used, how should each of them be defined, and what should the weighting of each be in designing the incentive compensation structure.

To align management interests with those of shareholders, some measure(s) of business performance should be the dominant driver of incentive compensation. Perhaps the best approach is to tie the measures directly to the business objectives which would be some earnings-per-share number or growth rate, or some derivative measure like net profit before or after taxes, or operating income before or after taxes. Similarly, the profitability target can be tied directly to the return-on-investment metric the company uses, or, perhaps, economic value added, if that philosophy is used in the business. It is also useful to use "benchmarking indices" against predetermined peer group companies to accommodate unforeseen economic developments as well as other distortions that are considered exogenous, like significant increases in the price of oil and reductions in interest rates, for example.

Individual objectives can be used to articulate the specific contributions that each executive needs to make during the period in question beyond the achievement of the corporate performance measures. These individual objectives need to be aligned with the strategic agenda, and cascaded down from the CEO to his direct reports, and then to the direct reports of the direct reports in order to achieve consistency and continuity of focus.

Cooperation incentives can be used to encourage coordination and integration across functions, geographies, and brands. These may be included in individual objectives, or singled out for special attention and emphasis as a separate category.

Finally, there can be incentives to contribute to various initiatives, particularly growth and strategic initiatives. These can be useful in gaining alignment and cooperation around the most critical initiatives when individuals do not have primary responsibility for them, but their support is essential.

The relative emphasis given to each component of the incentive compensation structure should be architected to ensure the type of individual and collective behavior that is most likely to result in the company achieving its objectives. It may be appropriate to make corporate performance account for 100 percent of incentive compensation. Or, it may make more sense to devote somewhere between

10 to 20 percent, perhaps even as much as 50 percent to results beyond performance metrics. There is no "magic formula," rather careful analysis and judgment should be employed. Whatever the system, incentive compensation . . . both bonus and equity grants . . . should be directly and strongly tied to, and determined, by business performance.

A major upside opportunity is to make growth and strategic initiatives part of the incentive structure for senior executives. This technique is very useful in making certain that the business does not become completely focused on quarterly and annual results and neglect doing those things that are necessary to prepare for future performance during the remainder of the planning period and beyond into T3.

Finally, care should be taken not to include too many different metrics in an incentive compensation system. This can dilute effort and attention, and thereby reduce the effectiveness of the system.

EXECUTIVE AND KEY PERSONNEL DEVELOPMENT

Do we have the executives and key personnel to execute the strategic agenda? Do we have adequate numbers of qualified people currently? Will we have adequate numbers of qualified people in the future, including T3? What development plans should be designed and implemented to make certain that we have the personnel resources that are needed currently, and will be needed in the future? These are some of the major issues that need to be addressed.

All senior executives and other key personnel, like perhaps scientists or engineers or high-level programmers, should be evaluated, generally on an annual basis. This should include an assessment of their technical and functional competence as well as their leadership abilities. Each person's evaluation can then be summarized using some type of scale or system like red, yellow, and green, or unacceptable, acceptable, and star.

Is this talent pool capable of achieving the strategic agenda? What improvements would be useful? Decisions should be made regarding the development program that is best suited for each person including formal training at universities, executive education programs at universities and/or within the corporation, job assignments including committees and task forces, coaching, mentoring, and the like.

Focusing on Key Positions, Functions and Processes.   While all functions and positions in a business are important, some are more important than others, generally those that are most essential in achieving a competitive advantage. These key positions should be identified and subjected to more intense evaluation and analysis. Development programs like those mentioned above should be focused on

these functions, positions, and people. Excellence in these areas should be achieved before the programs are expanded to other functions, positions and people.

Recruiting efforts should also be distorted to these key functions and positions. How many people will be needed in the future for each of these positions? How many backups should there be for each of these key positions? Keeping this pipeline filled with quality people . . . first in terms of recruiting, and then in terms of the appropriate development programs . . . is one of the single most important determinants of whether a company can successfully execute an aggressive strategic agenda. Deficits in the key functions and positions are the major reason why many companies do not do better, and why they can not achieve more aggressive profit growth rates.

Organizational Capabilities

The task here is to assess the current capabilities of the organization, evaluate their appropriateness in achieving objectives and strategies during the planning period in question and beyond into T3, and determine which ones need to be strengthened and which ones need to be initiated or added. This capability evaluation should have been covered in the previous phases of the strategy formulation process, but is resurfaced here to make certain that something important has not been omitted.

While the organizational capabilities that are important vary from one company to another, some of the most common ones include:

- Customer orientation. Focusing all of the activities of the organization around satisfying specific needs, wants, problems, preferences or expectations of specific customers in a targeted market segment.
- Profitability orientation. Understanding and managing to return-on-investment or economic value added.
- Leadership. Being outstanding in leadership and having exceptional leaders throughout the organization.
- Collaboration. Working across functions, geographies, brands, and/or other boundaries to improve efficiency and leverage.
- Innovation. Developing new and impactful products and processes.
- Testing and learning. Understanding the importance and role of testing in the organization and how to manage it.
- Talent. The quality level of people in the organization measured across the relevant dimensions of quality. Attracting, motivating and retaining competent and committed people.

Which of these, and/or other, organizational capabilities are most important in achieving the strategic agenda? How does the company rate on the most important capabilities, in general and relative to competitors? This type of analysis and thinking can be used to develop organizational development initiatives for the time frame in question.[92]

GOVERNANCE SYSTEMS

It is also important to review and assess the business governance system, and its appropriateness in achieving the corporate agenda for the future . . . objectives, strategies, corporate initiatives and strategic initiatives. While the appropriate governance system depends on the specific situation, in general it should include long-range planning and reviews of progress against the plan; annual fiscal year planning, including operating and capital budgets, and reviews of these plans and budgets, generally on a monthly basis; personnel reviews; and various meetings that deal with key functions, supply chain, capabilities and processes that are critical components of the business model. The governance systems spells out what these components are, who participates in them, what their objectives are, when they meet, and what happens with the decisions that are made in these meetings.

What changes should be made in the governance system to execute the growth initiatives? What changes need to be made to implement the strategic initiatives? Each growth and strategic initiative needs to be evaluated and reviewed in terms of its governance system requirements as well as its organizational design needs.

LEADERSHIP STYLES

It is also important to analyze and evaluate the leadership styles of the major executives in the organization in terms of the appropriateness of these styles for achieving business objectives, strategies, and growth and strategic initiatives. Are leadership style changes required? While it is difficult for executives to change, it is possible to increase their sensitivities and responses to certain conditions, people, and types of interactions, through proper coaching, often with outside specialists. This may be particularly important when there are major disruptive changes occurring like changes in values, major increases in the growth and/or profitability requirements, reductions in force, and mergers and acquisitions.

In thinking about the appropriateness of leadership styles, it may be useful to revisit Peter Drucker's view on the habits of effective executives.[93]

- They know where their time goes.
- They focus on results rather than work.

- They build on strengths: their own; the strengths of their superiors, colleagues and subordinates; and on the strengths in the situation. They do not build on weaknesses.
- They concentrate on the few major areas where superior performance will produce outstanding results. They set priorities and stick with them.
- The make effective decisions; the right steps in the right sequence. An effective decision is always a judgment based on dissenting opinions rather than on consensus on the facts.

Jim Collins has identified the characteristics of leaders who were able to elevate their company from good to great. He calls these people Level 5 leaders, and describes them:[94]

- They shift their ego away from themselves toward the goal of creating a great company. Their priority is for the institution, not themselves.
- They set up their successors for even greater success in the next generation.
- They attribute success to factors other than themselves, but take personal responsibility for failures.
- They almost always (90%) come from within the company.
- They are more plow horse than show horse.

Additional perspectives on leadership styles focus on the importance of creating and maintaining the proper organizational environment, rather than just decision making. This involves creating and communicating continuously a vision and mission that is both transcendent and directional, as well as values that guide the behavior of the company and its associates, and then achieving alignment between different parts of the business and the vision, strategy, organizational design, and the people. This approach enables more executives to make greater contributions to the success of the organization.[95]

THE ORGANIZATIONAL DESIGN AND DEVELOPMENT AGENDA

The output from this phase of the strategy formulation process should be a prioritized and sequenced list of changes that need to be made, if any, in the culture and values of the organization, the design of the organization, lateral linking mechanisms, incentive compensation, executive development and recruiting, organizational development, governance system and leadership styles. Only those changes that are necessary to achieve the business strategic agenda are important at this point.

CHAPTER 11

PRO-FORMA FINANCIAL STATEMENTS AND FINANCIAL STRATEGY AND STRUCTURE

The average corporate life expectancy is below 20 years. The maximum life is in the hundreds of years. One of the key characteristics of companies that survive is conservatism in financing.[96]

The final step in developing a long-term business strategy for a single-unit business is to develop pro-forma financial statements, and engage in a series of financing decisions. (Figure 11.1) For divisions of a multi-unit enterprise, this step includes preparation of the financial statements that are discussed, but not the financing decisions, since that responsibility lies in the corporate domain.

This phase of the process involves quantifying the business strategy, growth initiatives, and strategic initiatives into pro-forma profit and loss statements, balance sheets, and cash flow statements, for each year in the planning period . . . generally 3–5 years. Most existing businesses will have computer models constructed for these purposes; if not, it will be worthwhile to develop them, as this process usually involves many revisions and iterations.

PRO-FORMA PROFIT AND LOSS STATEMENTS

The core of the analysis is the preparation of the pro-forma income statements for the period covered in the plan. Every company has its own chart of accounts; a typical one is presented in Figure 11.2. The amounts entered for sales, gross profit, and operating expenses should reflect the best estimates of the financial results of

Figure 11.1 Developing business financial statements, financial strategy & financial structure

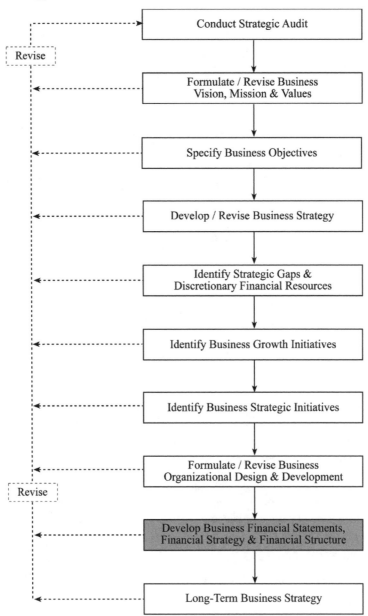

the business strategy, growth initiatives, and strategic initiatives that have been developed. In some instances, it may be best to stop the process at the operating income line, since completing the remainder of the statement may involve financing decisions that have yet to be made.

Since the purpose of this exercise is to quantify the preliminary strategic decisions that have been made and evaluate their financial adequacy relative to the

Figure 11.2(A) Pro-forma consolidated statements of income

	Year				
	1	2	3	4	5
Net sales	$	$	$	$	$
Cost of goods sold					
Gross profit	$	$	$	$	$
Operating expenses:					
General & administrative					
Special & nonrecurring					
Operating income	$	$	$	$	$
Interest expense					
Interest income					
Other income (loss)					
Income from continuing operations before income taxes	$	$	$	$	$
Income tax expense					
Net income from continuing operations					
Income from discontinued operations (loss)					
Net income	$	$	$	$	$
Basic net income per share:					
Net income per share - basic	$	$	$	$	$
Weighted average common shares - basic					
Diluted net income per share:					
Net income per share - diluted	$	$	$	$	$
Weighted average common shares - diluted					

objectives, it is generally best to error on the conservative side. That is, sales estimates should be conservative, and so should the cost of goods sold. Similarly, it is most useful not to overestimate the impact of various cost savings measures stemming from the strategic initiatives. More stringent targets can be set during the annual planning and budgeting cycle, but at this juncture the issues is whether there is enough "power" in the thinking to achieve the objectives.

Pro-forma Balance Sheets

Following the preparation of an income statement for each year, a balance sheet needs to be constructed. Again, the entries for balance sheets vary by company; a common classification is presented in Figure 11.2(B). Asset requirements can be estimated based on their historic relationship to sales as adjusted to reflect the relevant initiatives in the plan.

The asset requirements drive the current liability requirements, again based on historic relationships between assets and sales, adjusted for the impact of the business strategy initiatives. Other liabilities can be estimated based on their past relationship to sales, again modified by relevant initiatives. Anticipated earnings drive the equity section supplemented with anticipated options exercises. To close the loop for the computer model, cash should be allowed to accumulate at this point in the analysis. Since sales have been forecasted on the conservative side, the balance sheets should also reflect this posture.

Figure 11.2(B) Pro-forma consolidated balance sheets

	Year				
	1	2	3	4	5
ASSETS					
Current assets					
Cash & equivalents	$	$	$	$	$
Accounts receivable					
Inventories					
Prepaid expenses					
Other					
Total current assets	$	$	$	$	$
Property & equipment	$	$	$	$	$
Deferred income taxes					
Goodwill					
Other assets					
Total assets	$	$	$	$	$
LIABILITIES & SHAREHOLDERS' EQUITY					
Current liabilities					
Accounts payable	$	$	$	$	$
Customer prepayments					
Current portion of long-term debt					
Accrued expenses					
Income taxes					
Other					
Total current liabilities	$	$	$	$	$
Long term liabilities					
Deferred income taxes	$	$	$	$	$
Long term debt					
Commitments & contingencies					
Other					
Total long term liabilities	$	$	$	$	$
Total liabilities	$	$	$	$	$
Shareholders' equity					
Preferred stock	$	$	$	$	$
Common stock					
Paid-in-capital					
Retained earnings					
Less treasury stock					
Total shareholders' equity	$	$	$	$	$
Total liabilities & shareholders' equity	$	$	$	$	$

Pro-forma Cash Flow Statements

The final requirement is the construction of cash flow statements for each year in the planning period. An illustrative statement is presented in Figure 11.2(C). Again, most companies will have computer models to prepare these statements, usually in a more abbreviated form than shown.

Using the estimates contained in the pro-forma income statements and balance sheets, the added requirements here are principally to estimate capital expenditures by year, proceeds from the maturity of marketable securities, subsidiaries and joint ventures (if any), and dividend payouts using estimates that reflect the continuation of the current dividend policy into the future. Any changes in the dividend policy can be addressed at a later time.

Sensitivity Analysis

The three financial statements . . . profit and loss, balance sheet, and cash flow . . . for each year in the planning period with realistic estimates that err on the conservative side, constitute the "most likely case." The next step is to repeat the process from two different perspectives. One is to prepare a "best likely case" set of documents that reflect more aggressive estimates of sales, and more aggressive estimates of the results of strategic initiatives. The second is to prepare a "worst likely case" that is more conservative than the first, "most likely case."

With these three sets of estimates, the purpose is to capture the "band of possibilities" in terms of the financial consequences of the strategy and initiatives that have been developed. Catastrophic events like major epidemics or a series of terrorist's attacks are outside the scope of this thinking; the focus is on situations that have a much higher probability of occurring.

Performance Analysis

Figure 11.3 presents an illustrative format for evaluating the financial consequences of the strategy and initiatives that have been developed against the objectives. The major types of objectives that have been discussed in Chapter 5 are listed down the left hand column. The years covered in the plan form the next grouping of columns, ending with a column for compound annual growth rate entries, where appropriate. For each year three separate entries are made . . . worst likely case, most likely case, and best likely case.

Figure 11.2(C) Pro-forma consolidated statements of cash flows

	Year				
	1	2	3	4	5
OPERATING ACTIVITIES:					
Net income	$	$	$	$	$
Adjustments to reconcile net income to net cash provided by (used for) operating activities					
Depreciation & amortization	$	$	$	$	$
Amortization of deferred compensation					
Deferred income taxes					
Loss or disposal of assets & impaired assets					
Minority interest					
Special & nonrecurring items					
Changes in assets & liabilities					
Accounts receivable					
Inventories					
Accounts payable					
Accrued expenses					
Income taxes payable					
Other assets & liabilities					
Net cash provided by operating activities	$	$	$	$	$
INVESTING ACTIVITIES:					
Capital expenditures	$	$	$	$	$
Investments in marketable securities					
Proceeds from maturity of marketable securities					
Proceeds from sales of subsidiaries					
Proceeds from sale of joint ventures					
Net cash used for investing activities	$	$	$	$	$
FINANCING ACTIVITIES:					
Repayment of long term debt	$	$	$	$	$
Proceeds from issuance of long term debt					
Repurchase of common stock, including transaction costs					
Dividends paid					
Proceeds from exercise of stock options & other					
Net cash provided by (used for) financing activities	$	$	$	$	$
Net increase (decrease) in cash & equivalents	$	$	$	$	$
Cash & equivalents (beginning of year)	$	$	$	$	$
Cash & equivalents (end of year)	$	$	$	$	$

The first part of the analysis uses the most likely case estimates. The issue is quite simple: does the strategy and initiatives achieve the objectives, or not? If there are deficiencies against the objective(s), the question becomes "why?" The alternatives are to recycle and change the strategy and/or initiatives, or accept performance that does not achieve the targeted objective(s).

Figure 11.3 Pro-forma performance analysis against objectives

	Unit	Year 1			Year 2			Year 3			Year 4			Year 5			5 Year Compound Annual Growth Rate		
		WC*	MLC*	BC*	WC	MLC	BC	WC	MLC	BC	WC	MLC	BC	BC	MLC	BC	WC	MLC	BC
Scale:																			
Sales	$																		
Operating income	$																		
Net profit after taxes	$																		
Earnings per share	$																		
Cash flow	$																		
Cash flow per share	$																		
EVA	$																		
Growth:																			
Sales	%																		
Operating income	%																		
Net profit after taxes	%																		
Cash flow	%																		
Cash flow per share	%																		
EVA	%																		
Profitability:																			
Gross profit	%																		
Operating expenses	%																		
Net profit margin	%																		
Asset turnover	X																		
Return on assets	%																		
Financial leverage	X																		
Return on net worth	%																		
Return on invested capital	%																		
Cash flow return on assets	%																		
Cash flow return on net worth	%																		
Cash flow return on invested capital	%																		
Market share:																			
Units	%																		
Dollars	%																		
Internal Efficiency:																			
Inventory turnover	X																		
Accounts receivable turnover	X																		
Working capital tunover	X																		
Plant /equipment turnover	X																		
Capacity utilization	%																		
Sales per employee	$																		
Operating profit per employee	$																		
Flexibility:																			
% of sales to top customer	%																		
% of sales to top 5 customers	%																		
% of sales from patent X	%																		
Current ratio	X																		
Acid-test ratio	X																		
Debt/equity ratio	X																		

*WC= worst case, that has at least a 10% probability of occuring   MLC = Most likely case   BC= Best case, that as at least a 10% probability of occuring

FINANCING

Can the strategy and initiative agendas be financed comfortably? This requires an examination of the pro-forma balance sheets and critical balance sheet relationships such as debt/equity, current ratio, acid-test ratio and perhaps some of the other measures listed in Figure 11.3.

The analysis should focus on the impact of the strategy and initiatives on the balance sheet and these key ratios, under both the most likely case and the worst likely case scenario. Is additional capital needed? If so, what kind in what amounts? Is it available? What are the terms? Answers to these questions should be fed into the computer models, and the pro-formas recalculated along with the performance analysis sheet, and re-analyzed for sufficiency, appropriateness, and reasonableness.

If the capital requirements can be satisfied at reasonable terms, and if the financial risk is acceptable, the process is complete and attention shifts to annual plans and implementation. On the other hand, if the financial risk is not acceptable, the process recycles . . . including, perhaps, lowering the EPS growth or profitability objectives, eliminating or postponing certain growth and/or strategic initiatives, and/or other changes . . . until there is a combination of strategies, growth initiatives, and strategic initiatives that achieve EPS growth and profitability objectives in a way that seem sustainable and has a tolerable level of financing risk.

FINANCIAL STATEMENT, STRATEGY AND STRUCTURE AGENDA

The output of this final step in the strategy formulation process should be profit and loss statements, balance sheets, and cash flow statements that reflect the financial results of the strategies, growth initiatives, and strategic initiatives developed under three scenarios: most likely case, worst likely case, and best likely case. These financial results should demonstrate the achievement of the business financial objectives, or these objectives, and/or growth initiatives and strategic initiatives should be adjusted.

Using these financial statements, particularly the balance sheets, decisions are made regarding financial strategy and structure. If additional capital is required, decisions as to the amount, type, and timing are made. If excess capital is generated, decisions as to the amount, mix between dividends and stock repurchases, and timing are made. These issues are explored in greater depth in the closing section of Chapter 20.

PART III

DEVELOPING LONG-TERM CORPORATE STRATEGIES

T he focus now shifts to an enterprise with multiple operating divisions. Examples of these types of organizations would include Amgen, Microsoft, General Electric, Colgate Palmolive, Four Seasons, and Goldman Sachs. The operating divisions within these organizations can use the concepts and processes that have been developed in Chapters 3–10 to develop divisional business strategies. A corporate strategy includes the business strategies of the operating divisions, but it is not just the sum of them. Chapters 12–20 present the additional constructs and processes that are involved in architecting long-term corporate strategies for organizations with multiple operating divisions.

Chapter 1 presented a generic management system for a multiple operating division enterprise. (Figure 1.2) Referring to Figure 1.2, the anchor point for that system is a long-term corporate strategy. The major components of a corporate strategy are the same as those involved in a business strategy. Specifically:

- A Corporate Strategic Audit.
- Corporate Mission, Vision, and Values.
- Corporate Objectives.
- Corporate Strategies.
- Corporate Strategic Gaps and Discretionary Financial Resources.
- Corporate Growth Initiatives.
- Corporate Strategic Initiatives.
- Corporate Organizational Design and Development Initiatives.
- Corporate Pro-forma Financial Statements, Financial Strategy and Structure.

While the components of the process are the same for both business and corporate strategies, the latter involve a larger and different focus, as well as different considerations and content. Do not be fooled by the process component similarity.

Corporate strategy involves decisions regarding the composition of businesses in the portfolio. What does the ideal portfolio look like in terms of distribution of sales and operating income across businesses and geographies? What businesses should be added to and deleted from the portfolio? How should capital and talent be allocated to the businesses?

Successful corporate strategies *add value* to the operating divisions that comprise it. A corporate strategy that significantly improves the competitive advantage of each operating unit is extraordinarily potent. Often the power of a corporate strategy can be enhanced when a competitive advantage in one business unit is used to build competitive advantage in other operating divisions. In developing corporate growth options, a prospective new venture, or operating divisions, can gain competitive advantage from its association with the enterprise, or vice versa; that is, the new unit has a competitive advantage that can be leveraged across the existing business units of the enterprise. Adding value in these ways involves sharing knowledge, information, and activities, and transferring skills throughout the relevant part of the organization.

There are many other ways that the process of developing a long-term strategy for a multi-division business differs from the formulation of business strategies for the individual operating divisions. The template is presented in Chapters 12–20.

CHAPTER 12

CORPORATE STRATEGIC AUDIT

"In business you often don't see the cliff until you've already walked over it."

Andy Grove
Former Chairman & CEO
Intel

As Figure 12.1 indicates, the first step in developing a long-range corporate strategy for an enterprise consisting of multiple operating divisions is to conduct a corporate strategic audit. This involves:

- Industry analysis.
- Current market analysis.
- Competence analysis.
- Benchmarking and best practices analysis.
- Environmental analysis and forecasts.
- Competitive strategy analysis.
- Portfolio analysis.

The corporate strategic audit is a critical phase in developing a common point of view about the future. Achieving this common perspective among senior executives at the corporate level, as well as among the leadership of the divisions, provides a unifying framework for developing strategies for the divisions and the corporation as an entity. Preceding this common perspective should be serious, open debate among those involved in developing and implementing strategies. Once these differences have been heard and considered, the common perspective should prevail. Differences can continue to be voiced, but unless they rise to the level of modifying or revising the current common perspective, they should not become the basis for strategy.

Figure 12.1 Conducting a corporate strategic audit

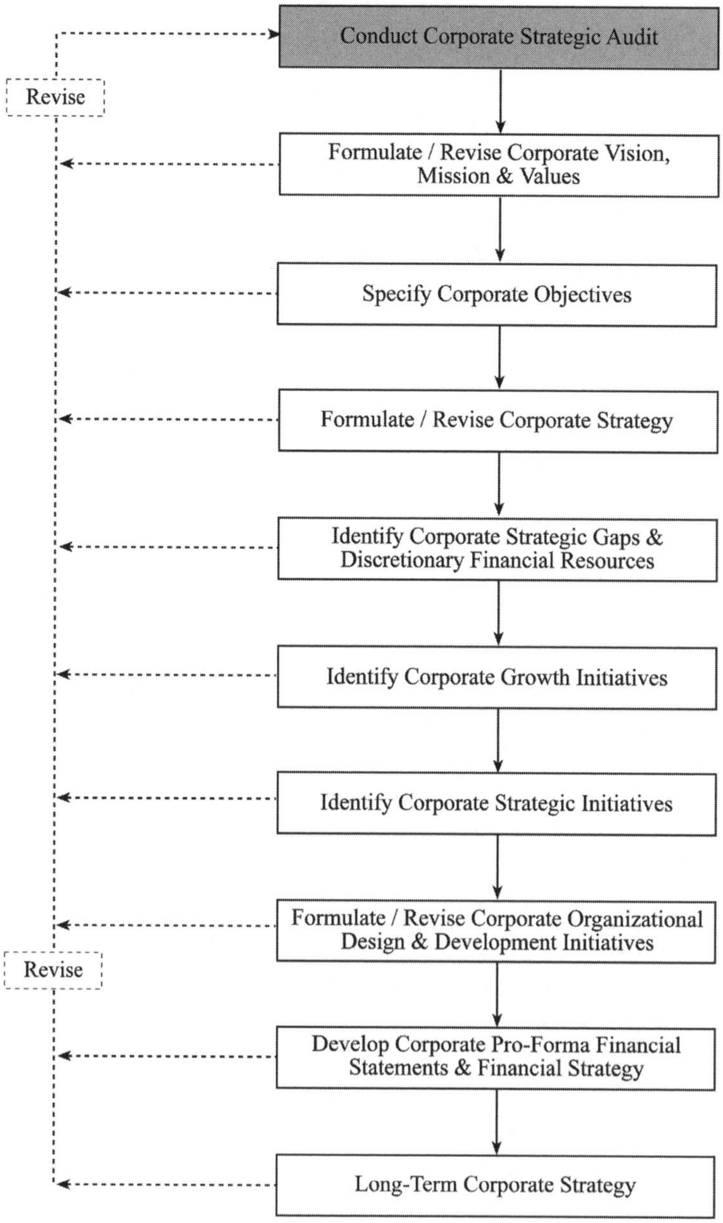

INDUSTRY ANALYSIS

While individual businesses within a company are almost always in some industry, the company in total may or may not be. Thus, while General Motors is primarily in the automobile industry, and Microsoft is primarily in the software industry, it is difficult to categorize General Electric as being in any specific industry. If the business in total can appropriately be considered to be in an industry, then it is useful to think about:

- Size of the market in dollars and units.
- Projected growth of the market in dollars and units.
- Market shares of the leading companies and trends in these shares.
- Availability and cost of resources.
- Price-elasticity of demand.
- Barriers to entry.
- Industry profitability and trends.

The analysis of these areas forms the basis for a summary and evaluation of the industry in terms of its status, problems, opportunities, and so on, for the strategy planning period.

CURRENT MARKET ANALYSIS

This section includes multi-year market share trends for each product and/or service in the company's business portfolio. It also summarizes the major factors contributing to each business's success or failure as well as an overview of the actions necessary to improve market share, and the costs and capital expenditure requirements, if any, to make these improvements. This evaluation provides the major input into the business portfolio analysis discussed in the last section of this chapter.

COMPETENCE ANALYSIS

This section of the strategic audit describes the strengths, weaknesses, and problems of the total company (not the individual divisions), and compares them with each of its major competitors. This includes an evaluation of the supply chain; all functions of the business; and all processes of the business, particularly core processes around competitive advantage(s).

With respect to the company's strengths, the challenge is how to use these most effectively in developing/revising strategies for the future. In terms of weaknesses, the issue is whether they should be corrected, and if so, how and when. This might involve internal development and/or the acquisition and development of resources. It might also involve outsourcing.

BENCHMARKING AND BEST PRACTICES

This type of benchmarking is focused on financial comparisons of the company (not the individual divisions) on every major line item in the income statement, balance sheet, and cash flow statement. Income statement comparisons should include cost of goods sold, gross profit, and operating expense ratios for every significant expense category. Key balance sheet comparisons are inventory turnover, day's sales outstanding, and fixed asset turnover.

Various return-on-investment comparisons are also useful. These include after-tax profit margins, asset turnover, return on assets, financial leverage, and return on net worth. Cash flow return on assets and cash flow return on net worth may also be appropriate. Some companies may prefer various measures of return on capital employed. A growing number of influential companies believe that economic value added is the most important construct and metric.

Growth comparisons should also be made. These might include multi-year comparisons of growth in sales, operating income, net profit before taxes, net profit after taxes, and earnings per share. Some company's use one, two, three, four, five, and ten-year comparisons for their multi-year analysis, but other periods may be more appropriate in specific situations.

The purpose of this benchmarking is to identify the company's strengths and weaknesses from a financial perspective. Where does the company do better than competitors? Where do competitors do better than the company? What are the reasons for these differences? What needs to be done so that the company can do better than competitors? These insights can become candidates for the strategic initiative agenda for the future that is discussed in Chapter 18.

Best practice analysis involves a different frame of reference. Here the question is who is best in the world at whatever is being discussed. These questions should be asked for every functional area, capability, and organizational process, particularly those that are key to satisfying customer's problems and achieving competitive advantage. This is the type of thinking that is most likely to generate breakthrough ideas and innovations. Truly innovative ideas often come from outside the industry rather than from within it.

ECONOMIC, ENVIRONMENTAL, AND MARKET FORECASTS

One of the services that corporate staffs provide their operating divisions is useful forecasts of the economic, environmental and market conditions that are likely to exist during the planning period. The corporate effort should generally focus on major macroeconomic trends, leaving more detailed and refined industry forecasts to the individual divisions involved. The corporate forecasts of the macro trends become the basis for both division strategies and the corporate strategy.

The areas that need to be covered in these macro forecasts include:

- The forecasts for economic growth and inflation in the countries in which the business operates.
- Interest rates projections.
- Personal consumption expenditures, broken out by categories relevant to the business.
- Major technological developments or trends.
- Major regulatory developments or trends.
- Patent expirations.
- Current and emerging changes in life-styles and their anticipated impact.
- Major demographic trends that will affect the size of the market and/or the company's business.
- Significant geo-political trends and developments.
- Major supply chain trends and developments.
- Significant changes in the structure of distribution and major companies in the distribution channel.
- Raw material and other resource availability and price forecasts.

Only those areas that are relevant to the company and its operating divisions need to be included. These should be summarized into:

- Significant trends and future events.
- Key threats and opportunities.
- The areas of uncertainty that have an impact on strategy.

COMPETITIVE STRATEGY ANALYSIS

This section of the corporate strategic audit attempts to identify the most likely moves that competitors will make, when they will make them, and the impact they will have on the company. The focus here is the corporation's major competitors. Some major factors to consider in making these assessments include:

- What are competitor's objectives and strategies?
- What are their strengths and weaknesses?
- What do they think our strengths and weaknesses are?
- Which of our strengths hurt competitors the most?

- How could competitors circumvent our strengths?
- How could they strengthen their competitive advantage(s)

These judgments about competitors' likely moves should be considered as a company formulates its strategy. Which moves could competitors make that would hurt the business the most, and what could be done to preempt or mitigate that move on their part?

Once the future strategy is designed or revised, it is useful to return to this issue and speculate as to how and when competitors will react, and then try to include elements in the strategy that will preclude or limit the effectiveness of their response. Countering the counter move in advance is a characteristic of strategic excellence.

PORTFOLIO ANALYSIS

The central component of corporate strategy is to determine the business portfolio, and how to allocate human and financial resources to the various businesses that comprise it. In order to make these judgments, it is useful to have some way of analyzing and summarizing the performance and future of businesses comprising the company's current portfolio. Three major techniques are presented below.

The GE/McKinsey Model.[97]   This approach, uses a matrix defined by two axes: industry attractiveness and competitive advantage. (Figure 12.2) Industry attractiveness is determined on the basis of an evaluation of the following factors:

- Size of market.
- Market growth rate over the past 10 years.
- Industry profitability as measured by three-year average net profit margin of the business and its competitors.
- Cyclicality as measured by average annual percentage trend deviation in sales.
- Ability to cover cost increases by higher productivity and/or increased prices.
- Globalization of market as measured by the ratio of international to domestic sales.

The competitive advantage of the division or business unit involves an evaluation of the following:

- Market position as measured by domestic market share, global market share, and market share relative to leading competitors.

144

Figure 12.2 The GE/McKinsey portfolio model

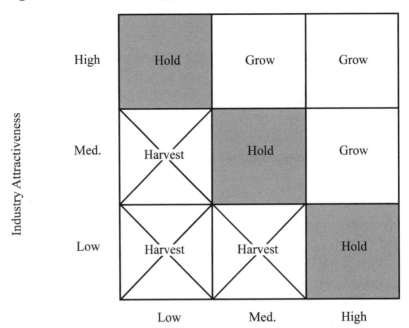

Business Unit Competitive Advantage

- Position relative to competitors on quality, technology, manufacturing, distribution, marketing, and costs.
- Net profit margins relative to competitors.

Using evaluations and judgments on these indices, each operating division or business unit can be plotted on the matrix based on its individual industry attractiveness and competitive advantage. The result is a strategic perspective on the company's current business portfolio with preliminary indications of possible future strategies:

- Businesses that rank high on both attractiveness and competitive advantage are candidates for continuing, and perhaps, accelerated, future growth.
- Those businesses that rank low on both attractiveness and competitive advantage are candidates for *harvesting,* that is managed to maximize cash flow with minimal incremental capital expenditures, or, perhaps divested.
- In-between businesses are candidates for a hold strategy, which means they are probably not major growth vehicles in the future.

The BCG Growth-Share Matrix.[98]   This matrix also uses industry attractiveness and competitive position to compare the existing businesses in the company's portfolio. The approach is simpler, however, in that it uses only one variable to measure each axis. Market growth rate is the proxy for industry attractiveness while market share relative to the largest competitor is used to calculate competitive advantage. (Figure 12.3)

This technique can be used to plot all of the company's businesses in the appropriate cell in the matrix, and thus gain a quick, if simplistic, overview of the company's product portfolio. The possible future strategies become:

- *Stars.* These businesses usually have strong, growing earnings. They are major growth candidates.
- *Cows.* These are businesses with high, stable earnings. They are candidates to be "milked."
- *Dogs.* These are businesses with low, unstable earnings and a low market share in a slow growth market. They businesses are serious contenders for divesture.
- *What?* These businesses usually have most earnings that may be growing at a modest rate, at best. The management judgment required here is whether these businesses can become stars, or whether they will become dogs and need to be divested.

Shareholder Value Analysis.[99]   Using this approach, the fundamental criterion to be applied to each business unit is whether the market value of the company is

Figure 12.3 The Boston Consulting Group growth-share matrix

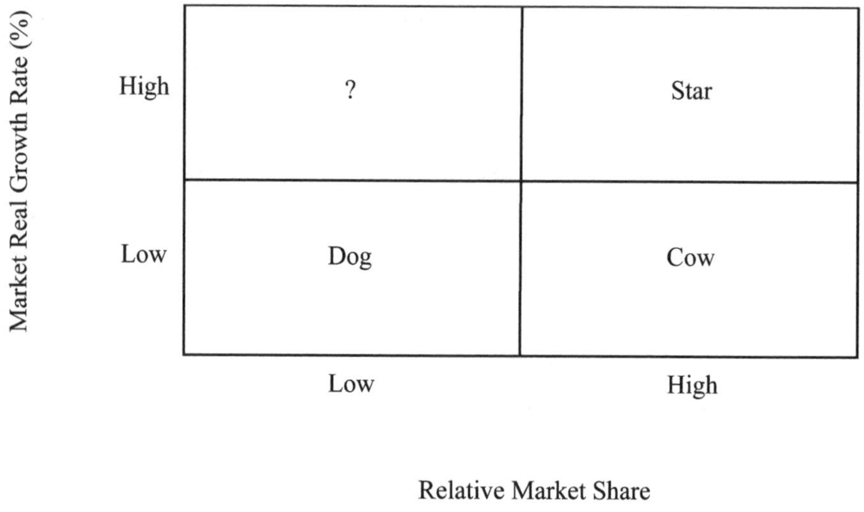

Market Real Growth Rate (%)		
High	?	Star
Low	Dog	Cow
	Low	High

Relative Market Share

146

greater with the business, or without it; that is after selling it to another owner or spinning it off as a separate entity via some sale mechanism.

While simple in concept, the determination of the market value of the unit to be divested, and the market value of the remaining business is extraordinarily complicated involving analyses of synergies lost and their impact on sales and costs, likely price-earnings multiples of the unit to be divested, and, the effect of the divesture on the PE multiple of the parent company, among other things. For these and other reasons, it is usually a good idea to use the services and recommendations of an investment banker for this exercise, and the banker's analysis should be cross-checked with others to ensure reasonableness.

Preliminary Screening.   The first two techniques . . . GE/McKinsey and BCG growth-share matrix . . . are useful ways of gaining a preliminary overview of the role that existing businesses will play in the prospective corporate strategy. Both analyses are simplistic and need to be augmented with other considerations which are discussed in Chapter 15. Shareholder value analysis performed internally on a "rough-cut" basis can be used to analyze further divisions that fall in the "questionable" category if the BCG matrix is used, and the "harvest" category if the GE/McKinsey matrix is used. Again, final decisions should be postponed until additional factors are considered as presented in Chapter 15.

THE CORPORATE STRATEGIC AUDIT

The results of the corporate strategic audit provide part of the input to operating divisions in preparing their long-term strategies, and also part of the input for developing the long-term strategy for the enterprise in total. The analyses that comprise this audit should be confined to issues that are relevant to the company. They should be formatted in a manner that facilitates the strategy formulation process:

- Identification of the significant trends and expected developments.
- The key threats and opportunities.
- The areas of uncertainty that can have a significant impact on strategy.
- Results of the portfolio analysis.

Often this type of analysis can extend to hundreds of pages, which dilutes the effectiveness. A more useful, crisp presentation should take only a few pages.

CHAPTER 13

CORPORATE MISSION, VISION AND VALUES

"What was your greatest thrill in baseball, Joe?"
"Being a Yankee. Wearing the pinstripes."

Joe Di Maggio

Joe Di Maggio is one of the greatest baseball players of all-time. During his 13 year career, he had a .325 batting average, and averaged 118 runs batted in per year. He was a 13 year All Star, was MVP 3 times, and won 10 World Series. Ted Williams, the famed Red Sox slugger, and the last man to hit over .400 in a season, called Joe the greatest baseball player he had ever seen.

But Di Maggio's greatest thrill wasn't all the records and championships; it was "being a Yankee." In sports, the Yankees in baseball, like the Packers in football under Vince Lombardi, or the UCLA Bruins in college basketball under John Wooden created exceptional organizations that were successful over long periods of time, and transcended people, including the greatest stars that played with them. How many businesses are able to reach and maintain the stature of these sports organizations? Unfortunately, not many. One of the reasons is that most businesses do not have a vision, mission and values that inspires and uplifts its associates.

The second step in developing a long-range corporate strategy for a multi-division corporation like GE or P&G is to develop a mission, vision and values. (MVV) (See Figure 13.1). The task is to evaluate whether the existing MVV is appropriate given anticipated changes in the environment and competitive conditions in the future.

Mission, vision and values define, in general terms, what the enterprise and its operating divisions is, or is trying to become, and how it will operate. As such, the MVV provides guidance and direction for the operating divisions and is also the defining step in the strategy formulation process for the entire corporation.

Figure 13.1 Formulating/revising corporate vision, mission & values

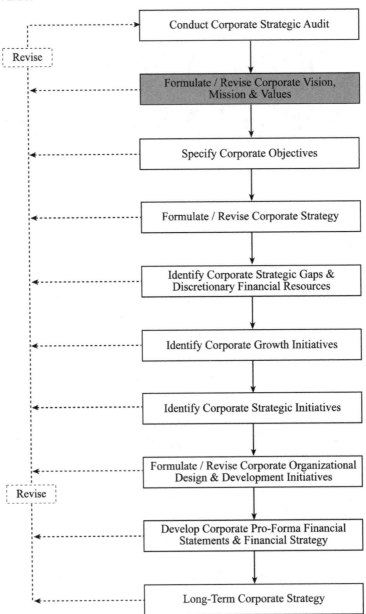

Developing/Revising a Mission and Vision

It most useful to combine a vision and mission into one statement, rather than separate them and engage in endless debates about which is which.

Mission Defined

A mission is a *long term vision of what the enterprise is or is trying to become*. The most useful mission statements have two components;

- What businesses or industries or "spaces" are we in?
- What are the standards of performance for acceptability?

As an example, consider Limited Brands which owns Victoria's Secret, Bath& Body Works, Henri Bendel, and other businesses. They view themselves as "a family of the world's best fashion brands." While the company originated as a retailer, they think of themselves as owners of brands, not retail stores. Secondly, the company is interested in *fashion* brands, not brands in general. This means that they are interested in products that have, or can have, an emotional content, as well as physical and functional characteristics. Limited Brand's mission statement provides direction for what types of businesses it is interested in, and how it manages the businesses it owns. Their standard of performance is as challenging and complex as it is simple: "the world's best."

When Limited was founded, their original mission was "to be the fastest growing, most profitable women's apparel specialty retailer in America." Their mission has changed to reflect the additional product categories that they are involved in . . . personal care items and women's lingerie . . . as well as a different perspective about how to best compete in the current environment; i.e., as brands rather than just stores.

Corporate vs. Business Missions

Corporate missions set the direction for the entire enterprise, on the one hand, and also provide a template for the missions of business units comprising the corporation. In the case of Limited Brands, each brand has its own mission that reflects its own consumer market segment and competitive scenario. While the missions of the individual brands are different because they reflect the individual circumstances that each brand faces, they are all consistent with the overall corporate mission of "a family of the world's best fashion brands."

Formulating a Corporate Mission

The chances of high-yield performance are probably greater if a company has a challenging mission. A good mission should be motivational, and stretch the performance standards of people in the organization. It should be a creative, imaginative, and demanding. It should be a fun journey that encourages people to spend their careers with the enterprise. It should help create a "near obsession"with winning at all levels of the organization.[100]

A useful corporate mission should be founded on solving the problems and expectations of customers. It should also consider the needs, requirements, and expectations of other stakeholders; e.g., managers and other associates, suppliers, stockholders, non-owner sources of capital including banks, brokers, and other lenders, and society.

The mission should also take into consideration the present and future anticipated environment of the enterprise. Anticipated global trends, the economic environment, political, legal and regulatory trends, and cultural and life style trends should all of considered. "Sustainability" is also important so that the business is an outstanding corporate citizen in terms of energy usage and efficiency, environmental practices, and "green" behavior. Sound environmental practices are no longer an option, but rather a requirement, in framing the mission of a responsible organization.

Core, or distinctive, competences should play a defining role in designing a thoughtful mission. Core competences are resources and/or capabilities that a company does well, preferably better than competitors. All businesses think of themselves in terms of the products or services that they provide as well as the markets they serve. A company should also think of itself in terms of the distinctive competences that it possesses, and ask the question: "where are the other spaces that these competencies can be used to enable the company to be successful?" New constellations of opportunities may become visible.[101]

For example, one of PepsiCo's distinctive competences is their strong delivery systems. The latter include direct-store-delivery, where their own associates load and set up the shelves; warehouse systems, where retailers store and replenish product; and dedicated teams to supply foodservice and vending customers. Pepsi might think about their mission in terms of where and how they might capitalize on their delivery systems; that is what additional industries, products, and services might be growth opportunities because one of their success requirements is the kind of delivery system that PepsiCo possesses.

EXAMPLES OF CORPORATE MISSIONS

Vision/mission statements and philosophies of some leading companies:

- **UPS.** To help coordinate their customers' distribution systems, supply chain, and order management cycles so they can compete better in an expanding global economy.
- **Williams Sonoma.** To "own the home" through multi-channel retailing, including stores, catalogues, and e-commerce with their brands: Pottery

Barn; Pottery Barn Kids; Williams-Sonoma; Williams-Sonoma Home, West Elm; and PBteen.

- **Google.** To organize the world's information and make it universally accessible and useful in order to make the world a better place.
- **Motorola.** To create seamless mobility so people have easy, uninterrupted access to information, entertainment, communication, monitoring and control.
- **Ebay.** To pioneer communities built on commerce, sustained by trust, and inspired by opportunity.
- **Merck.** To provide society with superior products and services by developing innovations and solutions that improve the quality of life and satisfy customer needs, and to provide employees with meaningful work and advancement opportunities, and investors with a superior rate of return.
- **Microsoft.** To help people and businesses throughout the world realize their full potential.
- **Nike.** To bring inspiration and innovation to every athlete in the world.

CULTURE AND VALUES

A company's culture is a set of values, beliefs, and norms of behavior shared by the associates of that company that affect their behavior. A new strategy that is perceived as contradictory to a company's culture and values will often not be accepted, or accepted reluctantly and suffer execution problems. On the other hand, a compatible culture can accelerate the achievement of a strategy. Values and culture that focus on the importance of the customer, foster interfunctional and interdivisional cooperation, and deal constructively with those activities and processes that constitute a company's competitive advantage are the most critical.[102]

It is important to specify expected relationships between the company and shareholders, suppliers, associates, government, community, environment and other important parties in the businesses' sphere of operations. In each of these relationships, a company should state what it contributes to the party, what it holds itself responsible and accountable for, on the one hand, and what it expects from that party, including its responsibilities and deliverables.

Equally important is an explicit statement of values and beliefs about how the company functions internally, its internal relationships, and relationships between the operating divisions and staff functions. This should include statements concerning expected relationships between the company and its associates, interpersonal relationships among associates and activities and behaviors that are encouraged, discouraged, and prohibited.

So, the questions here are what are the values of the company? Are these values appropriate for the future? What changes in values and culture are needed in order to compete effectively in the future?

EXAMPLES OF BELIEF AND VALUE SYSTEMS

Chico's is a company selling women's apparel and lingerie to niche markets through three major businesses: Chico's, White House/Black Market, and Soma by Chico's. Their core values are teamwork, energy, commitment, courtesy, respect, honesty, and giving back to their communities through Chico Charities, Inc. which focuses on their core giving areas of women and children's causes, education, health, community, environment, and the needs of their associates.

The largest retailer in the world, Wal-Mart, describes their culture as built from the foundation of integrity, respect for one another, continual improvement, and service to the customer. Wal-Mart is making a concerted effort to work more collaboratively with the communities in which they operate by being more flexible in individual store designs to accommodate local tastes and preferences, and being a good local citizen. They are the largest cash contributor to local community organizations and causes in corporate America.

3M, a diversified technology company, describes their core values:

- Provide investors an attractive return through sustained, quality growth.
- Satisfy customers with superior quality, value, and service.
- Respect our social and physical environment.
- Be a company employees are proud to be part of.

General Motors calls their core values "what the company stands for." Those values are:

- Customer enthusiasm.
- Integrity.
- Teamwork.
- Innovation.
- Continuous improvement.
- Individual respect and responsibility.

PepsiCo refers to its core values as guiding principles. They are:

- Care for customers, consumers and the world we live in.
- Sell only products we can be proud of.
- Speak with truth and candor.

- Balance short term and long term.
- Win with diversity and inclusion.
- Respect others and succeed together.

Amgen, a leading biotechnology company, describes its values:

- Be science-based.
- Compete intensely and win.
- Create value for patients, staff and stockholders.
- Be ethical.
- Trust and respect each other.
- Ensure quality.
- Work in teams.
- Collaborate, communicate, and be accountable.

Anheuser-Busch, brewer of the world's largest selling beers, Budweiser and Bud Light and other beers, articulates their values as:

- Quality in everything we do.
- Exceeding customer expectations.
- Trust, respect and integrity in all of our relationships.
- Continuous improvement, innovation and embracing change.
- Teamwork and open, honest communication.
- Each employee's responsibility for contributing to the company's success.
- Creating a safe productive and rewarding work environment.
- Building a high-performing, diverse workforce.
- Promoting the responsible consumption of our products.
- Preserving and protecting the environment and supporting communities where we do business.

These corporate examples are stated in highly abbreviated form that does not communicate the breadth and depth of thought and commitment. General Electric, for example, has a *Citizenship Report* that is 89 pages long and may be worth reviewing for inspiration, if not content. However brief, the examples illustrate the types of things that should be included in a company's values and culture.

CREATING AN ENABLING AND UPLIFTING CULTURE

In his study of companies that have gone from good to great, Jim Collins discovered that great companies preserve their core values and purpose while their business strategies and operating practices continuously adapt to a changing world. Core values serve as an anchor point connecting the past, present and future while companies stimulate change, improvement, innovation and renewal in everything else.[103]

The role of values and culture is not only to provide a foundation for strategy, but also to unify and inspire the efforts of all associates and everyone else that is involved. Values should be enabling and uplifting, bringing out the best efforts and behavior from everyone. Well designed cultures are simple, pure and honest. They teach people, and encourage them to learn. They motivate them to strive and become something they never thought they could be, inspire them to make everyone around them better, and encourage them to want to give back to those who have helped them, including the community and institutions that facilitate their lives.

These types of cultures are what prompted Joe Di Maggio to say that his greatest thrill in baseball was "Just being a Yankee." These cultures underlie the successes of great organizations. They are the cultures that great executives create from whatever they inherited, and this is the ultimate legacy that they can leave.

THE MISSION, VISION, AND VALUES AGENDA

The output of this stage in the formulation of a long-term corporate strategy should be a brief, but insightful and profound, statement of the corporation's mission, vision and values for the future.

CHAPTER 14

CORPORATE OBJECTIVES

"Big thinking precedes big achievement."

Wilferd A. Peterson

T he third step in developing/revising a corporate strategy for a multi-division business like Johnson & Johnson or American Express is to specify the objectives that the strategy needs to achieve, consistent with the mission, vision, values and culture. Figure 14.1 shows the relationship between objectives and the other components of the strategy formulation process.

Most multi-division businesses are publicly-held, and the overarching objective generally is to increase shareholder value. The most important types of objectives are earnings-per-share growth goals and profitability targets. Other objectives are concerned with market share, internal efficiency, and flexibility objectives. These objectives will be the focus of this chapter, and, since they do not differ materially from their counterparts in single-unit businesses, the discussion here will be an abbreviated version of what was discussed in Chapter 5. Following this dialogue, we will review the objectives of some illustrative companies, and then consider the task of setting divisional objectives and guidelines for the business units of the enterprise.

The most effective objectives setting process involves the interaction and collaboration of a "top-down" and "bottoms-up" approach. Both approaches must consider the other. Here we begin with the former and end with the latter.

SETTING STRETCH OBJECTIVES

In the last chapter we spoke about the importance of establishing a bold, uplifting, and inspiring mission, and developing the values and culture to support and nurture it. The driving logic is that this type of environment has a higher probability

Figure 14.1 Specifying corporate objectives

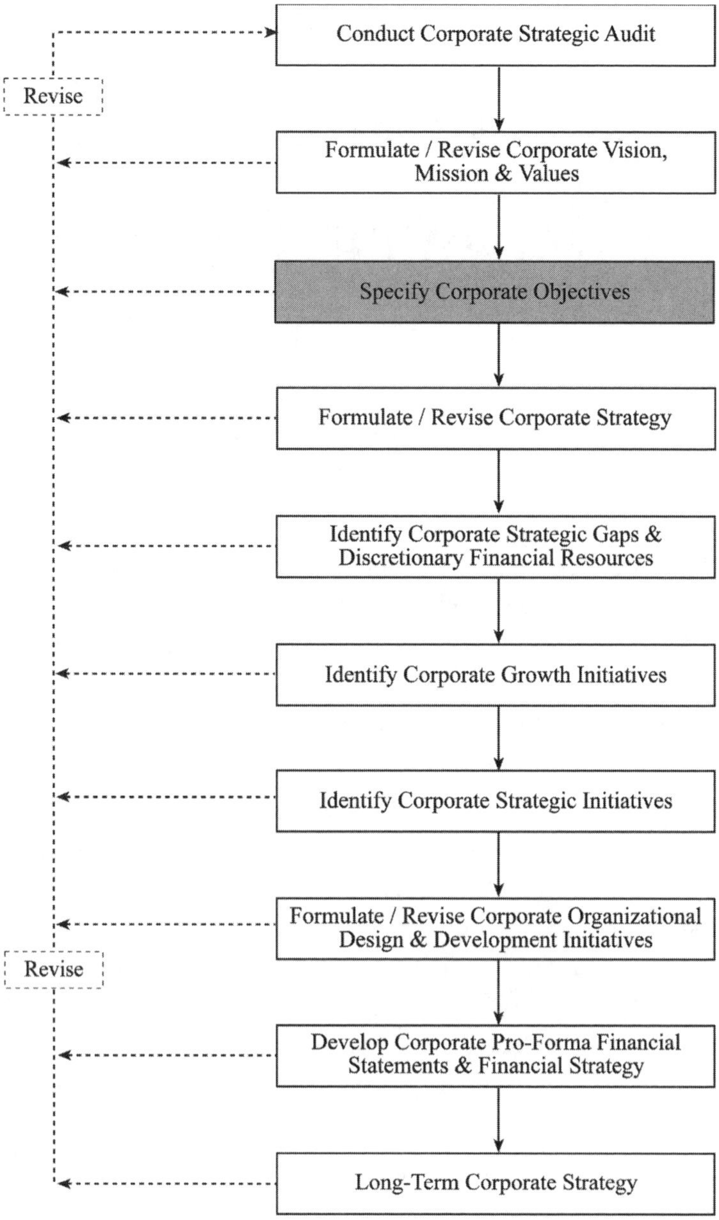

```
 ┌ ─ ─ ─ ─ ─ ─ ─ ─ ─ ─ ─ ─ ─ ─ ► ┌─────────────────────────────────┐
 │                                │  Conduct Corporate Strategic Audit │
 │  ┌ ─ ─ ─ ┐                     └─────────────────────────────────┘
 │    Revise                                      │
 │  └ ─ ─ ─ ┘                                     ▼
 │ ◄ ─ ─ ─ ─ ─ ─ ─ ─ ─ ─ ─ ─ ─   ┌─────────────────────────────────┐
 │                                │  Formulate / Revise Corporate Vision, │
 │                                │         Mission & Values          │
 │                                └─────────────────────────────────┘
 │                                                │
 │                                                ▼
 │ ◄ ─ ─ ─ ─ ─ ─ ─ ─ ─ ─ ─ ─ ─   ┌─────────────────────────────────┐
 │                                │    Specify Corporate Objectives   │
 │                                └─────────────────────────────────┘
```

Conduct Corporate Strategic Audit

Revise

Formulate / Revise Corporate Vision, Mission & Values

Specify Corporate Objectives

Formulate / Revise Corporate Strategy

Identify Corporate Strategic Gaps & Discretionary Financial Resources

Identify Corporate Growth Initiatives

Identify Corporate Strategic Initiatives

Formulate / Revise Corporate Organizational Design & Development Initiatives

Revise

Develop Corporate Pro-Forma Financial Statements & Financial Strategy

Long-Term Corporate Strategy

of unifying people in the organization and motivating them to a level of achievement that exceeds their individual and collective expectations.

For the same reasons, it is important to set aggressive objectives. They should stretch the performance of the business and the people in it, to the edge of sustained attainability. Stretched objectives will produce superior results as long as they are not extended to the point of being perceived as unbelievable, unattainable, or unsustainable, or to the degree that they involve types and degrees of risk that are unreasonable. Stretched objectives will attract and retain people who want to be part of a winning team that wins big, and wins in an exemplary way. "Big thinking precedes big achievement," as Mr. Peterson put it.

EARNINGS-PER-SHARE GROWTH RATE OBJECTIVES

The EPS growth rate target is one of the most important decisions that a CEO, his executive team, and the board of directors make. The faster the market believes a company can grow its earnings per share on a consistent basis with reasonable risk, the higher the company's price-earnings multiple and the higher its total market capitalization

Historically a general rule of thumb was that there should be a one-to-one relationship between the anticipated EPS growth rate and the price-earnings multiple. In other words, the so-called PEG ratio should be 1, so that a company with an EPS growth rate of 15 should have a PE multiple of 15, while a company with a 20 percent EPS growth rate should have a PE ratio of 20.

In today's world, the relationship between EPS growth rates and PE multiples is more complicated. For example, as of the date of this writing, PEG ratios of the 30 companies comprising the DJIA varied from .9 to over 3.0 with the median being 1.7. Companies with above-median PEG ratios tend to be perceived as having less risk and less earnings volatility. Despite these complications, the general rule holds that the higher a sustainable EPS grown rate, the higher the PE multiple.

Setting an Earnings-per-Share Growth Rate Target.

Most companies have a limitation on their growth rate imposed by a variety of factors, including the growth rates of the industries in which they operate, the earnings growth rate possibilities of their operating divisions, their capacity to finance growth, the capabilities of the organization and people to grow, and many other factors. One of the most important roles of the CEO is to have an understanding of the rate at which the company can grow, and what, if anything, can be done it facilitate an increase in the growth rate in the future.

Given all these considerations, to maximize shareholder value, it is important to have an aggressive EPS growth rate target for the enterprise. Aggressive usually means the first or second highest rate in the industry, or the company's peer group, whichever reference point is most meaningful. Growth rates that are in the upper-quartile or at least above the median may be acceptable in certain situations. If an enterprise can not grow its earnings at an above-average rate, at least after a period of time to accommodate adjustments in strategy and/or execution, **it** may be appropriate to have a conversation about the future of the enterprise in its current configuration.

Most members of a Board of Directors are too far removed from the day-to-day operations of a business to have the sensitivity required to challenge EPS growth rate objectives unless they are obviously sub-standard compared to the industry and/or peer group average, industry leaders, or companies in other industries that may be meaningful reference points. Therefore, it is usually wise for a Board to support the CEO's EPS target, unless it is obviously too high or too low, or the rate of improvement is unacceptable for financial or other reasons.

The penalty for missing earnings targets is generally severe in terms of reduction in share price. For this reason, and others as well, the "publicly stated" EPS growth objective, or "street guidance," should usually be lower than the one that is used for strategy formulation purposes.

PROFITABILITY OBJECTIVES

Another important objective is some profitability goal. The profitability objectives of most companies should be expressed in terms of return-on-investment, or some variation or refinement of it. Figure 5.4 in Chapter 5 presented a schematic illustration of a basic return-on-investment model that is used in this discussion. Other ROI measures are defined in Appendix A, and may be equally, or more, appropriate in specific situations.

ROI is important because it affects the net profit of the business, and therefore the earnings per share, stock price, and market capitalization. The rate of return also determines the rate at which the company can grow without changing its capital structure. A higher ROI has a positive impact on shareholder value.

Setting a Return-on-Investment Target.   In selecting a target ROI rate for the company it is obviously important to consider the specific circumstances that the business faces, including its current rate of profitability, its financial profile, competitive conditions and pressures, organizational capabilities, and so on.

Within the company's industry, or peer group if that comparison is more meaningful, an enterprise should be, or strive to become, in the upper quartile, preferably the first or second most profitable business as measured by return on assets, or the measure of profitability that is most commonly accepted. In situations where an organization is achieving below-average profitability, achieving these levels may require several years of improvement. In these situations, the question is whether the organization is making, or can make, reasonable progress toward an acceptable rate. If such progress is not being made, or cannot be made, then the issue is whether the current leadership should continue, and/or whether an investment banker should be hired to recommend strategic options, including a sale.

ECONOMIC VALUE ADDED OBJECTIVES

As described in both Chapter 5 and Appendix A, economic value added is derived from subtracting the dollar cost of capital from the net operating profit after taxes. Many people would argue that economic value added (EVA) is the best measure of corporate performance. However, since earnings per share and return on investment are universally accepted measures, we are proposing EVA *in addition to*, rather than instead of, the EPS and ROI metrics.

EVA produces a dollar number. Growth rate objectives can obviously be expressed as some percentage increase in EVA, and profitability objectives can be stated in dollar terms. This same procedure and process can be applied to operating divisions and other segments and aggregations of a business. Executive bonus and stock option programs can also be tied to EVA, which, in the opinion of many experts, is a major advantage of this approach.

EVA will probably enjoy more widespread usage in the future and could become the dominate growth and profitability objective in the future. At the present time, however, earnings-per-share and return-on-investment are the most common metrics, and, for that reason, EVA has been assigned a supplementary role.

OTHER OBJECTIVES

Competitive Strength.   Most common are growth objectives stated in terms of specific annual rates of increase in sales and operating income for the enterprise. For example, a target EPS growth rate of 20 percent might be translated into derivative growth rates as follows:

Target EPS growth rate	=	20%
Stock buyback program	=	2%
Operating income growth rate target	=	18%
Sales growth rate target	=	10%

In this hypothetical example, the company has an ongoing stock buyback program which retires 2 percent of the shares annually, therefore the target operating income growth rate is 18 percent Since the company has ongoing initiatives that generate significant economies of scale, a 10 percent sales growth rate is required to achieve the 18 percent increase in operating income. These sales and operating income growth rates become key objectives in developing and evaluating strategies.

Market share is another type of competitive strength objective. Since most multi-business companies are operating in several industries, one market share objective for the enterprise does not make sense. Instead, market share objectives are set for the individual operating divisions to reflect their individual circumstances. For multi-business companies operating totally or primarily in a single industry, a combined market share objective may be meaningful.

Also common are various objectives focused on the stability of the enterprise. Examples would include target maximum rates of fluctuations in sales, earnings, and capacity utilization.

Internal Efficiency. These types of objectives are more detailed metrics that make meaningful contributions to profitability. Examples include profit margins or contribution to profit, while supporting ones would be turnover of working capital, net worth, inventory, accounts receivable, and the debt/equity ratio.

Other objectives might focus on the quality of fixed assets. For example, a manufacturer might have a target age for various types of plant and equipment, while a retailer might be concerned with the percentage of its store fleet that has the most current or productive store design.

Productivity measures can also be used as internal efficiency objectives. Sales, gross profit, and/or operating income per dollar of fixed asset investment, and/or sales and/or operating income per employee, or full-time equivalent are often very useful measures.

Flexibility. These types of objectives are concerned with such things as the maximum percentage of sales and/or profits that can be derived from a single customer, or customer segment, or product, or product group. Similarly, it is sometimes important to target maximum proportions of sales and/or profits from certain technological processes, or patents. Strategies can then be designed to achieve or make progress toward these targets.

Financial flexibility can be engineered by specifying various liquidity targets. The most common indices would be an acceptable range for the current ratio, the acid-test ratio, and the debt-equity ratio.

EPS GROWTH RATES VS. PROFITABILITY: THE TRADEOFFS

Of the types of objectives discussed, earnings growth and profitability are the most important in most instances. Which of these two are most important? Does the greatest potential for increased shareholder value lie in more earnings growth or higher profitability?

Obviously, it is important for a company to understand the specific relationship between earnings growth and profitability before designing a strategy to maximize shareholder value. However, in general, while adding a point or more of sustainable growth may be harder to achieve than improving operating margins, the largest profits usually result from the fastest growth, *due primarily to the compounding effect*. For some companies, investing in growth generates more shareholder value that cost cutting does.[104] For other companies, the opposite may be the case; that is improving profitability may increase shareholder value more than accelerating growth.[105] Obviously, it is critical to understand which avenue is most productive in improving shareholder value in the specific situation that the company faces.

EXAMPLES OF CORPORATE OBJECTIVES

The stated objectives of some blue ribbon publicly-held companies based in the United States are:

- **American Express.** Earnings-per-share growth of 12 to 15 percent; 8 percent revenue growth; and return on equity of 28–30 percent on average and over time.
- **General Mills.** Low single-digit growth in net sales, mid single-digit growth in operating profit, high single-digit growth in earnings-per-share, consistent double-digit returns to shareholders.
- **Proctor & Gamble.** Sales growth of 4–6 percent; 10 percent or better earnings-per-share growth, and free cash flow productivity equal to or greater than 90 percent of earnings.
- **Citigroup.** Return on equity of 18–20 percent; mid to high single-digit organic revenue growth; organic income growth that exceeds organic revenue growth.
- **General Electric.** More than 10 percent annual earnings growth and 20 percent return on total capital.

Since these are publicly stated objectives, the objectives used for strategic formulation purposes are probably higher.

DIVISIONAL OBJECTIVES AND GUIDELINES

As was mentioned earlier, the best planning process is a collaborative one featuring "bottoms-up" and "top-down" processes of discussion. Growth, profitability and other objectives for the total enterprise should reflect a rigorous understanding and evaluation of the capabilities of each operating division and the contributions that each can make, as well as contributions from other sources. However, the target objectives and guidelines for each operating unit should generally be more aggressive that the division executives would voluntarily commit to. Best practices are to "stretch" every division, but stretch fairly and equitably so that no division feels they are being taken advantage of. "Tough but fair," should be the operative attitude.

THE CORPORATE OBJECTIVES AGENDA

The output of this stage in the strategy formulation process should be a concise statement of corporate objectives including earnings-per-share target growth rates, some return-on-investment rate target, growth rate targets for sales and operating income, and whatever internal efficiency and flexibility objectives are important. Shareholder value will be increased if these objectives are stretched, but are also attainable and sustainable, and involve a tolerable level of risk. These objectives, covering a three, five, or some other time period, when combined with the vision, mission, and values statement, establish the goals and direction for the corporate strategy.

CHAPTER 15

CORPORATE STRATEGY

"Everyone sees the tactics by which I conquer, but what none can see is the strategy from which victory is evolved."

Sun Zsu
The Art of War
1500 BC

As Figure 15.1 indicates, the next phase of the strategy formulation process is to specify the corporate strategy that will be used to achieve the objectives within the context of the corporate mission, vision, and values.

BUSINESS VS. CORPORATE STRATEGY

Corporate strategy is different from business strategy that was discussed in Chapter 6. Competition occurs at the business unit level, and business strategy, as we discussed, is concerned with identifying the needs, wants problems, preferences, and/or expectations of customers in a target market segment. A compelling and integrated value proposition, business model, and profit model are designed to satisfy the problems and expectations of customers in the target market segment in a way that enables the company to achieve a competitive advantage that is differentiated from competition and sustainable for a reasonable period of time given the context and dynamics of the industry involved.

A successful corporate strategy should reinforce the business strategies of the operating divisions that comprise it. Sometimes the corporate strategy evolves from the business strategy, other times the opposite is the case. But, in both cases, corporate strategy is rarely a larger version of business strategy.

Adding Value. The most successful multi-division enterprises *add value* to the business units that comprise it. Each business unit of an enterprise should be better

Figure 15.1 Formulating/revising corporate strategy

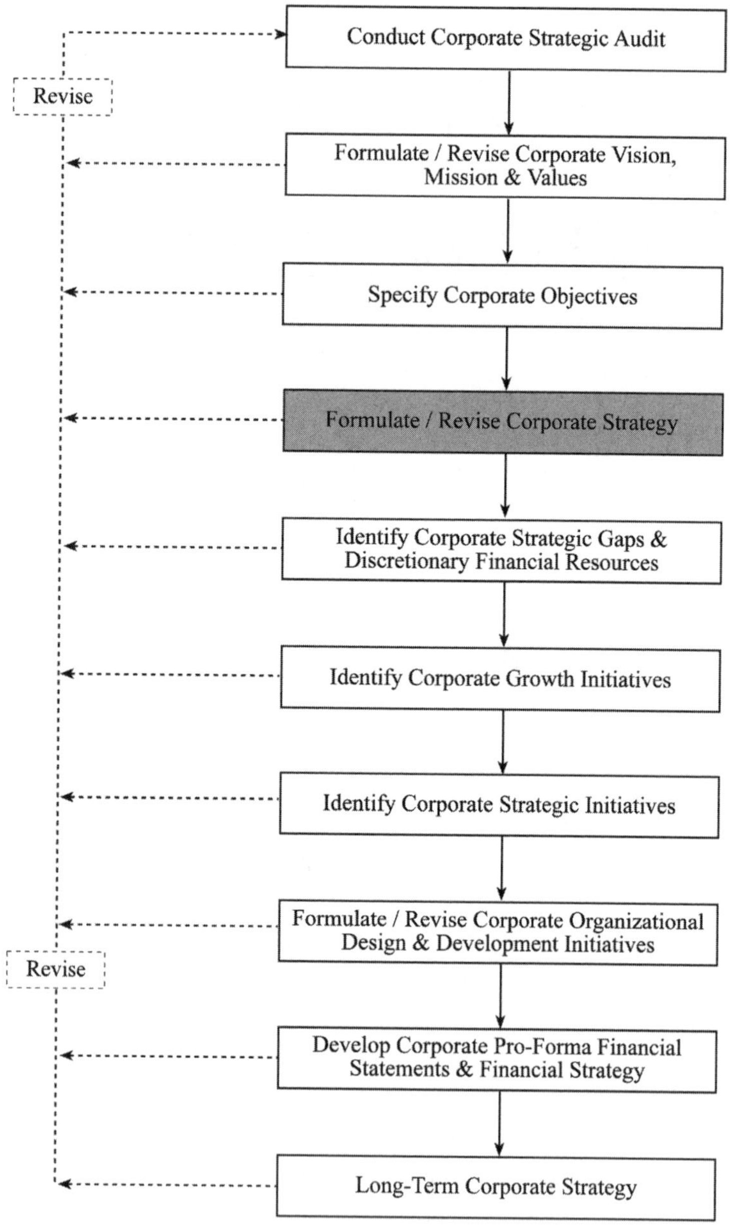

```
                              ┌─────────────────────────────────────┐
              ┌ ─ ─ ─ ─ ─ ─ ─│   Conduct Corporate Strategic Audit  │
              │               └─────────────────────────────────────┘
   ┌ ─ ─ ─ ┐  │                              │
   │ Revise│  │                              ▼
   └ ─ ─ ─ ┘  │  ┌─────────────────────────────────────┐
              │◀─│  Formulate / Revise Corporate Vision, │
              │  │         Mission & Values              │
              │  └─────────────────────────────────────┘
              │                              │
              │                              ▼
              │  ┌─────────────────────────────────────┐
              │◀─│      Specify Corporate Objectives     │
              │  └─────────────────────────────────────┘
              │                              │
              │                              ▼
              │  ┌─────────────────────────────────────┐
              │◀─│   Formulate / Revise Corporate Strategy │
              │  └─────────────────────────────────────┘
              │                              │
              │                              ▼
              │  ┌─────────────────────────────────────┐
              │◀─│   Identify Corporate Strategic Gaps &  │
              │  │   Discretionary Financial Resources    │
              │  └─────────────────────────────────────┘
              │                              │
              │                              ▼
              │  ┌─────────────────────────────────────┐
              │◀─│   Identify Corporate Growth Initiatives│
              │  └─────────────────────────────────────┘
              │                              │
              │                              ▼
              │  ┌─────────────────────────────────────┐
              │◀─│  Identify Corporate Strategic Initiatives│
              │  └─────────────────────────────────────┘
              │                              │
              │                              ▼
              │  ┌─────────────────────────────────────┐
              │◀─│ Formulate / Revise Corporate Organizational│
   ┌ ─ ─ ─ ┐  │  │   Design & Development Initiatives     │
   │ Revise│  │  └─────────────────────────────────────┘
   └ ─ ─ ─ ┘  │                              │
              │                              ▼
              │  ┌─────────────────────────────────────┐
              │◀─│  Develop Corporate Pro-Forma Financial │
              │  │   Statements & Financial Strategy      │
              │  └─────────────────────────────────────┘
              │                              │
              │                              ▼
              │  ┌─────────────────────────────────────┐
              └◀─│     Long-Term Corporate Strategy       │
                 └─────────────────────────────────────┘
```

off being part of the enterprise than it would be if it was independent, or part of an-other enterprise.[106]

Value adds are likely to occur when the enterprise's skills and resources fit well with the needs and opportunities, and particularly the competitive advantage requirements, of each business unit. A corporate strategy that significantly im-proves the competitive advantage of each business unit is optimum. The power of the strategy can often be enhanced when a competitive advantage in one business unit can be used to build competitive advantage in other units.

Adding value in these ways involves sharing knowledge, information and activities, and transferring skills throughout the relevant parts of the organization.[107]

Management Perspectives on Corporate Strategy.   The major management perspectives that underline our approach to corporate strategy are:

- Corporate value is created at the strategic level as well as the business-unit level.
- The business portfolio structure of an enterprise can create shareholder value.
- Corporate-divisional relationships are driven by business unit needs *and* corporate-level strategic considerations.
- Companies can achieve success with varying degrees of relatedness between divisions, based on individual circumstances. The preferred relatedness is when the skills, processes, assets, and capabilities required to achieve competitive advantage are the same, or similar, across several, or ideally all, operating divisions.
- Corporate headquarters is the ultimate authority, but it is also a support service for the businesses by multiplying the resources available, both human and financial, and spreading best practices.
- Corporate executives should help make business units stronger by transferring the best ideas, the most developed knowledge, and the most valuable people between businesses in a way that maximizes shareholder value.
- Corporate executives in general and the CEO in particular, are the drivers of strategic and organizational change.[108] However, ideas for change are encouraged from all parts and levels of the enterprise.

From these perspectives, the major components of corporate strategy in a multi-division business are:

- The composition of the company's portfolio of businesses, including decisions concerning expansion, diversification, and divestment.
- Redefining and repositioning existing businesses and operating divisions.
- Competitive advantage requirements.
- Core competence requirements.
- Strategic priorities.

- Allocation of capital and human resources among the company's various divisions.
- Designing organizational structures.
- Controlling business unit performance.

These components of strategy will be discussed in the remainder of this chapter and continued is subsequent chapters, primarily Chapters 17, 18 and 19.

Effective corporate strategy is concerned with three time periods simultaneously, what we have previously referred to as T1, T2, and T3. The major focus in T1 is about maximizing performance over the next fiscal year. The second focus, T2, is on developing and deploying resources and capabilities for competing over a longer time period, generally three to five years. T3 is concerned with the time horizon beyond the three to five years; this may reach 10 or more years into the future. T3 forces a consideration of the issues of scale, scope, capabilities, and competences that must be developed during T2 in order to be attain the goals and objectives during T3.

BUSINESS PORTFOLIO

A McKinsey study of the performance of the 200 largest United States companies from 1990 to 2000 found that those that actively managed their business portfolios through acquisitions and divestitures created substantially more shareholder value that those that passively held their businesses. The actively managed companies increased shareholder value by about 30 percent over passive companies.[109]

The central question is what businesses should be in the business portfolio going forward? What businesses, if any, should be deleted? What businesses, or growth platforms, should be added? This process begins with the notion of the ideal business portfolio.

Ideal Business Portfolios.   There is no business portfolio that is "ideal" in a generic sense. Rather, ideal is a company-specific issue that depends on a variety of factors including the mission, vision, and values, growth and profitability objectives, the company's existing core competences, and so on. There are, however, four major issues that are worthy of consideration:

- *Business/Industry Characteristics.* What are the growth rates, profitability, and competitive characteristics of businesses and industries that the company wants to be in? Generally, it is desirable to focus the company in high-growth, high-profitability, businesses, and industries characterized by limited competition.

- *Balance.* Is it appropriate to have some diversity in the distribution of sales, operating income, and investment across businesses, product categories, market segments, and geographies? How many businesses or operating divisions should there be and what should be the maximum and minimum percentage of operating income that any one division accounts for?
- *Cash Generation.* How important is it to have a mix of cash-generating vs. cash-using businesses?
- *Stage in Life Cycle.* How important is it to have businesses in various stages of their life cycle, as opposed to being heavily concentrated in one or two stages? If you divide the life cycle into introduction, rapid growth, maturity, and decline, what is the ideal life cycle profile for the businesses comprising the portfolio?

Examples of Business Portfolios. Cisco Systems, with a revenue in excess of $26 billion, attributes its success to the balance achieved in nearly all of their product families, customer market segments, and geographies. Cisco's six advanced technologies have the highest revenue growth of their product groups, and they introduced more than 50 new products white maintaining the leading market share position in most product categories. They have also experienced balance across all key customer market segments, with solid growth in the service provider, enterprise, and commercial segments. In addition, they have experienced solid revenue growth in all five geographic areas they serve. They recently completed 17 acquisitions to extend their talent and technology opportunities for both their core routing and switching products as well as their advanced technologies.

With sales in excess of $37 billion, Caterpillar's 22 autonomous profit center business units manufacture and market large machines, engines and turbines, and are supported by eight service center units providing financing, insurance, and parts and other logistical products and services. These business units are focused on major market segments—global mining, global energy, and infrastructure development—throughout the world. All market segments have strong growth opportunities.

Wal-Mart is the largest retailer in the world with revenues in excess of $315 billion. Their business portfolio consists of four retail formats—Super centers, Discount Stores, SAM'S CLUBS and Neighborhood Markets. Each of these retail formats has a different consumer or customer market segment target, and a different product mix, and each has a variety of store sizes and configurations. Most sales are from US units, although the company does operate in many international markets and is emphasizing global expansion, but not without difficulty. Each of the four formats are at differing stages in their life cycle, and collectively have the ability to power the large sales and income increases involved in growing an enterprise of this enormous size.

General Electric, with sales in excess of $150 billion, has reconfigured its business since the departure of Jack Welch into six business segments: Infrastructure, Commercial Finance, Consumer Finance, Healthcare, NBC Universal, and Industrial. Each business has scale, market leadership and solid customer offerings. This reconfiguration involved $65 billion of acquisitions, and announced or completed divestitures of approximately $30 billion, since 2002. GE's non-U.S. revenues are growing at about a 16 percent rate, and represent nearly 49 percent of total corporate sales. About 50 percent of their global revenue is in the "developed world" of Western Europe and Japan, with the remainder in developing markets, principally the Middle East, India, and Japan, which, collectively, are growing in excess of 20 percent annually. GE's portfolio is probably the most diverse in the world across products, market segments, and geographies. And, like Wal-Mart, GE has designed a portfolio that provides growth opportunities of sufficient size for an organization of this scale.

Divestitures.   Another finding of the McKinsey study alluded to earlier was a strong bias against divestiture. Fewer than half of the 200 companies divested three or more substantial businesses during that decade. Moreover, in studying 50 of the largest divestitures, more than 75 percent of them occurred late. Most of the divestitures were not just done under strained circumstances; they happened only after extended delays when problems became so obvious that action became unavoidable. For the majority of divestitures, an earlier sale would have generated significantly higher returns. Historically, there has been a strong tendency to divest too little, too late.[110]

All of the capital, management time, and support-function capacity that are released through a divestiture can be reinvested in improving shareholder value. This may involve reducing debt, increasing dividends, creating a special dividend, or buying back stock. It may also involve expanding existing businesses and/or investing in attractive new growth opportunities.

Candidates for divestiture can be identified through the types of analyses discussed in Chapter 12's Strategic Audit, namely the GE/McKinsey Model, the BCG Growth-Share Matrix, and Shareholder Value Analysis. Final decisions regarding disposition and the timing of divestiture might not be appropriate until repositioning and growth options have been analyzed and quantified in terms of their impact on sales, net income, and return-on-investment.

REDEFINING AND REPOSITIONING EXISTING BUSINESSES

Another major component of corporate strategy is redefining and/or repositioning existing businesses. The need and opportunity for this type of activity should also flow from the analyses suggested in Chapter 12's Strategic Audit. The impetus for redefining and repositioning can come from a variety of sources including changes in the environment, life styles, consumer behavior, technology, government regulations, and competitive activity, to name a few.

Ideally, the operating business that is involved sees the need for and opportunities of repositioning and includes the appropriate responses in its business plan. Often, however, this is not the case, because business unit executives tend to be more focused on meeting the current year's objectives, and often less focused, and perhaps less skilled, in identifying transformational trends. Sometimes the operating unit is experiencing extraordinary success which often has a tendency to blind people to paradigm shifts.

In some cases the transformational change can have profound effects on several operating divisions. In this case it may be more effective and efficient to have a corporate-led initiative to redefine and reposition these divisions simultaneously.

Examples of Redefining and Repositioning.   With sales in excess of $35 billion, PepsiCo has a business portfolio that is balanced across product categories, market segments, and geographies, with domestic beverages accounting for 30 percent of operating profit; Quaker Foods, 8 percent; Frito-Lay 38 percent, and international businesses 24 percent. PepsiCo's largest share of sales and profits come from Frito Lay which consists of Lay's and Ruffles Potato Chips, Doritos and Tostitos Tortilla Chips, Fritos, Cheetos, Sun Chips, Rold Gold pretzels, and many other snack foods. Unfortunately, obesity is a major issue gaining increased attention and importance in the U.S. and many other nations. PepsiCo views this as a challenge and an opportunity. Their perspective is that the solution to consumers' health and wellness needs, and the obesity epidemic in particular, lies in the concept of energy balance; that is, finding balance between the calories consumed and the calories burned. Accordingly, they have reformulated their products with lower sugar, fat and sodium, and added new or additional ingredients that deliver health benefits Collectively these products constitute what they refer to as "Smart Spot" designated items, currently numbering over 250 products which represent 40 percent of the revenues of products that can contribute to healthier lifestyles. All of this repositioning has been accomplished since 2003.

In the mid 1980's, Leslie Wexner, founder and chairman of Limited Brands, was intrigued with personal care items for young women of the type that bought clothes in the retail chains in Limited's portfolio of apparel and lingerie stores. After testing the idea in a few of his Express stores, he started a new chain called Bath & Body Works, and by 1989 there were 6 of these new test stores. After proving the concept, Limited expanded it at a rate faster than any other chain in the history of retailing. By 1999 there were 866 BBW stores doing $1.2 billion in sales and generating $319 million in operating income. Like the apparel stores, virtually all of the beauty and personal care items sold in BBW were private label, designed and formulated in- house. This success did not go unnoticed, and by the early years in the new millennium Wal-Mart, Target, and others were offering similar products at substantially lower prices. BBW management did not consider this to be a significant strategic issue. Faced with the intensifying need to reformulate and reposition the product lines, and the ineffectiveness of BBW's efforts to accomplish this initiative, Limited Brand executives up-scaled the product line, and BBW management turned over. Wexner invented BBW, grew it rapidly, and then reinvented it and grew it again, so that by the end of fiscal 2006 there were 1546 stores generating $2.6 billion in sales and $456 million in operating income.

COMPETITIVE ADVANTAGE REQUIREMENTS

Another dimension of corporate strategy is to identify the sustainable competitive advantage requirements that are necessary for the enterprise to achieve its objectives within the context of its vision, mission and values. This process begins with the identification of the sustainable competitive advantage requirements for each of the businesses in the portfolio. Some advantage requirements will apply to all businesses, some to many units, and, perhaps, one or more to only a few divisions or brands.

Those businesses that have unique competitive advantages within the portfolio should be strategically conspicuous. This condition raises a "red flag" as to the appropriateness of the business in the portfolio going forward. Combining this analysis with the portfolio analysis described in Chapter 12 provides additional information that is useful in deciding whether the business(s) in question is a candidate for divestiture.

One of the most important characteristics of an ideal business portfolio is when all businesses in the portfolio have the same sustainable competitive advantage requirements, or at least when there is substantial and material overlap. This competitive advantage alignment can provide a basis for creating strategic leverage across all businesses and allow the corporate strategy to truly add value.[111]

Examples of Competitive Advantage. Citigroup is a large global financial services company based in the United States with sales in excess of $85 billion. Compared to other financial services companies, Citigroup believes they have five competitive advantages:

- The most global presence. They believe they have the best presence in the United States of any international financial services company, and the best international footprint, servicing more than 100 countries.
- Unmatched distribution. Through thousands of banks, consumer finance, and Smith Barney branches; ATM's; trading desks; online ser-

vices etc., they calculate that they serve more people every day than any other financial services company.

- Strongest brand. They maintain that their brand franchise helps attract and retain talented people as well as customers.
- Unmatched scale and efficiency. They maintain that this produces strong margins and capital generation which finances growth and partially insulates the company during difficult economic environments.
- The broadest product offering. They believe their broad product offering facilitates one-stop shopping and increases their ability to cross-sell products and services.

Cisco Systems, profiled earlier, describes their competitive advantages more succinctly: a unique balance of financial strength, product leadership, and global presence.

To review, this component of the corporate strategy identifies the types of competitive advantages that businesses in the portfolio (current businesses as well as prospective businesses) should have or should develop.

CORE COMPETENCY REQUIREMENTS

The most important type of corporate core competencies are those designed to strengthen competency requirements that are common across businesses in the portfolio. Here the corporate strategy adds value through additional resources in the form of people and capital, sharing information, experiences, and best practices, and other activities all focused on increasing the effectiveness of resources and core processes of individual business units that are necessary for those units to sustain competitive advantages in the individual markets that they serve. These corporate core competencies should elevate the level of performance of the divisions in these areas and also achieve cost and/or investment synergies for the enterprise in total.

The second type of corporate core competency is remedial in nature, focusing on those competences that are deficient in more than one operating division. A third category should focus on those competitive advantages that will allow several operating divisions to compete more successfully in the future by building new advantages, devaluing the incumbent's advantages, adapting quicker and more effectively to changing opportunities, and so on. Both the second and third types of corporate core competencies should also elevate performance and achieve cost and investment synergies, and thereby add value.[112]

Examples of Corporate Core Competencies. With revenues exceeding $60 billion, Proctor & Gamble, like GE, Cisco, Wal-Mart, Caterpillar, and PepsiCo, has a business portfolio that has a balanced mix of businesses, brands, markets, customers, and geographies. Their core competencies are branding, innovation, ability to go-to-market quickly and efficiently, and scale. P&G is the global leader in all four core categories of their business . . . Baby Care, Feminine Care, Fabric Care, and Hair Care . . . with market shares in each category exceeding 20 percent. They have 17 brands with sales volumes in excess of $1 billion each. In recent years they have accelerated consumer-centric innovation at affordable prices creating attractive value for customers. Their retail partners rank them first in six of eight categories: clearest strategy, most innovative, most helpful consumer and shopper information, best supply chain management, best category management, and best consumer marketing. They create scale in purchasing, distribution, business services, etc. at the corporate level, enabling business units to keep operating costs low, to bring innovation to market at competitive prices, and to invest more than competition in R&D and marketing.

PepsiCo has a set of core competencies similar to P&G. Strong brands, world-class innovation, and powerful go-to-market systems are the competencies they use to drive their corporate strategy.

Toyota believes their corporate core competencies are consumer orientation, quality, speed to market, pricing and service. Within a decade they will have moved from the fourth to the largest car company in the world.

So, this component identifies the corporate core competencies that the enterprise has, or is trying to develop, and their respective roles in formulating the corporate strategy for the future.

STRATEGIC PRIORITIES AND RESOURCE ALLOCATION

The next dimension of corporate strategy is to develop strategic priorities and then allocate resources, both human and financial, in a way that enables the enterprise to achieve these priorities. One set of strategic priorities should focus on the business portfolio, identifying those businesses that are targeted for serious growth, those that are to be harvested, and those that are in a "hold" position, meaning they are not growth vehicles at this time. Input for these decisions comes from the portfolio analyses described in Chapter 12. These are still preliminary decisions, pending the results of a detailed analysis of divestiture options in terms of their feasibility, likely proceeds, timing and so on. The other decision having a bearing on the strategic priorities of the business portfolio is the output of the growth initiatives evaluation, in terms of the potential volume and profit opportunities, the capital requirements, the timing, and so on. These will be discussed in Chapter 17.

The other set of strategic priorities should focus on the core competences that need to be strengthened and those that need to be developed in order to compete more profitably in the future. This set of priorities seldom receives the same degree of analysis and thinking that business portfolios do, and this is both a major error on the one hand, and a significant opportunity, if addressed rigorously, on the other hand.

Examples of Strategic Priorities and Resource Allocation.   P&G is focused on building existing core businesses into stronger global leaders. Their strategic priorities are faster-growing, higher-margin, more asset-efficient businesses with global leadership potential. They concentrate on growing their leading brands, large countries, and the most important retail customers.

Colgate, with sales in excess of $12 billion has similar strategic priorities in terms of their business portfolio. They give priority to their high-margin, fast-growing oral care, personal care and pet care businesses in key consumer markets around the world including the United States, Brazil, China, India, Mexico and Russia.

Colgate's strategic priorities in the core competences area, common in many companies, focus on increasing efficiency. Their initiatives focus on developing a global supply chain with fewer, more sophisticated global and regional manufacturing centers. Additionally, business support functions for subsidiaries around the world are being consolidated into global and regional shared service centers. Another initiative focuses on globalizing procurement, which is achieving significant savings for raw and packaging materials, as well as personal computers, telecommunications, printed materials, and advertising and promotion. Colgate uses the savings from these initiatives to further increase marketing spending, accelerate innovation, and increase profitability.

The Corporate Strategy Agenda

Specifying the ideal business portfolio, including divestitures and acquisitions; repositioning existing businesses; identifying competitive advantage requirements; specifying core competences requirements; establishing strategic priorities and allocating financial and human resources are the major components involved in developing a corporate strategy for an enterprise consisting a several operating divisions. Sophisticated corporate strategies create the right balance of resources and businesses, because the enterprise's corporate capabilities and core competences enhance the competitiveness of every business in the portfolio, in the present as well as the future. The corporate strategy adds value.

Chapters 17, 18, and 19 further dimensionalize corporate strategy by identifying growth initiatives; strategic initiatives focused on core competencies, innovation and learning; and organizational design and development initiatives.

CHAPTER 16

CORPORATE STRATEGIC GAPS AND DISCRETIONARY FINANCIAL RESOURCES

"Strive for excellence and, as you come close to accomplishing your goals, push them out a little further and see what happens. You'll be amazed at what you can really do."

Sandy Weill
Former CEO
Citigroup

As Figure 16.1 indicates, the next step in developing/revising a corporate strategy for an enterprise with multiple operating divisions is to identify and measure strategic gaps and discretionary financial resources. Strategic gaps quantify the challenges that must be satisfied in achieving the corporate objectives for the planning period, while the discretionary financial resources measure the approximate amount of money that will be available to close the gaps and achieve the objectives. The concepts are similar to those described in Chapter 7's discussion of single business companies but the techniques are a little different in order to accommodate the complexity of multiple operating divisions.

CORPORATE STRATEGIC GAPS

Strategic gaps measure the difference between the levels of performance specified in the corporate objectives (see Chapter 14), and the levels attainable through the continuation and improvement of businesses in the current portfolio, or the current portfolio minus any divestitures that are anticipated at this point. Because there are usually multiple objectives, there are usually multiple gaps.

Figure 16.1 Identifying strategic gaps & discretionary financial resources

```
          ┌─────────────────────────────────────────┐
     ┌─── │      Conduct Corporate Strategic Audit   │
     ┊     └─────────────────────────────────────────┘
 ┌ ─ ─ ┐                        │
 ┊Revise┊                       ▼
 └ ─ ─ ┘   ┌─────────────────────────────────────────┐
     ┊◄─── │    Formulate / Revise Corporate Vision,  │
     ┊     │          Mission & Values                │
     ┊     └─────────────────────────────────────────┘
     ┊                          │
     ┊                          ▼
     ┊     ┌─────────────────────────────────────────┐
     ┊◄─── │      Specify Corporate Objectives        │
     ┊     └─────────────────────────────────────────┘
     ┊                          │
     ┊                          ▼
     ┊     ┌─────────────────────────────────────────┐
     ┊◄─── │   Formulate / Revise Corporate Strategy  │
     ┊     └─────────────────────────────────────────┘
     ┊                          │
     ┊                          ▼
     ┊     ┌─────────────────────────────────────────┐
     ┊◄─── │   Identify Corporate Strategic Gaps &    │
     ┊     │     Discretionary Financial Resources    │
     ┊     └─────────────────────────────────────────┘
     ┊                          │
     ┊                          ▼
     ┊     ┌─────────────────────────────────────────┐
     ┊◄─── │    Identify Corporate Growth Initiatives │
     ┊     └─────────────────────────────────────────┘
     ┊                          │
     ┊                          ▼
     ┊     ┌─────────────────────────────────────────┐
     ┊◄─── │   Identify Corporate Strategic Initiatives│
     ┊     └─────────────────────────────────────────┘
     ┊                          │
     ┊                          ▼
     ┊     ┌─────────────────────────────────────────┐
     ┊◄─── │ Formulate / Revise Corporate Organizational│
 ┌ ─ ─ ┐   │   Design & Development Initiatives        │
 ┊Revise┊   └─────────────────────────────────────────┘
 └ ─ ─ ┘                        │
     ┊                          ▼
     ┊     ┌─────────────────────────────────────────┐
     ┊◄─── │  Develop Corporate Pro-Forma Financial   │
     ┊     │   Statements & Financial Strategy        │
     ┊     └─────────────────────────────────────────┘
     ┊                          │
     ┊                          ▼
     ┊     ┌─────────────────────────────────────────┐
     └───► │      Long-Term Corporate Strategy        │
           └─────────────────────────────────────────┘
```

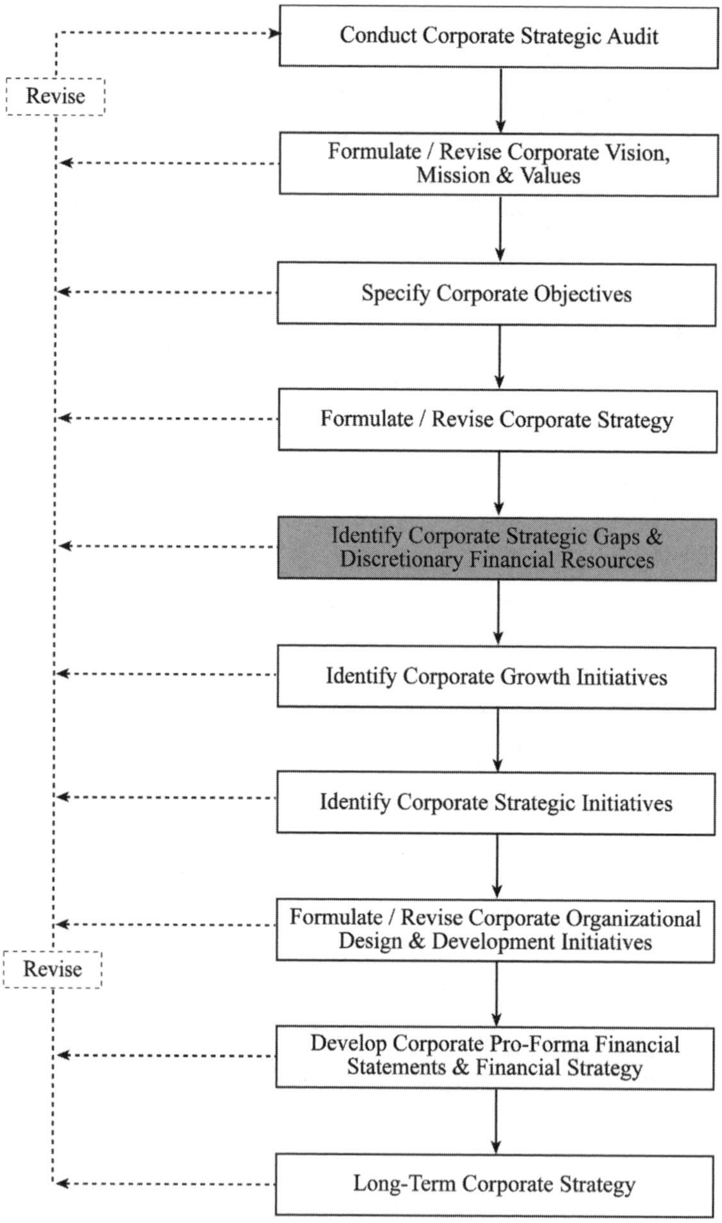

Earnings-per-Share and Sales Gaps

Figure 16.2 presents a process for identifying EPS and sales gaps in multi-division businesses. This process assumes each of the divisions has followed the processes outlined in Chapters 3–11 for developing a business strategy for a single division in a multi-division enterprise.

Figure 16.2 Illustrative strategic gaps (000)

	Base Year	1	2	3	4	5	Comment
			Planning Period, Year				
1. Earnings-per-share objective	$1.00	$1.20	$1.44	$1.73	$2.07	$2.48	Objective is 20% CAGR
2. Shares outstanding	# 100,000	98,000	96,000	94,000	92,000	90,000	Assume 2% annual buyback
3. Net profit after taxes objective	$100,000	117,000	138,240	162,620	190,400	223,200	(Line 2 x Line 1)
4. Net profit before taxes objective	147,000	172,050	203,290	239,150	280,000	328,230	Assume 32% tax rate
5. Other income (expense)	10,000	13,500	15,000	17,000	18,500	20,000	Interest income & expense, net
6. Operating income objective	157,000	185,550	218,290	256,150	298,500	348,230	(Line 4 + Line 5)
7. Operating income projections from existing business units:							
A Division	100,000						
B Division	70,000						
C Division	60,000						
D Division	<3,000>						
Corporate overhead	<70,000>						
7. Total	$157,000	$184,000	$215,000	$249,000	$289,000	$332,000	(Sum of A + B + C + D + E)
8. Strategic operating income gap	0	$1,550	3,290	7,150	9,500	16,230	(Line 6 - Line 7)
9. Sales gap for planning purposes	0	$15,500	32,900	70,150	95,000	162,300	(Assumes 10% operating income for sales gap planning purposes) vs 15.7% earned by existing businesses

The starting point is to lay out the EPS objective. In this case, the hypothetical company's objective is to increase earnings-per-share by 20 percent per year compounded. Starting with the estimated EPS of $1.00 in the base year, this results in a requirement of $2.48 for the last year of the planning period.

The second step is to determine the number of shares outstanding. We assume that the company, like many other publicly-held companies, has an on-going stock buy-back program. In this case we assume 2 percent per year, so the shares are reduced by this amount per year from the base of 100 million.

The net profit after- taxes objective is simply a math calculation involving multiplying the EPS objective by the number of shares outstanding for each year.

The net profit before- tax objective is simply the after-tax number adjusted for taxes, which in this case, are assumed to be 32 percent.

Other income is the net of interest income, interest expense and other items that a company classifies as such. The numbers shown are hypothetical but realistic in the context of the example.

The operating income objective is simply the mathematical sum of net profit before- taxes plus the net of other income. This is the amount of operating income that the enterprise must generate to achieve its objective of a 20 percent compound annual growth rate (CAGR) in EPS. The operating income growth rate requirement is less than 20 percent CAGR, due principally to the share buyback strategy of 2 percent compounded annually.

The next step is to insert the operating income estimates and projections of the operating divisions in the prospective product portfolio. These estimates should include the improvement in operating income that each of the operating divisions have signed up to, although it may be appropriate to reduce these numbers somewhat to be on the conservative side depending on the circumstances and the personalities involved.

The difference between the operating income objective and the sum of the operating income projections for each of the existing business units is the *strategic operating income gap*. In this illustration, the operating income gap grows from $1.5 million in year 1, to $16.2 million in year 5.

Since it is often easier to think in terms of sales, the operating income gap can be converted into a sales gap by adjusting the former for the estimated operating income rate. In the example, the core businesses are operating at about a 16 percent operating income rate, but in calculating the sales gap, only a 10 percent operating rate has been assumed. The more conservative number of 10 percent results in a larger sales gap than would be the case of a 16 percent operating income rate were used. Generally, it is better to have too many profitable growth options, as opposed to too few, so some conservatism is prudent. In the example, the 10 percent operating rate assumption results in a sales gap of $15.5 million in year 1 and a $162.8 million gap in the fifth year.

In the case, the operating income gap of $16.3 million in year 5 represents about 4.6 percent of the total operating income requirement if the enterprise is to achieve its objective of increasing EPS by 20 percent compounded. In many instances this would be a reasonable expectation. If it were too high, management could decide to try to make greater improvements in the current businesses, perhaps increase the share buyback, or reduce the EPS objective below the current 20 percent rate.

Conversely, the operating income gap may be too low, which may suggest that the enterprise is capable of growing EPS at a rate faster than 20 percent. Understanding the rate at which a business can grow is one of the most important and difficult challenges facing the CEO and senior management. The challenge is to accelerate earnings growth to the edge of sustainability and tolerable risk

ADDITIONAL GAPS

Gap analysis also needs to be performed for the other corporate objectives for the planning period. Among the most important are the profitability objectives used in the business; operating income, pre-tax income, after-tax income, after-tax profit margins, asset turnover, after-tax return on equity, cash flow, cash flow return on assets and equity, economic value added, and so on.[113] Additional objectives can be "gapped" in the same manner using, among other things, the benchmarking analyses completed during the Strategic Audit described in Chapter 12.

SCOPING

It is also useful at this juncture to scope the business out over an extended time period, say 10 or more years, depending on the situation. Scoping should usually be focused on identifying sales and operating income gaps that result if a firm intends to achieve a respectable EPS growth rate over this extended time period.

As a corporation grows in size, its growth rate usually declines. Part of this is inevitable due to the law of large numbers. Part of it, though, is the result of not thinking in the right scale. Scoping will create very large gaps, and result in different thinking about what needs to be done now, and during the remainder of the planning period, to be able to achieve reasonable EPS growth rates during the period following the current planning period.

Given the very long-term focus of scoping, it is primarily a math exercise with educated rough guesses about the rate that existing operating divisions can grow operating income during the scoping period. Consequently, the time and other resources devoted to calculating these scoping gaps should be limited, and the number of people involved severely restricted. The results of the scoping exercise and their strategy implications should be exposed to the wider audience.

Scoping will add new and different perspectives to dealing with the immediate challenges, as well as the number and types of growth options, including acquisitions, that should be considered. Properly used, it should enable the enterprise to achieve higher long-term EPS growth rates, and hence greater shareholder value, than would otherwise be possible.

DISCRETIONARY FINANCIAL RESOURCES

This step involves a preliminary evaluation of the financial resources that are available, or could be available, to the enterprise for closing the strategic gaps. This, in turn, involves both operating expenses and capital requirements.

OPERATING EXPENSE REQUIREMENTS

The operating expense requirements for closing strategic gaps need to be funded, one way or another, by the operating divisions. This expense contribution can be made via any combination of volume increases, gross margin rate increases, and/or operating expense rate improvements.

Returning to Figure 16.2, a *strategic gap fund* line could be added as line 6a which estimates the operating incremental operating expenses the enterprise needs to close its strategic gaps. Adding the strategic gap fund to the operating income objective yields a revised operating income objective that would be higher than the amount shown on line 6 of Figure 16.2. This, of course, would increase the size of both the strategic operating income and strategic sales gap.

Alternatively, in Figure 16.2 a strategic gap fund line could be added to line 7, or added into the amount estimated for corporate overhead. This would have the same effect as the previous processes: both the strategic operating income and strategic sales gap would increase. Other variations, are of course, possible, but the point is that existing businesses must provide the funds to close strategic gaps by generating operating income to supply this expense requirement as well as satisfy EPS requirements.

CAPITAL REQUIREMENTS

The capital required for closing strategic gaps can be funded through cash flow or possibly changing the capital structure of the business.

Cash flow can be increased by improving the profitability of the existing businesses. Increasing operating expense margins, increasing asset productivity, improving the relationship between inventory, payables and receivables, and reducing or time-extending capital expenditures are the most common approaches to improving cash flow.

Utilizing existing lines of credit and/or increasing lines of credit are common ways of financing strategic gaps. Other methods include additional credit vehicles, long-term debt, and issuing additional capital stock of some type. If closing strategic gaps involve acquisitions, the acquired company may have excess cash and/or unused debt capacity.

The result of this is a rough estimate of the amount of money that is available to cover operating expenses and capital requirements involved in closing strategic gaps. Obviously, the magnitude of the amount available affects the types of strategic options that can be considered. If the pool of financial resources is not adequate, and/or if the cost and investment required would threaten the financial stability of the business, the objectives may again be revised upward. If the resources are available, the process moves to the next phase: identifying specific growth initiatives

THE STRATEGIC GAP AND DISCRETIONARY FINANCIAL RESOURCES AGENDA

The first output from this exercise should be quantitative measures of the sales, operating income and profitability gaps that must be closed through new growth and strategic initiatives if the enterprise is to achieve its stated EPS and profitability objectives for the planning period.

The second output is a quantification of the level of financial resources that will be available to close the gaps. If the amount of financial resources is not adequate, and/or if the cost and investment required would put the financial stability of the business at risk, the objectives may be revised downward. If the resources are available, the thinking moves to identifying the best growth initiatives that will close the gaps within the constraints of the available finances.

CHAPTER 17

CORPORATE GROWTH INITIATIVES

*"Iconic success is sometimes just around the corner. The difficulty is
in seeing around corners."*

David T. Kollat

As Figure 17.1 reminds us, the next step in developing a long-term business strategy for a multi-division business is to generate and evaluate corporate growth initiatives. Collectively, these initiatives should satisfy the EPS growth requirements, profitability requirements, and any other objectives of the enterprise for the planning period in question, in a way that is consistent with the vision, mission, and values. Identit,ing corporate growth initiatives involves the following major activities:

- Selecting the best growth options from the growth option agendas of the operating divisions in the enterprise.
- Determining whether additional growth options should be pursued that are *not* on the growth options agendas of the operating divisions.
- Identifying additional growth options (if needed).
- Evaluating the additional growth options.
- Developing the growth initiative and divestiture agenda.

EVALUATING THE GROWTH OPTION INITIATIVES OF OPERATING DIVISIONS

Chapter 8 presented an approach where each operating division prepares an agenda of growth options that allow it to achieve the operating income and profitability targets assigned to it for the planning period in question. Each growth option initiative on this agenda should have been rigorously evaluated based on:

- Sales and operating income potential, including forecasts by year.
- Profitability measures including operating margins, return on assets or capital employed, economic value added, discounted cash flow, etc.

Figure 17.1 Identifying corporate growth initiatives

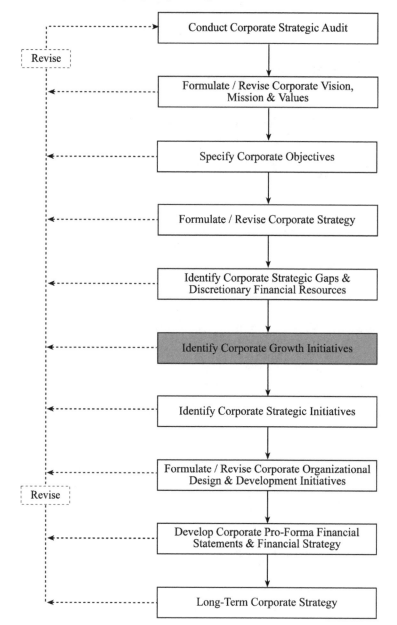

- Potential as a growth platform for future growth initiatives.
- Ability to achieve and sustain an acceptable competitive advantage.
- An acceptable degree of strategic vulnerability.
- Capital requirements.
- Other criteria, as appropriate.

186

The growth option agendas of the operating units can be compiled and summarized into a master growth option agenda which facilitates a fresh evaluation from a broader perspective. Some growth options may have appeared desirable when viewed within the context of an individual operating division, but now may seem questionable given the broader context of alternatives. Other evaluative criteria and judgments can also be made at this juncture including the relative workloads of each division, the relative competences and capabilities of the executives running each division, the relative probabilities of success of each option, the relative power of various new growth platforms, the relationship of each option to the strategic priorities of the enterprise, and so on.

Based on these, and other analyses that may be important in individual situations, a master growth option agenda list is created.

ARE ADDITIONAL GROWTH OPTIONS APPROPRIATE?

The master growth option agenda needs to be compared against several criteria to determine whether it is appropriate to identify additional growth options, to be generated at operating divisions, within the corporate group, or both.

First, the growth option agenda needs to be evaluated from the perspective of the target business portfolio. Adding the current portfolio and the growth options that are on the agenda yields the total portfolio that would result from successful implementation. This total portfolio needs to be compared with the target business portfolio to determine whether appropriate progress is being made toward the attainment of the target portfolio Target business portfolios, you recall, are often described in terms of distribution of revenue and net income across industries; balance across products, geographies, and customers; cash-generators vs. cash-users; response to business and industry cycles; stage in business life cycle; longevity of patent or legal protection; and so on.

Second, the growth option agenda needs to be evaluated in terms of its earnings and profitability potential. This earnings and profitability potential needs to be compared with the EPS and profitability objectives for each year in the planning period, and, particularly in the case of EPS objectives, should exceed the requirement by a substantial margin, 10 percent or more not being unreasonable. The earnings and profitability potential of the growth option agenda also need to be compared with the earnings and profitability requirements for the extended time period as derived from the scoping exercises described in Chapter 14. This is often a more stringent requirement, but critically important if the enterprise is to achieve accelerated earnings growth over an extended time horizon of ten or more years. This evaluation is more obtuse and judgmental, but the prudent course is to maintain a comfortable cushion.

Third, the growth option agenda should be evaluated in terms of how it affects the core competencies and competitive advantage requirements of the enterprise. Do all of the options use existing core competencies? Does the agenda strengthen core competencies and key competitive advantage requirements, particularly those that are common to several operating divisions? Does the agenda add new competencies that do not currently exist that are competitive advantage requirements in one or more operating divisions? Will this growth agenda strengthen the competitive advantage of the enterprise relative to competitors, or weaken it?

Using these criteria, and others that may be important in specific situations, the decision can be made to either finalize the current growth option agenda or generate corporate growth options.

IDENTIFYING CORPORATE GROWTH OPTIONS

The consulting company, Bain & Co. conducted a five year study of the growth strategies of 2000 companies worldwide. They found that the most risky decision a company can make is to stray from its *core*. In the study, Bain defines core business as that set of products, capabilities, customers, and geographies that defines the essence of what the company is, or aspires to be, to achieve its grown mission. Their research identifies five steps that companies can use to evaluate the real risks and payback of any strategic growth initiative:[114]

- Define the boundaries of your core business and gain consensus on those boundaries.
- Decide which cores have the most potential for growth based on their competitive positions and profitability.
- Determine whether the strongest cores are close to their full growth potential or whether there is more potential to tap.
- Map out the opportunities, or adjacencies, surrounding the strongest cores and determine the order in which these opportunities should be addressed.
- Assess whether market leadership is possible in the proposed areas, and evaluate the cost of getting there.

The Bain study found that companies that profitably outgrow their competitors on a consistent basis develop a formula for expanding those boundaries in predictable, repeatable ways. They found that the average company succeeds only 25 percent of the time in launching new initiatives successfully. Companies that have a repeatable formula have success rates of twice that, and some have rates as high as 80 percent. Repeatability allows the company to systematize the growth, and, in so doing, enjoy the benefits of learning-curve effects.

When a company expands beyond the core, Bain found that the most sustained, profitable growth comes when a company pushes out the boundaries of its core business into an *adjacent* space.[115] Figure 17.2, is one way of thinking about these adjacent spaces, except for the diversification option which is not considered adjacent, and it is often the most risky option.

Market Penetration Options.   This approach to generating corporate growth initiatives focuses on achieving EPS and profitability objectives by doing better with current businesses in the markets these businesses currently serve. (Figure 17.2) Generally this is the least risky strategy. Moreover, as the Bain study confirmed, most management teams underestimate the growth potential of their core and fail to mine all of the hidden value growth. In fact, the best core businesses are often the greatest underperformers relative to their true potential.[116]

Proctor & Gamble uses this strategy. For many years, P&G's growth strategies strayed away from its core products in favor of attempting to develop new exciting

Figure 17.2 A generic system for identifying corporate growth options

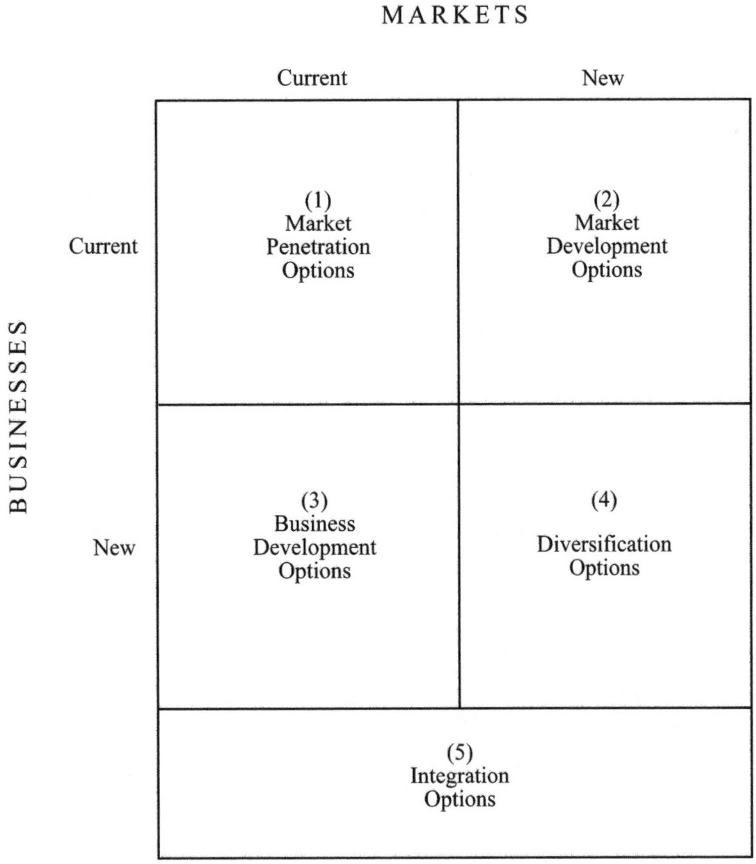

MARKETS

	Current	New
Current	(1) Market Penetration Options	(2) Market Development Options
New	(3) Business Development Options	(4) Diversification Options
	(5) Integration Options	

BUSINESSES

breakthrough products. After A.G. Lafley took over as CEO, the company returned to building basic big brands. He and his team selected P&G's best brands going forward and made them the focus. P&G's organic sales growth objective is 6 percent per year. During their most recent fiscal year, volume was up 7 percent, on average, for the Company's 17 billion dollar brands, including such names as Tide, Charmin, Bounty Pampers, Head & Shoulders, Pantene, Crest, Pringles, Braun, and Gillette.

Another example of this strategy is Performance Food Group, one of the fastest-growing, most profitable companies in America. The Company markets and distributes over 66,000 national and proprietary brand food and non-food products to approximately 44,000 customers in the foodservice industry which includes restaurants, hotels, cafeterias, schools, healthcare facilities and other institutional customers, as well as multi-unit chain restaurants. PFG has focused on increasing sales to existing customers within existing markets. The Company's goal is to become the principal supplier to all of its customers. PFG developed a value-added services program which helps customers control costs via computer communications, more efficient deliveries, and consolidation of suppliers. These enhancements make PFG more attractive in its efforts to increasing sales per delivery, sell higher-margin 'center of the plate' products, and secure a maximum market share in all existing regions.

In retail companies, the term for this strategy is increasing "same store sales" or "comparable store sales". In other words, increasing the sales per store of existing stores in existing markets. Thus, a company like Wal-Mart focuses on maintaining their price leadership position; merchandising more aggressively; and improving their in-stock position in order to prevent lost sales; and motivate and incentivize their associates. Similarly, Williams Sonoma's portfolio of brands including Williams-Sonoma, Williams-Sonoma Home, Pottern Barn, Pottery Barn Kids, PBteen and West Elm all have individual programs designed to increase their respective sales per store over the levels attained last year.

Companies can sometimes rescue businesses in the maturity phase of their life cycles and return them to the growth phase via two major types of strategies:[117]

- Reverse positioning. This involves stripping away some product attributes while adding new ones. An example would be JetBlue which supplements its basic essentials offering with leather seats, high-end personal entertainment systems with satellite television, and extra leg room in the rear two-thirds of the plane.
- Breakaway positioning. This strategy associates the product and business with a category that is perceived as different from the current one. For example, Swatch provided an alternative to watches as a form of jewelry by defining watches as playful fashion accessories.

Market Development Options. This approach to generating additional growth initiatives focuses on expanding existing businesses into new markets, including new market segments and new geographic markets both domestically and internationally. (Figure 17.2) In this option the risk is in understanding the market and the appropriateness of the business model to the new market. Sometimes these issues are formidable, other times they are not.

Retailers rely heavily on this strategy for growth. For example, Wal-Mart will add more that 500 new stores to their portfolio each year. This includes adding up to 250 more supercenters, 45 new Discount Stores, 40 new SAM'S CLUBS, and 30 new Neighborhood Markets in the United States. Internationally, they will add as many as 165 new locations. In total they will add about 55 million square feet of selling space, expanding their total square footage by 8 percent, a rate that is not unusual percentage wise, but nearly incomprehensible from an absolute size perspective

Starbucks, with over 13000 stores, is expanding rapidly, both domestically and internationally toward its long-term goal of 40000 stores. In 2007 it will expand its store base about 20 percent adding around 2400 new stores, 700 of them in international locations.

FedEx Corporation, one of the most admired companies in America, provides a broad portfolio of transportation, e-commerce and business services with companies that operate independently and compete collectively under the FedEx brand. Market development is the major strategy that the Company has used to grow its business. FedEx was the first all-cargo carrier to enter the China in 1984, and now operates more all-cargo flights to and from China than any other U.S. airline. In 2005, FedEx launched the express industry's first direct flight from mainland China to Europe. In other parts of the world, FedEx recently launched overnight service to Mexico, and began serving Iraq and Kazakhstan. With operations in 220 countries and territories, FedEx appears well positioned to capitalize on the twelve fold increase in global trade that is anticipated over the next 30 years.

Citigroup has extraordinary market development growth options. They have opportunities to add retail bank branches, consumer finance branches, Smith Barney branches, and automated loan machines in the more than 100 countries that they have some type of presence in. Citigroup allegedly has the best international footprint of any U.S. financial services company.

Business Development Options. This approach to generating additional corporate growth options focuses on developing new businesses to serve customers and/or consumers in the markets that the business currently addresses. (Figure 17.2) Here the risk resides in developing businesses that the current market will accept, and in a way that does not have negative or unintended consequences for the company's existing businesses.

As an example, Toyota's primary growth strategy is to maintain its leading position in the development of environmental technology, and positioning its technologies as the industry standard. The Company has dedicated considerable resources to the development of its breakthrough hybrid technology. The launch of the highly successful Toyota Prius has lead to the development of an entire fleet of hybrid cars, trucks and SUV's. The Company continues to aggressively research and develop other environmentally sound technologies including fuel cells and other non-traditional power sources. How this strategy will play against the backdrop of the geopolitical dynamic, oil prices, consumer life styles and preferences, and the development of new "clean diesel technology" by Chrysler, is, of course, the question.

For years Nestle was a global leader in many packaged goods categories, but struggled to compete with Kraft Foods and General Mills in the United States. In the early 2000's they initiated a series of moves designed to correct their U.S. market share deficiency. The acquired Ralston Purina to add to their existing Friskies and Alpo brands making them the leading U.S. pet food maker. To complement their Haagen-Dazs brand of premium ice cream, they purchased Dreyers Ice Cream with its Edy's, Starbucks, and Godiva ice cream brands. And, they acquired Chef America, the maker of Hot Pockets and other frozen snacks to complement their Lean Cuisine and Stouffer's brands. These acquisitions helped Nestle become either the first or second company in each food category and simultaneously achieve significant operating efficiencies.[118]

In 2002, K2 was a successful manufacturer of skis selling 125,000 pair a year in the U.S., but with minimal prospects for growth. The CEO observed the consolidation that was occurring in sporting goods retailing and determined that major retailers would prefer to deal with fewer venders so they could streamline the supply chain and reduce distribution costs. After successfully adding ski poles to their assortment of skis and fishing equipment, they acquired 17 companies, and now have a portfolio of businesses that include water sport activities, baseball, softball, snowboards, in-line skating, lacrosse, paintball, apparel and sportswear so that K2 can offer in-season products all year long.[119] Sales to existing customers have nearly tripled.

Retailers frequently use market development options to accelerate growth and profitability. Leslie Wexner, for example, started Limited Stores in 1963 as an apparel store offering moderately priced clothing to fashion-conscious women, primarily in the 18–34 year old age category. Several years later he acquired a company with three stores and a catalogue that offered lingerie to the same customer, and then expanded it dramatically to a sales volume in excess of $5 billion . . . Victoria's Secret. Similarly, he invented Bath & Body Works, a company offering fashionable personal care products at masstige prices to the same female customer, and has developed it into a $2.5 billion business.

Diversification Options.   This approach to generating new corporate growth initiatives focuses on identifying new business opportunities that serve markets that are new to the company. (Figure 17.2) In other words, the company has no experience in the business, or in the markets, that the business serves. Not surprisingly, diversification is generally the most risky method of growth and should be treated accordingly.

The experience of generations of businesses is that diversification is dicey. The critical issue is to avoid the errors of the past through better understanding and strategic analysis of diversification decisions. Economies of scope provide the financial rationale for diversification, but, at the same time, the economies of scope that are realized are often insufficient to ensure that diversification creates shareholder value. The economies of scope that exist can often be exploited more efficiently and with less risk through collaborative relationships with other companies rather than through diversification.[120]

Where diversification has been effective, it has been based on economies of scope among businesses that are related in terms of technologies or markets. More broadly diversified firms have not performed well. While mergers have increased shareholder value, these increases have largely gone to the shareholders of acquired firms. Over a longer time frame, active diversifiers have divested many of their acquisitions.[121]

There are several critical questions that need to be answered appropriately in order to increase the chances for a diversification to be successful:[122]

- What are the distinctive competences of our company?
- What core competences are necessary to be successful in the diversification opportunity?
- What distinctive competences does our company lack in order to be successful in the diversification opportunity?
- If an acquisition, does the company to be acquired have *every* strategic asset necessary to establish a competitive advantage?
- If a strategic asset is missing, can it be purchased, or developed in-house, or can it be negated?
- Will diversification break up any of our strategic assets that need to be kept together?
- Will we simply be a player in the new market, or will we emerge a winner?
- Can competitors outmaneuver us by imitating our strategic assets, purchasing them, or replacing them?

- What can our company learn by diversifying, and are we sufficiently organized to learn it?
- Can the new business help improve existing ones? Alternatively, can the new business act as a bridge to desirable industries that are currently out of reach?
- Can the new business improve our organizational efficiency?

Proctor & Gamble's acquisition of Gillette is an interesting example of the application of these insights. P&G viewed Gillette as an extension of P&G's own core business; as the vehicle to expand into male personal care. Gillette already had over a 70 percent market share in men's razors and blades, and a notable innovation capability. And, the male grooming market is growing at an attractive rate of 14 percent. With its enormous distribution network, P&G believes it will be able to expand the Gillette brand into developing markets such as China, Brazil, and India as well as offer Gillette products beyond the big cities and into smaller and rural areas in these countries. With Gillette, P&G will own 21 brands that each generate at least $1billion in annual sales, which means that it will own more mega brands than any company in the world.[123] The acquisition should create greater economies of scale and scope, provide a brand platform for innovation into future male personal care products, and extend P&G's research and technology capabilities into new areas.

Integration Options.   A fifth approach to generating corporate growth options is to integrate into the supply chain, either backwards toward the sources of basic materials, products, supplies and services; or forward toward the ultimate consumer; or both backward and forward (Figure 17.2). This type of strategic option often increases quality, reduces cost, and improves time-to-market. A major disadvantage is it can reduce flexibility in responding to changes in customer demand.

(1) Backward integration.   Like many others, the automotive industry has long engaged in backward integration into a wide variety of parts and components. More recently, however, Toyota has established a fully operational bank in the U.S. under the name Toyota Financial Savings Bank. With the success of their automotive business, TFS has become the third largest captive loan operation in America after General Motors Acceptance Corp. and Ford Motor Credit Co. Now TFS plans to gradually introduce a broad range of services from credit cards, to cash management, to unsecured loans. Eventually, they have a vision to be a one-stop shop for financial services. But, their core strategic priority is to enhance brand loyalty among their existing 2.3 million auto loan and enhanced warranty customers with a convenient way to manage their finances.[124]

(2) Forward integration. This type of integration is more visible. Examples would include Timberland owning some of its own shoe stores, Ralph Lauren operating his own apparel and home furnishings stores, Apple selling their products through their own stores, Estee Lauder selling their cosmetics brands through a portfolio of their own store formats including Origins and Aveda, Peet's operating their own coffee stores, and Coach selling their handbags, shoes and leather accessories through their own stores. For consumer goods companies in most industries, forward integration of some sort in a prerequisite for being able to compete effectively because it allows a company to achieve greater market impact and improved operating efficiencies.

White Space Options. The final corporate growth strategy option, one not shown on Figure 17.2, is to move into the "white space," or unserved or underserved market, with a business built around a strong capability. According to the Bain & Co. study cited earlier, this is the rarest and most difficult growth option to execute.

Examples might include IBM's movement into the personal computer market when it was a "mainframe company." Apple's invention of iTunes and the iPod is another example. Limited Brand's invention of Pink lingerie is also illustrative of identifying white space options.

Here the strategy is to leverage some of the company's core competences into providing products or services to a market that did not exist or was underserved, when these competences correspond to the success requirements for servicing that market.

EVALUATING CORPORATE GROWTH OPTIONS

Potential corporate growth options that have been generated via the techniques described above, and in any other ways, should be evaluated and compared against each other, and also with the division growth options using the same criteria as before:

- The sales and operating income potential, including pro-forma sales and operating income over the planning period.
- Appropriate profitability calculations, including return on assets, or return on capital employed, or economic value added, or some other measure that is most useful.
- The sales volume and operating income potential of the growth platform that the initiative can create.

- The competitive advantages embedded in the growth initiative.
- Synergies.
- The strategic vulnerability of having the competitive advantages eliminated or weakened seriously.
- Capital expenditure requirements.
- Other criteria, as appropriate.

Using these criteria, and others that may be useful in individual situations, additional corporate growth options, if any, can be selected. Those chosen can then be added to the divisional growth options that are still under consideration, and this master list can again be evaluated on the basis of:

- *Target business portfolio.* After combining the master list of growth initiatives with the enterprises' current portfolio, how does the combined business portfolio compare against the target? Is there the right balance across brands, industries, countries, and customers? Is there the proper balance between cash generating and cash-using businesses? Is there the right balance between sensitivities to the business cycle? Is there the correct distribution when businesses are analyzed by stage in the product life cycle? If the answer is "no" to any of these questions, then the issue becomes, is an appropriate degree of progress toward that goal being made? If the answer to that is "no", then additional corporate options may be necessary.
- *Earnings and profitability potential.* Does the combined portfolio satisfy the EPS and profitability targets over the planning period with a reasonable cushion of 10 to 20 percent? Does the combined portfolio lay the necessary foundation to achieve the earnings and profitability requirements over the *scoping period* (T3) with a sensible cushion? If the answer is "no", then additional or different growth options need to be developed.
- *Core competencies.* Does the combined portfolio strengthen the core competencies and competitive advantages of existing businesses? Does it add new competences that are or can become competitive advantages? If the answer to either of these questions is "no", then additional re-thinking of the growth initiatives may be useful in the sense of asking how these criteria can be satisfied.

In making these evaluations, it may be useful to remember the findings of the Bain & Co. study of more than 2000 technology, service and product companies in a variety of industries. Defining core business as that set of products, capabilities, customers, and geographies that defines the essence of what the company is or aspires to be, they conclude:[125]

- Very few companies actually grow profitably and sustainably, although all plan to do so.
- Building unique strength in a core business, no matter how small or narrowly focused, is the key to subsequent growth.
- The best core businesses are often the greatest underperformers relative to their true potential.
- Most successful companies achieve most of their growth by expanding into logical adjacencies that have shared economics and reinforce the core business, not from unrelated diversifications or moves into "hot" markets.

THE GROWTH INITIATIVES AND DIVESTITURE AGENDA

Using the evaluation and analytical processes just described, a master list of growth initiatives can be compiled by combining those initiatives generated by the operating divisions with the initiatives generated by corporate teams working independently or with operating division personnel. This becomes the growth initiatives agenda for the planning period.

Against this agenda, businesses that have been under consideration for divestiture should receive final review. These divestiture candidates were surfaced using the GE/McKinsey, or BCG growth-share matrix, or Shareholder Value analysis methods described in Chapter 12's Strategic Audit, or via other techniques that may be more useful in individual situations. The effects of these divestitures should now be evaluated in terms of how they impact the target portfolio and core competencies issues described above. Finally, they should be evaluated in terms of their impact on the EPS and profitability objectives for the planning period. The results of these analyses determine whether in fact each of the candidates should in fact be divested and when.

In thinking about divestitures, it may be useful to remember the McKinsey study of the performance of the 200 largest U.S. companies from 1990 to 2000. The analysis indicated that:[126]

- Companies that actively manage their business portfolios through acquisitions and divestitures create substantially more shareholder value that those that passively hold their businesses. They did about 30 percent better in terms of shareholder returns.
- There was a strong bias against divestiture. Fewer than half of the 200 companies divested three or more substantial businesses.

- In studying 50 of the largest divestitures, more than 75 percent occurred late. Most of these were not just done under strained circumstances; they happened only after long delays, when problems become so obvious that action became unavoidable.
- For the vast majority of divestitures, an earlier sale would have generated much higher returns.
- Clearly, companies divest too little, too late.

With these historical observations in mind and using the processes and evaluative techniques described above, the next step is to prepare a growth initiatives and divestiture agenda that is time-phased over the planning period.

While there is a method and logic to this process, it should not be mechanistic. Breakthrough ideas generally involve creative, "blue-sky" thinking involving a lot of intuition and judgment, and this type of behavior should be encouraged. Transformational changes should be explored. And, the process should be robust.

The scope and magnitude of this dimension of strategy is illustrated by the activity of General Electric since 2001 when Jeffrey Immelt replaced Jack Welch as CEO. Over this time period, the Company has exited the following businesses:[127]

- Insurance.
- Motors used in appliances and heating, ventilation and air-conditioning systems.
- Industrial diamonds used in manufacturing.
- Business outsourcing unit based primarily in India.

Simultaneously, they have entered the following new businesses since 2001:

- Hispanic television.
- Movies.
- Health-care information technology.
- Homeland-security systems.
- Water treatment.
- Home mortgages.
- Digital Media.

During this time period, sales have increased from $130 billion in 2000 to $163 billion in 2006. EPS has grown from $1.27 to $2.00. Net profit margins have increased substantially from 9.8 to 12.7 percent, but return on assets has remained constant at 3 percent reflecting a higher investment in assets.

The Company believes that this reconfiguration of its business portfolio has positioned it to capitalize more fully on future market opportunities and competitive dynamics. Time will tell.

Finally, it is appropriate to remember that the average corporate life expectancy is below 20 years. The maximum life is in the hundreds of years. Companies that survive are very good at "management for change." Every single company that has survived long-term has changed its business portfolio at least once.[128]

Adding the divestitures to the growth initiatives produces the growth initiatives and divestiture agenda for the planning period in question.

CHAPTER 18

CORPORATE STRATEGIC INITIATIVES

"I start where the last man left off."

Thomas Edison

D uring his 84 years on earth (1853–1931), Mr. Edison was awarded 1,093 patents, the last one the year before he passed away. During one segment of his career, he was granted 400 patents in eight years, nearly one per week. Some of his inventions include electricity, the phonograph, the light bulb, motion pictures, the Dictaphone, the mimeograph, the storage battery, and a system for generating electric light, heat and power.

Historians consider him the most influential figure of our millennium. Mr. Edison attended formal schools only four years of his life. He had what would probably be called attention deficit disorder today, as well as a hearing problem, and, according to some, something more complicated medically than a hearing disorder. Thomas Edison thought about things in different ways. He was always asking "why?" He changed the world.

'Starting where the last man left off' is what strategic initiatives are all about. As the pace of change accelerates and competition intensifies, the need for continuous improvement in all areas of the enterprise has become a necessity. As one company says in its advertising: "The relentless pursuit of perfection."

As Figure 18.1 reminds us, developing strategic initiatives is the next phase in developing a long-range strategy for a company with multiple operating divisions. In multi-division businesses, the most obvious types of strategic initiatives focus on sharing resources and transferring capabilities among the different businesses within the enterprise, thereby achieving what are commonly called synergies.[129] Equally important, and, in many respects, more impactful, are strategic initiatives that strengthen the competitive advantages of existing business units, improve core competencies, and develop new capabilities that will enable existing business units and the enterprise to compete more profitably in the future. All of these types of initiatives are the subject of this chapter.

Figure 18.1 Identifying corporate strategic initiatives

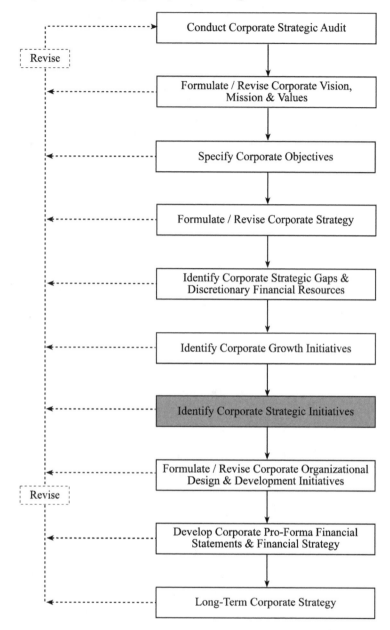

EVALUATING AND CONSOLIDATING THE STRATEGIC INITIATIVES OF OPERATING DIVISIONS

Each operating division of the business should develop its own strategic initiatives as part of the long-range strategy for that division. (Chapter 9) These initiatives should be reviewed, challenged and critiqued by the CEO and his or her team as part of the oversight process.

At this point it is useful to consolidate the strategic initiatives from all of the operating divisions and then re- evaluate the composite agenda. The evaluation should include:

- Are there strategic initiatives that are common across several operating divisions?
- Are there strategic initiatives that *should be* common across several operating divisions?
- Have any significant strategic initiatives been omitted?

The output of this analysis should be the revised composite agenda of strategic initiatives for the operating divisions for the planning period in question. The major focus here should be on identifying opportunities to add value by achieving synergies in implementing strategic initiatives that are common across all, or several, operating divisions. These can become corporate-wide programs backed by the appropriate level of resources to achieve the improvement potential. Examples include major quality improvement programs, cost reduction programs, initiatives designed to accelerate speed-to-market, brand building programs, building innovation skills, and so on. Implementation mechanisms can include task forces, corporate-wide educational programs and so on. Well-managed companies generally have these, and/or similar, types of programs.

IDENTIFYING CORPORATE STRATEGIC INITIATIVES

Here the focus changes from operating divisions to the enterprise as a whole. Insightful companies view the enterprise as more than simply the sum of the operating divisions. Well-run enterprises add value to operating divisions and create additional value as well. Corporate strategic initiatives are the mechanisms that initiate this process.

Competitive Advantage Requirements.   Here the operative question is what competitive advantages does the enterprise have, or desire to have, relative to its competitors? Depending on the degree of homogeneity of the operating divisions, the enterprise might have one major set of competitors, or multiple sets.

Proctor & Gamble, for example, is focused on four major competitive advantages: branding, innovation, go-to-market capability, and scale. In this instance their corporate initiatives might focus on improving their branding and/or innovation capabilities. This focus might lead to initiatives different from, and beyond, those proposed by operating divisions.

Toyota's competitive advantage aspirations are becoming the number one automaker in the world in quality, speed-to-market, pricing, and service. There corporate initiatives are focused on fast-forwarding process innovation to shorten development lead times, as well as increasing their lead in the development of environmental, safety, and other next-generation technologies.

These are the most important type of corporate strategic initiatives and they deserve the appropriate thought, insight and resources that is commensurate with their criticality.

Core Competence Requirements. These types of corporate strategic initiatives focus on improving the resources, capabilities, and assets that are common to more than one operating division of the businesses. One of the characteristics of enterprises that truly add value is that they have a portfolio of businesses that have common core competency requirements. This commonality provides the opportunity to commit resources to achieve a degree of excellence at a cost and investment level that competitors can not match. Accordingly, these are the second most important type of corporate strategic initiatives.

For example, Williams-Sonoma has the single vision: to "Own the Home" through multi-channel retailing targeted at the highly fragmented home-furnishings market. Their portfolio consists of core brands, Pottery Barn and Williams-Sonoma, as well as emerging brands, including West Elm, Williams-Sonoma Home, and PBteen. Their multiple channels include stores, catalogues, and ecommerce.

One core competence requirement for Williams-Sonoma is supply-chain operations. Accordingly, strategic initiatives at the corporate level focus on implementing "Daily Store Replenishment" processes and systems, and furniture hub operations. Other initiatives focus on their direct-to-customer order management and inventory management systems, as well as new retail store inventory management systems.

Gross Margin Enhancement. These corporate strategic initiatives focus on opportunities to lower the cost of goods sold of several operating divisions. This might be achieved through initiatives dealing with purchasing, sourcing and/or manufacturing facilities including the number, location, size, operating practices, and so on. Additionally, there may be opportunities in the freight area by combining shipments, redesigning routes, and/or backhauling. Different warehousing strategies and practices may be another source of new efficiencies. These types of initiatives can often result in significant reductions in the total cost of goods sold by reconfiguring these types of activities and processes.

Economies of Scale, Scope, and Focus. These corporate strategic initiatives provide a major opportunity to add value in a multi-division business. They center on sharing resources and transferring capabilities among different operating divisions.

Are there opportunities to centralize some functions and processes that are common to several divisions? For example, is it appropriate to provide core support activities such as strategic planning, finance, legal, and/or human resources for operating divisions? Additionally, is a shared services organization responsible for research, engineering, information technology, and/or purchasing of core items, supplies and services, appropriate? What about opportunities for sharing manufacturing facilities, or research laboratories, or advertising, or distribution systems, or service networks? [130] The broader question is: "Have we achieved uniformity and standardized all those things that we should?" Conditions obviously change, and so what might not have been appropriate in the past, may be now, and vice-versa. All of these areas may be appropriate sources for corporate strategic initiatives.

Nearly every well-managed company has a continuing series of strategic initiatives designed to improve efficiency and productivity and achieve economies of scale, scope, and focus. For example:

- American Express has reengineering initiatives that have produced annual savings of over $1 billion in each of the past five years. Their initiatives are designed to provide a disciplined approach to enhancing quality, costs and revenues through reengineering and Six Sigma process improvements.

- Caterpillar has ongoing initiatives to include 6 Sigma disciplines into their daily work, particularly in the areas of employee safety, product quality, and product availability. Additional initiatives have increased the production capacity of existing facilities and helped suppliers break through capacity bottlenecks.

- Colgate has a four-year program of strategic initiatives focused on increasing efficiency everywhere. They are developing a global supply chain with fewer, more sophisticated state-of-the-art global and regional manufacturing centers. Additionally, business support functions for subsidiaries around the world are being consolidated into global and regional shared services centers. Another group of initiatives is focused on globalizing procurements for raw and packaging materials as well as indirect purchases such as personal computers, telecommunications, printed materials, and advertising and promotion. The last set of initiatives has increased savings more than tenfold.

- General Electric, like many other companies, attempts to lower cost and improve margins every year. They recently launched an initiative called *Simplification* to attack "non-growth" cost. Overhead cost as a percentage of revenue was 11 percent; their target is to reduce that to 8 percent. This improvement represents a reduction of $6 billion and the savings will be deployed into growth and profit enhancement.

Increasing Balance Sheet Productivity. These types of strategic initiatives focus on increasing the productivity of current and fixed asset investments, as well as the relationship between current assets and current liabilities, so that the asset turnover of the entire enterprise improves (sales/average assets). Generally, the largest opportunities are in improving inventory turnover and accounts receivable turnover, so these areas may be strategic initiatives across multiple, or all, operating divisions. Other potential areas for strategic initiatives in these areas include:[131]

- Eliminate or reduce categories or classes or SKU's of inventory. Install an open-to-buy system.
- Reduce asset investment through sales, sales and lease-backs, and/or outsourcing.
- Increase the number of days or hours that assets are used.
- Pool some assets with those of other firms.
- Increase space utilization by using vertical space (the cube).
- Profitably delay payments to others.
- Accelerate case receipts from customers.
- Increase customers' frequency of payment.
- Accelerate the customer's ordering cycle.
- Automate customer payment processes.
- Offer customers an electronic-payment option.

Hopefully, operating divisions have surfaced these types of opportunities for profit enhancement and have included them in their respective business strategic initiatives. Many times, however, they are overlooked. And, in many cases it may not be economically justifiable for a single operating division to incur the costs and capital investment requirement to implement these types of initiatives, but the enterprise can do it profitably because of the larger scale involved in implementing it across multiple operating divisions.

The most obvious way that these kinds of opportunities become apparent is through comparative analyses of the financial results, characteristics, and ratios of the enterprise against it peers. But, even if the company is best in every measure, opportunities still arise and should be pursued aggressively because organizations change and develop "artery-clogging" inefficiencies continuously.

Proctor & Gamble provides an example of a company focused on improving expense and balance sheet productivity throughout the organization:

- They have increased sales per employee nearly 40 percent over the past five years.
- Even though research and development has increased over the past five years, R&D as a percentage of sales has declined from 4.8 percent in

2000 to 3.4 percent in 2005. More than 80 percent of initiatives succeeded in creating shareholder value, an improvement of 25 percent over the past three years.

- They have decreased P&G's Global business Services costs by more than 15 percent on base business services since 2000.
- They have grown the productivity of P&G's Product Supply organization at a high single-digit rate since 2000.
- They have reduced capital spending as a percentage of sales since 2000 from nearly 8 percent to less than 4 percent, without foregoing any apparent strategic investment in growth.
- They have added an incremental growth point to sales over the past two years with marketing return-on-investment initiatives.

New Capabilities.   These corporate strategic initiatives focus on developing new capabilities that will be needed to attain corporate objectives, implement strategies, and compete in the future. The key questions are:

- How is the future going to differ from the present?
- How are competitors going to behave in the future?
- What are we going to have to do differently to compete?

For example, some likely scenarios for the future would include:

- "Environmental correctness" as a requirement, not a choice.
- The globalization of markets and globalized competition.
- Continuing increases in the prices of oil and oil-related products, and the growing importance of alternative energy sources.
- Continuing increases in the cost of raw materials.
- Continuing increases in fringe-benefit costs.

The issue is which of these scenarios is relevant, which others are critical, how will competitors respond, and what corporate strategic initiatives should be developed and implemented as a result?

THE CORPORATE STRATEGIC INITIATIVES AGENDA

Using the analytical techniques and processes described above, a master list of corporate strategic initiatives can be compiled by combining those business strategic initiatives generated by the operating divisions with the corporate initiatives developed by corporate teams working independently and with operating division personnel. This becomes the corporate strategic initiatives agenda.

CHAPTER 19

CORPORATE ORGANIZATIONAL DESIGN AND DEVELOPMENT INITIATIVES

"It is the willingness of people to give of themselves over and above the demands of the job that distinguishes the great from the merely adequate organization."

Peter F. Drucker

The next step in developing a long-range strategy for an enterprise with multiple operating divisions is to identify corporate organizational design and development initiatives (Figure 19.1). These initiatives should focus on enabling and enhancing the enterprise's ability to achieve its strategic agenda . . . its mission, objectives, strategies, growth initiatives and strategic initiatives. This involves:

- Evaluating and consolidating the organizational design and development initiatives of the operating divisions.
- Gaining culture and value alignment.
- Organizational design.
- Lateral linking mechanisms.
- Incentive compensation design.
- Executive development.
- Organizational capabilities.
- Governance systems.
- Leadership styles.

Figure 19.1 Formulating/revising organizational design & development initiatives

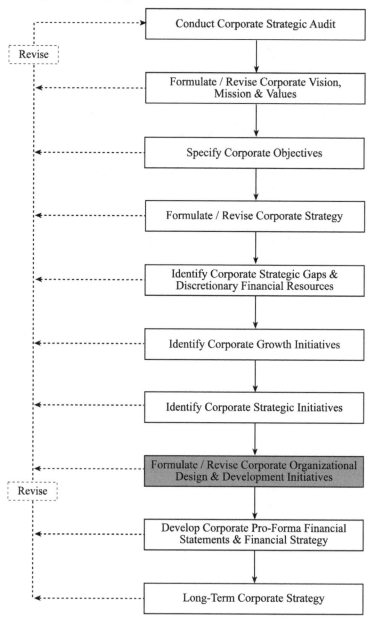

This template mirrors the one that has been used in the operating divisions. This is important in gaining alignment on what the key initiatives should focus on. At the same time, the perspective on these subjects at the corporate level is not only broader, but different in many respects.

Evaluating and Consolidating the Organizational Design and Development Initiatives of Operating Divisions

Each operating division of the business should develop its own organizational design and development initiatives (ODDI) as part of the long-range strategy for that division. (Chapter 10) These initiatives should be reviewed, challenged and critiqued by the CEO and his or her team as part of the normal review of the operating division's strategic plan.

It is useful to consolidate all of the ODDI from all of the operating divisions and then evaluate the composite agenda. The evaluation should include:

- Are there lateral linking mechanisms that are common to more than one operating division? Should there be?
- Are there executive development initiatives that are similar in more than one operating division? Should there be?
- Are there organizational development initiatives that are the same or similar in more than one operating division? Should there be?
- Are there governance system initiatives that are the same or similar in more than one operating division? Should there be?
- Are there any leadership style initiatives that are common to more than one operating division? Should there be?

The purpose of this evaluation should be to determine whether there is the opportunity to achieve operating efficiencies in implementing these initiatives by combining efforts across more than one division.

A second issue is whether there is an opportunity to share best practices in these areas, if that is not already being done. Some divisions will always be better than others is some things, but rarely in all things. There are almost always major improvement opportunities in spreading best practices in organizational design and development from one operating division to another.

The other issue is whether there are additional ODDI initiatives the enterprise should pursue that are not on the composite agenda for the operating divisions. These additional initiatives may be omissions by the operating divisions, and/or they may be things that become necessary as a result of the new corporate strategic agenda.

Culture and Value Alignment

Culture trumps strategy almost every time. Consequently it is critical to have culture and value alignment with the strategy of the enterprise. This involves the following dimensions:

- Are the corporate culture and values consistent with the corporate vision, mission, objectives, strategy, growth initiatives, and strategic initiatives?
- Are the corporate culture and values consistent or compatible with those of the operating divisions? Do they facilitate and enhance the types of interactions that are most productive to the enterprise in total?
- Are the cultures and values of operating divisions consistent enough, or compatible enough, to enable the divisions to interact and work together in the ways that they are supposed to?
- Does the corporate and division culture and values help or hinder the ability of the enterprise to attract, motivate, and retain the type of talent that is required to achieve the corporate agenda?

The corporate landscape is cluttered with problems resulting from culture and value incompatibilities. The AOL and Time Warner merger, for example, was less successful than anticipated partly because of culture and value clashes. The most recent merger of Gillette and P&G, while apparently very successful to date, still experiences operational inefficiencies resulting partly from different analytical, presentation, and decision making styles and time frames.

The first challenge is to figure out whether there are cultural and value differences that are meaningful. If there are significant differences, there obviously needs to be a plan and program to make the needed adjustments. The two most common errors are to either ignore the alignment requirement, or to underestimate the effort and time that it takes to achieve workable compatibility. Culture and value change, when successful, usually requires a continuous program spanning several years.

ORGANIZATIONAL STRUCTURE

Organizational structure should at least assist, and hopefully enhance, the achievement of corporate objectives, strategies, and initiatives. If the objectives, strategies, and/or initiatives are changing, a thoughtful review of organizational structure is definitely in order. But, even if these changes are only slight modifications from the past, a review should be conducted to make certain that an alternative structure would not be more effective, because changes in a variety of factors like relative sizes and profitability of divisions, the importance of global markets, the capabilities of senior executives, and so on, might shift the balance toward an alternative structure.

Figure 19.2 presents four organizational structures that are most common among multi-divisional enterprises. The first option, Figure 19.2(A), presents a basic multi-divisional structure for a company that markets its products domestically. In this case, the business is broken into 12 operating divisions with each division or-

Figure 19.2(A) Illustrative multidivisional structure*

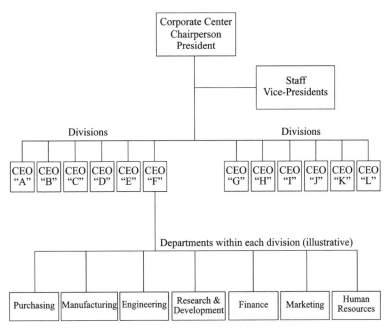

* Adapted from Phillipe Lassere, *Global Strategic Management*. (New York: Palgrave MacMillan, 2003), pp. 72-91.

ganized into departments across functional lines. The alternative, of course, is to organize by function, with each function responsible for its activities and results across all products in the company's business portfolio. Organizing by divisions rather than functions is generally more effective, because, among other things, it enhances accountability and communication.[132]

If the enterprise is global, but has only one, or a few, divisions marketing its products globally, it may be best to attach an international responsibility to the division(s) involved. If, however, many, most, or all, divisions are global, there are three basic choices, identified as Figure 19.2(B), (C), and (D). Here the options are to organize globally by division, or to organize divisions by global area, or a "matrix" that attempts to combine the two approaches. The advantages of one structure are the disadvantages of another, and vice-versa, so there is no perfect solution. The matrix approach attempts to reconcile these pros and cons, but often results in making matters even worse, because many executives end up having two bosses which create another layer of problems, including lack of speed and responsiveness, and compromises that can produce the "worst of both worlds."

The major challenge is how to gain global coordination and efficiencies on the one hand, and local responsiveness . . . particularly in sales, marketing, and

Figure 19.2(B) Illustrative multidivisional global product division organizational structure*

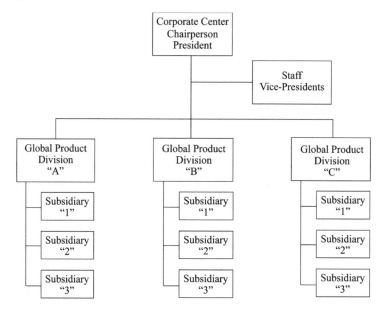

STRUCTURE:
- Each division is responsible for a product or service globally
- Subsidiary CEOs (i.e.: region or country) report to division CEOs
- R&D initiated by product divisions
- Each division develops its own marketing approach

ADVANTAGES:
- Global efficiencies & coordination

DISADVANTAGES:
- Duplication of effort across subsidiaries & potential lack of coordination across divisions
- Limited local responsiveness

* Adapted from Phillipe Lassere, *Global Strategic Management.* (New York: Palgrave MacMillan, 2003), pp. 72-91.

human resources . . . on the other hand. These should be the most powerful issues that drive the choice of structure.

Among the most insightful structural responses to this basic dilemma between global scale and efficiencies and local responsiveness, is the so-called *transnational corporation.*[133] This involves analyzing each division at the functional and activity level, rather than in toto. Scale-sensitive activities are centralized to achieve economies of scale, while other activities, where local

Figure 19.2(C) Illustrative multidivisional global geographical organizational structure*

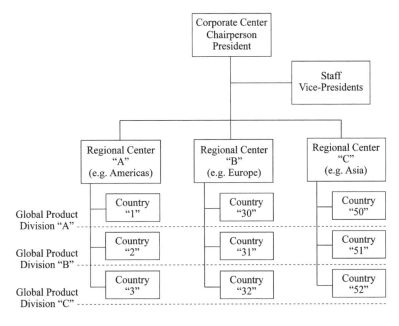

STRUCTURE:
- Each region, & its country subsidiaries, has complete responsibility for all products & services in their geographic area
- Products & marketing programs are adapted to local conditions
- Central global functions & product divisions have a "dotted-line" relationship to regional executive

ADVANTAGES:
- Adaptive to local conditions
- Optimization of results at local level

DISADVANTAGES:
- Lack of global efficiencies and coordination

* Adapted from Phillipe Lassere, *Global Strategic Management*. (New York: Palgrave MacMillan, 2003), pp. 72-91.

responsiveness is critical, are decentralized geographically. For example, production may be centralized while marketing is decentralized to individual markets. This may be the best option.

The output of this process should be to determine which organization structure best enhances the ability of the enterprise to achieve its strategic agenda. This may involve no changes from the current structure, minor changes, or a significant redesign. There are, however, no "magic bullets," every structure is a compromise.

Figure 19.2(D) Illustrative multidivisional matrix organizational structure*

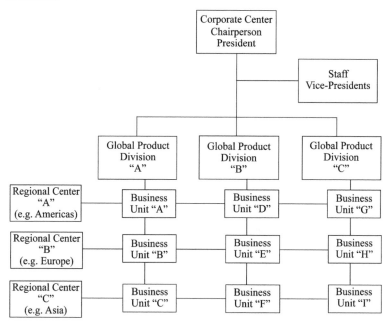

STRUCTURE:
- Global product divisions lead global product development. Regional/country executives adapt products locally
- Mix of global & local factories & operational units
- Global marketing direction with local integration of product lines
- Dual strategic plans; shared information systems

ADVANTAGES:
- Potential for both global efficiency & local adaptation
- Potential for synergies across businesses by Region CEOs

DISADVANTAGES:
- Dual reporting relationships result in conflicts necessitating various mechanisms to resolve them which consume both time & money. Compromises can also be costly

* Adapted from Phillipe Lassere, *Global Strategic Management.* (New York: Palgrave MacMillan, 2003), pp. 72-91.

LATERAL LINKING MECHANISMS

Lateral, or horizontal, linking mechanisms include task forces or teams, communities of practice, liaisons, centers of excellence, and integrators. These mechanism vary in terms of specificity of purpose, duration, decision-making authority, and whether members have other responsibilities, or are focused entirely on the issues in question.[134]

These mechanisms can be used for many purposes including supply chain programs, total quality management, six sigma, business process reengineering, and other things. Our interest in them at this point is to use them to implement the strategic initiatives that have been discussed in Chapter 18, the organizational development initiatives that are common across operating divisions, and corporate organizational development initiatives that are discussed below. The focus should be on establishing lateral linking mechanisms for each of the following:

- Competitive advantage requirement initiatives that affect more than one operating division.
- Core competence requirement initiatives that are common to more than one operating division.
- Economies or scale and scope initiatives designed to enhance gross margins and/or increase operating expense leverage that are common to several operating divisions.
- Balance sheet productivity improvement initiatives that are shared by more than one operating division.
- New capabilities initiatives that involve the same capability requirement for several operating divisions.
- Executive development initiatives that are shared by several operating divisions.
- Organizational development initiatives that are common to several operating divisions.
- Governance system initiatives that are shared by multiple operating divisions.
- Leadership style initiatives that affect several operating divisions.

For each individual corporate initiative, in each of these nine categories, the challenge is to identify the most appropriate horizontal linking mechanism and populate it with the right executives from the operating divisions and the corporate center. Effective and efficient lateral linking mechanisms covering these areas is a major vehicle for adding value in multi-division companies.[136]

Incentive Compensation Design

The incentive compensation structure of the enterprise (cash and equity) should be analyzed to determine whether it promotes the type of behavior required to achieve corporate objectives, strategies, growth initiatives, and strategic initiatives. The major elements of the incentive compensation structure might include:

- Corporate performance.
- Divisional performance.
- Individual objectives.
- Cooperation incentives.
- Incentives to contribute to various initiatives.

The issues are to select the elements to be used, how they should be defined, and their weighting in constructing the total incentive compensation structure. The overriding goal is to align the interests of executives and shareholders.

Most enterprises use some measure(s) of corporate performance in the incentive compensation package. One approach is to tie the measures directly to the corporate objectives. Thus, there is usually some profit target expressed in earnings-per-share, or EPS growth rates, or some derivative measures like net profit before or after taxes, or operating income before or after taxes. Similarly, the profitability target can be tied directly to the return-on-investment measure the company uses, or, perhaps, economic value added, if that philosophy is used in the business. In some cases it may be useful to use "benchmarking indices" against predetermined peer group companies on EPS growth and profitability measures. These indices are particularly useful in accommodating unforeseen geopolitical and/or economic developments and other distortions that are considered exogenous.

Divisional performance can be measured similarly. The profit target should usually by the budgeted operating income target, the profitability measure can be the divisions' return on assets, or return on capital employed, or economic value added, or whatever measure is used by the company to measure its corporate performance. Competitive benchmarking indices against an agreed upon list of the divisions' peer group in terms of operating profit growth and profitability measures can also be used.

Individual objectives can be used to emphasize the specific contributions that each executive needs to make during the period in question, beyond the achievement of the corporate performance measures. These individual objectives need to be aligned with the corporate objectives, strategies, and growth and strategic initiatives, and cascaded down from the CEO to his direct reports, and then to the direct reports of the direct reports in order to achieve consistency and continuity of focus.

Cooperation incentives can be used to encourage cross-functional, and/or cross-divisional integration of initiatives and other activities that are important. These may be included in individual objectives or singled out for special attention and emphasis.

Finally, there can be incentives to contribute to various initiatives, particularly growth and strategic initiatives. These can be useful in gaining alignment and cooperation around the most critical initiatives, particularly when individuals do not have primary responsibility for them, but their support and cooperation is essential for success.

The relative emphasis given to each component of the incentive compensation structure should be architected to ensure the type of individual and collective behavior that is most likely to result in the company achieving its strategic agenda. Some companies decide to make corporate performance account for 100 percent of incentive compensation. Others will make corporate performance account for 50–90 percent of the incentive compensation, with the remaining percent being focused on individual objectives. This mix can vary across corporate functions and levels in the organizational hierarchy.

Care should be taken not to include too many different metrics in an incentive system. This tends to dilute effort and attention and thereby reduces the effectiveness of the system in focusing on key issues.

After deciding on the components of the incentive compensation structure and their relative importance, the next step is to establish the quantitative relationships between the structure's metrics and the level of both cash and equity incentive compensation. For example, if the structure is based totally on corporate performance, and the measure is EPS, then it would be necessary to specify the relationship between different amounts or levels of EPS and the cash incentive compensation and equity compensation that will be earned. If the structure is based on more than corporate performance, it is necessary to determine how the composite will be calculated, and then the specific relationship between various composite results and the amount of cash and equity incentive that will be earned.

Establishing this relationship between corporate performance and incentive cash and equity compensation is critical in aligning the interests of management with those of shareholders. There is no "magic formula," rather careful analysis and judgment should be employed. But, whatever the formula, the principle should be that corporate performance determines the amount of incentive cash and equity compensation, and this relationship should be precise and transparent.

EXECUTIVE DEVELOPMENT

All senior executives of all operating divisions, and the corporate center, should be evaluated, generally on an annual basis. For each executive, this should include an assessment of their functional competence, as well as their leadership abilities.

Each executive's evaluation can then be summarized using some type of scale or system like "red, yellow or green," or "unacceptable, acceptable, and star."

In addition, each of these executives should be evaluated in terms of advancement potential. Some type of time horizons scale may be useful, like "within 1 year; 1–2 years; 2–3 years; longer than 3 years; and never."

Decisions should be made regarding the development program that is best suited for each individual including formal degree programs at universities, executive education programs at universities and/or within the corporation, mentoring, coaching, future job assignments, and the like.

While all functions and positions in a business are important, some are more important than others. These key, or "skilled" positions vary from one industry and company to another, and may change within a company as new strategies are developed. It is important to identify these key positions and subject them to even more intense evaluation and analysis. In addition, it may be useful to use concepts like "substitute-to-star" ratios to measure the depth of talent for each of these positions. Development programs for individuals in these key positions, and individuals that have the potential to mature into these positions, deserve special attention.

Finally, it is important to identify "high-potential" individuals within the organization. These people should receive special attention with detailed executive development programs that nurture and accelerate their progress.

All of these evaluations and career development recommendations for division executives should be made by personnel within that division, and approved by the division CEO. These recommendations should then be evaluated by appropriate people at the enterprise level, and approved by the CEO of the enterprise. This process enables the enterprise CEO to make certain that:

- Senior executives are being used in a way that maximizes shareholder value. Specifically, it allows him or her to determine that the right executives are working in the right positions in the right operating divisions.
- Executives have development programs specifically tailored to their specific circumstances so that the development program is developing the right executives for the right positions with the right skills that will maximize shareholder value in the future.
- The enterprise has identified the key positions correctly, has the right people in these skill positions, has the right development programs for people in these skill positions, has identified future incumbents for these skill positions, and has effective development programs in place to allow future incumbents to acquire the functional and leadership skills they will need to be successful in these skill positions.

- The enterprise has an appropriate number of people in skilled positions, has an appropriate number of qualified future incumbents, and has a recruiting and development effort and pipeline that will enable the company to achieve its strategic agenda, both in T2 and T3.
- The company has the appropriate number of "high-potential" individuals, has appropriate development programs for them, and has a recruiting and development effort that will produce the right number and quality of executives required to achieve the strategic agenda in T2 and T3.

This is one of the major ways that corporations can add value to the performance of operating divisions, and increase the performance of the enterprise in total. Accordingly it is one of the most important responsibilities of the CEO and his team. At General Electric, CEO Jeff Immelt spends one-third of his time on these issues, including the entire month of April each year.

ORGANIZATIONAL CAPABILITIES

Another major task is to assess the current capabilities of the organization, evaluate their appropriateness in achieving the corporate strategic agenda, and determine which ones, if any, need to be strengthened.

Important organizational capabilities differ from one industry and company to another. Some common ones include:

- *Customer orientation*. Focusing all of the activities of the organization around satisfying specific needs, wants, problems preferences or expectations of specific customers in a targeting market segment. Are all operating divisions really customer oriented?
- *Profit orientation*. Understanding and managing to return-on-investment or economic value added. Do all executives in all operating divisions really manage this way? Do they understand profitability, as opposed to profits?
- *Leadership*. Does the enterprise have exceptional leaders in all parts of the business?
- *Collaboration*. Is the enterprise effective and efficient in working across divisions, functions, geographies? What about relationships between the corporate center and the operating divisions?
- *Innovation*. How does each operating division compare with its competitors in terms of innovation? How does the enterprise compare with its peer group?
- *Speed-to-market*. How does each operating division compare with its competitors in terms of speed-to-market? Faster? Slower?

- *Analytical rigor and decisiveness.* How do the operating divisions and the corporate staff rate on these capabilities?
- *Testing and learning.* Understanding the role and importance of testing in the organization and how to manage it. How good are the operating divisions at this?
- *Creativity.* The ability to generate innovative solutions to important problems on a timely basis.

The issue is which of these, or other, organizational capabilities are most important in achieving the corporate strategic agenda. How does the company rate on each of these characteristics, in absolute terms, and relative to competitors? The most important improvement opportunities can become organizational development initiatives.[137]

GOVERNANCE SYSTEMS

It is also important to review and assess the enterprise governance system and its appropriateness in achieving the corporate strategic agenda during T1, T2, and T3. While governance systems vary from one organization to another, at the corporate level they usually should include long-range planning and reviews, fiscal year management including operating and capital budgets and budget reviews, executive evaluation and development plans reviews and communications agendas and vehicles for identifying, evaluating, and managing key strategic issues facing the enterprise.

General Electric's Governance System. Every year senior executives vote GE the most admired, or one of the most admired, companies in the world. The primary reason is that no other company has been so dominant for such a long period of time. The characteristics that executives most admire are GE's intellectual leadership in developing innovative management ideas and practices. GE is also admired for its ability to reinvent itself and change directions, and for developing people. GE's corporate governance systems consists of the following components:[138]

- The Corporate Executive Council (CEC) which meets quarterly.
- Session C, the annual leadership and organizational reviews.
- S-1 and S-2, the strategy and operating reviews.
- Boca Raton, Florida: the annual meeting where operating managers meet to plan the coming year's initiatives and re-launch current initiatives.

The CEC meetings run two and one-half days. The top 35 leaders review all aspects of their businesses, assess the external environment, identify their businesses' greatest opportunities and problems, and share best practices.

The Session C meeting is an 8–10 hour meeting where the corporate CEO and the Human Relations head meet with the business leaders and the senior HR executive of each business unit. They review the unit's talent pool and its organizational priorities.

The S-1 strategy meeting occurs toward the end of the second quarter. The Corporate CEO, CFO, and the members of the office of the CEO meet with each unit head and their team to discuss the strategy for the next three years, including the initiatives agreed upon by the CEC, and the fit between the strategy and the people executing it.

The S-2 meeting, held in November, is the operating plan meeting that focuses on the coming 12–15 months, linking strategy to operational priorities and resource allocation.

Between these meetings other governance mechanisms are at work. In April, GE surveys some 11000 employees online for feedback on how well the initiatives are being implemented throughout the organization, in their view. In October, the senior 150 corporate officers review the progress of the initiatives, initiate the operating plan process for the coming year, and participate in executive development courses.

Each GE operating division has its own governance system that is consistent with, and links to, the corporate governance system.

Obviously, governance systems need to be tailored to the specific circumstances that a company faces. GE's system is certainly not the right one for everyone. But everyone should have a governance system, and it should usually include the same components as GE's, and it should assist the company it achieving its strategic agenda.

Strategy Management. Another governance issue is how to manage all of the strategic activities of the corporation. It may be appropriate to consider an *office of strategy management* that is on the same level as the other senior corporate staff offices, and has the responsibility for managing and coordinating all of the key strategy management processes. These might include:

- Strategic planning assumptions and guidelines for the corporation and the major operating divisions.
- Strategic planning at both the corporate and division levels.
- Strategy reviews at the corporate and division levels.
- Strategy communication.
- Growth initiatives management.
- Strategic initiatives management.

- Integration and coordination of the strategic plan into annual planning and budgeting (in support of the CFO).
- Best practices communication.

In addition to the senior executive heading the group, 5–7 additional people may be required depending on the size and complexity of the enterprise. In addition, operating divisions may have a strategy management executive, with or without a small staff.[139]

LEADERSHIP STYLES

It is also useful to analyze and evaluate the leadership styles of the major executives in the organization in terms of their appropriateness for achieving the corporate strategic agenda. Other factors may also suggest the usefulness of a change in leadership styles: changing social and economic conditions; changes in people's expectations concerning the "proper" work environment; the need to be effective in many cultures, and so one. While it is difficult to get executives to change their leadership styles, it is possible to increase their sensitivities and behavior to certain conditions, people, and types of interactions through proper coaching, often with outside experts.

In thinking about the appropriateness of leadership styles, it may be useful to review one more time Peter Drucker's amazingly simple but insightful views relative to the habits of effective executives:[140]

- They know were their time goes.
- They focus on results rather than work.
- They build on strengths: their own; the strengths of their superiors, colleagues and subordinates; and on the strengths in the situation. They do not build on weaknesses.
- They concentrate on the few major areas where superior performance will produce outstanding results. They set priorities and stick with them.
- They make effective decisions; the right steps in the right sequence. An effective decision is always a judgment based on dissenting opinions rather than on consensus on the facts.

Jim Collins has identified the characteristics of leaders who were able to elevate their company from good to great. You may remember that he calls these people Level 5 leaders, and describes them:[141]

- They shift their ego away from themselves toward the goal of creating a great company. Their priority is for the institution, not themselves.
- Most come from inside the company (90%).
- They set up their successors for even greater success in the next generation.
- They are more plow horse, than show horse.
- They attribute success to factors other than themselves, but take personal responsibility for failures.

General Electric has one of the best, if not the best, executive development centers in the world. The current set of leadership traits that they are teaching to their executives:[142]

- External focus.
- Decisiveness.
- Imagination and courage.
- Inclusiveness.
- Domain expertise.

Whatever leadership styles are most appropriate; their effectiveness can be enhanced by creating the proper organizational environment. This involves creating and communicating, on a continuous basis, a vision and mission that is both transcendent and directional, as well as values that guide the behavior of the company, and then achieving alignment between different parts of the enterprise and the vision and strategy. This type of environment increases the ability of more executives to make greater contributions to the success of the enterprise.[142]

In addition to the appropriate leadership styles and the proper organizational environment, it is most useful for executives to have a well developed *emotional intelligence*. This includes:[143]

- *Self-awareness*. Understanding your own emotions, strengths, and weaknesses.
- *Self-management*. Integrity, conscientiousness, and achievement orientation.
- *Social awareness*. Understanding the emotions of others, the attitude of the organization, and customers' problems and attitudes.
- *Social skills*. Influencing and inspiring others; communicating, collaborating, and building relationships with others; and managing change, conflict and disappointments.

Using these and other insights the question is: "Do we have the right leadership skills to achieve the strategic agenda?" Needed changes should be identified in general, and by specific executive, and then action plans developed to make the necessary changes through executive development programs, mentoring, coaching and/or other techniques.[144]

THE ORGANIZATIONAL DESIGN AND DEVELOPMENT AGENDA

The output of this stage in the corporate strategy formulation process should be an agenda of changes that need to be made to the culture, organizational structure, horizontal linking structure, incentive compensation system, executive development and recruiting plans, organizational capabilities enhancements, governance systems, and leadership styles.

CHAPTER 20

PRO-FORMA FINANCIAL STATEMENTS & FINANCIAL STRATEGY & STRUCTURE

"To win . . . you've got to stay in the game."

Claude M. Bristol

The last step in developing a long-term corporate strategy for enterprises with several operating divisions is to develop pro-forma financial statements, and then formulate the financial strategy and structure of the business. (Figure 20.1). This involves evaluating the financial expectations for the various operating divisions, and then combining them with the corporate strategy, growth initiatives, and strategic initiatives into pro-forma profit and loss statements, balance sheets, and cash flow statements for each of the years in the planning period. Using these statements, particularly the pro-forma balance sheets, the financial strategy and structure of the enterprise can be formulated.

The central question in this exercise is whether these strategies and initiatives at the operating division and corporate levels achieve the corporate objectives. If so, the process is complete. If not, the process either recycles to produce additional strategies and initiatives, or the probable achievement of lesser objectives is accepted.

OPERATING DIVISION ANALYSIS

A useful starting point is to review projected sales by operating division for each year in the planning period. (Figure 20.2(A)). Here it is instructive to review the relative size of operating divisions and the sales growth expectations for each. First, and most obviously, does the plan produce the sales growth necessary to achieve

Figure 20.1 Pro-forma financial statements, financial strategy & financial structure

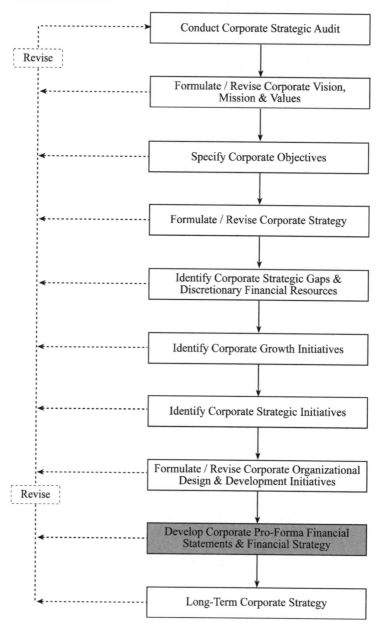

the corporate objectives? Which operating divisions are most critical to the success of the enterprise? How likely is it that each division will be able to achieve its sales objectives? Where are the real stretches and challenges? Is there too much pressure being placed on some divisions and not enough on others? While each of the operating divisions has been thoroughly reviewed, it is useful to look at and analyze the composite picture.

Figure 20.2(A) Sales by operating division

Operating Division	Actual sales					Forecasted sales					Compound annual growth rate
	Y-4	Y-3	Y-2	Y-1	Y	Y+1	Y+2	Y+3	Y+4	Y+5	%
A	$										
B											
C											
D											
E											
.											
.											
.											
X											
Total	$										

Growth
vs Prior
Year %

Next it is important to review operating income by operating division. (Figure 20.2(B)) The same types of questions should be asked. Does the plan in total produce the operating income growth that is necessary to achieve the corporate earnings-per-share growth target for each year? If not, why not, and what should be done about it? Which operating divisions are most important to the success of the enterprise in meeting its total operating income target for each year? Where are the most significant challenges? Should the requirements of other divisions be increased to help deal with the potential exposure of some divisions? This is one of the most important, if not the most important, analysis in the entire strategic planning process, and the discussion should have the appropriate rigor, intensity, and thoroughness.

Figure 20.2(B) Operating income by operating division

Operating Division	Actual operating income					Forecasted operating income					Compound annual growth rate
	Y-4	Y-3	Y-2	Y-1	Y	Y+1	Y+2	Y+3	Y+4	Y+5	%
A	$										
B											
C											
D											
E											
.											
.											
.											
X											
Total	$										

Growth
vs Prior
Year %

It is also important to analyze the projected profitability by operating division. Figure 20.2(C) looks at profitability in terms of return on invested capital, but additional and/or alternative metrics may be useful in individual situations, including return on assets, or cash flow return on assets, or economic value added . . . for example. Looking at it in terms of return on invested capital, the most obvious question is does the strategy meet the profitability objectives for the enterprise for each year, and if not, why not. This analysis also examines where the enterprise is earning its greatest returns, and where the returns are lower. A circle is used to flag each year in which an operating division is expected to not earn the weighted average cost of capital for the total enterprise. Obviously attention should be focused on those operating divisions not earning the cost of capital, including what needs to be done to remedy the situation, if, in fact, it can be remedied. From the opposite perspective, those divisions earning the highest returns can be challenged in terms of whether more pressure should be applied to achieve even greater returns.

It is also useful to look at a summary presentation of capital expenditures by operating division (Figure 20.2(D)). Is the allocation of capital consistent with the strategy? Does the capital allocation being proposed make sense in terms of the sales and operating growth requirements of each division and the risks involved? Special attention should be focused on those operating divisions not earning the cost of capital that are receiving additional capital. Is the additional capital improving the return? If not, why should the underperforming divisions receive any additional capital until they demonstrate that they can add economic value?

Shifting the focus to the entire planning period, in this case five years, Figure 20.3(A) presents a waterfall showing the cumulative operating income contribution of each operating division. This presentation makes it relatively easy to see where the enterprise must be successful if it is to achieve its earnings per share objective over

Figure 20.2(C) Return on invested capital by operating division

	Actual return on invested capital					Forecasted return on invested capital				
Operating Division	Y-4	Y-3	Y-2	Y-1	Y	Y+1	Y+2	Y+3	Y+4	Y+5
A	%									
B										
C										
D										
E										
.										
.										
.										
.										
X										
Total	%									

☐ = Denotes year in which opertaing division is earning below weighted average cost of capital for the total enterprise

230

Figure 20.2(D) Capital expenditures by operating division

			Actual capital expenditures				Forecasted capital expenditures					Compound annual growth rate	
Operating Division	Y-4	Y-3	Y-2	Y-1	Y	Y+1	Y+2	Y+3	Y+4	Y+5	CAPEX	Operating Income
A	$											
B												
C												
D												
E												
.												
.												
.												
.												
X												
Total	$											

☐ = Denotes year in which operating division is earning below weighted average cost of capital for the total enterprise

the five year period. This reopens the useful discussion of whether too much dependence is being placed on some operating divisions, and not enough on others.

Finally, Figure 20.3(B) is a waterfall presentation of the cumulative earnings-per-share contribution by what might be called "functional area" or "EPS driver." This analytic raises the issue of whether too much emphasis is being placed on some drivers and not enough on others. For example, is enough focus being placed on cost-of-sales reduction techniques? Should more emphasis be placed on unit volume growth? How much contribution is expected from the stock buy-back program?

Figure 20.3(A) Cumulative operating income contribution by operating division

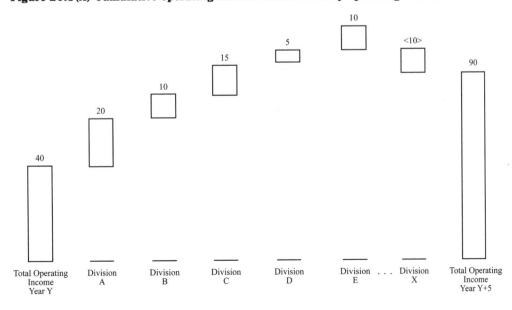

231

Figure 20.3(B) Cumulative earnings-per-share contribution by functional source

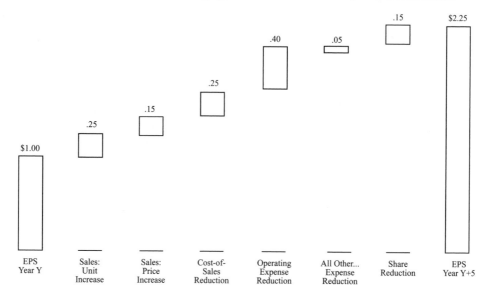

This type of analysis can and should be broken out separately for each operating division, but looking at it in total may also be very useful.

While every operating division has been dealt with in great detail, it is useful to look at the composite picture in terms of the financial metrics that have been used. Quite often this exercise will produce some "surprises" and suggest refinements in strategies and initiatives.

CORPORATE PRO-FORMA PROFIT AND LOSS STATEMENTS

Looking now at the combined strategies for all entities of the enterprise, the starting point is a pro-forma profit and loss statement for each year in the planning period. Every company has its own chart of accounts; a common one is presented in Figure 20.4(A). The amounts entered for sales, gross profit, and operating expenses should reflect the best estimates of the financial results of the business strategy, growth initiatives, and strategic initiatives that have been developed for each operating division, and then the corporate center.

Since the purpose of the analysis at this point is to quantify the preliminary strategic decisions that have been made, and evaluate their adequacy relative to the major objectives relating to earnings-per-share growth and profitability, it is best to estimate on the conservative side. Sales estimates should be conservative, and so should figures for the cost of goods sold. It is also important not to overestimate the impact of various cost savings initiatives. In addition, it is common

Figure 20.4(A) Pro-forma consolidated statements of income

	Year				
	1	2	3	4	5
Net sales	$	$	$	$	$
Cost of goods sold					
Gross profit	$	$	$	$	$
Operating expenses:					
General & administrative					
Special & nonrecurring					
Operating income	$	$	$	$	$
Interest expense					
Interest income					
Other income (loss)					
Income from continuing operations before income taxes	$	$	$	$	$
Income tax expense					
Net income from continuing operations					
Income from discontinued operations (loss)					
Net income	$	$	$	$	$
Basic net income per share:					
Net income per share - basic	$	$	$	$	$
Weighted average common shares - basic					
Diluted net income per share:					
Net income per share - diluted	$	$	$	$	$
Weighted average common shares - diluted					

to include an "adjustment factor" that provides an additional cushion against being overly optimistic.

CORPORATE PRO-FORMA BALANCE SHEETS

After the preparation of an income statement for each year, a balance sheet needs to be constructed. While the entries for balance sheets vary by company, a typical classification is presented in Figure 20.4(B). Asset requirements can be estimated based on their historic relationship to sales, adjusted, if necessary, to reflect the relevant initiatives in the plan.

The asset requirements drive the current liability requirements, again based on historic relationships, adjusted, if necessary, for the impact of the strategy and initiatives in the plan. "Other liabilities" can be estimated based on their past relationship to sales, again modified by applicable initiatives. Forecasted earnings

Figure 20.4(B) Pro-forma consolidated balance sheets

	Year				
	1	2	3	4	5
ASSETS					
Current assets					
Cash & equivalents	$	$	$	$	$
Accounts receivable					
Inventories					
Prepaid expenses					
Other					
Total current assets	$	$	$	$	$
Property & equipment	$	$	$	$	$
Deferred income taxes					
Goodwill					
Other assets					
Total assets	$	$	$	$	$
LIABILITIES & SHAREHOLDERS' EQUITY					
Current liabilities					
Accounts payable	$	$	$	$	$
Customer prepayments					
Current portion of long-term debt					
Accrued expenses					
Income taxes					
Other					
Total current liabilities	$	$	$	$	$
Long term liabilities					
Deferred income taxes	$	$	$	$	$
Long term debt					
Commitments & contingencies					
Other					
Total long term liabilities	$	$	$	$	$
Total liabilities	$	$	$	$	$
Shareholders' equity					
Preferred stock	$	$	$	$	$
Common stock					
Paid-in-capital					
Retained earnings					
Less treasury stock					
Total shareholders' equity	$	$	$	$	$
Total liabilities & shareholders' equity	$	$	$	$	$

from the previous spreadsheet drive the equity section supplemented with antici-pated stock option exercises.

In constructing the computer model to make these calculations, it is best to allow cash to accumulate at this point in the cash account. This will become one of the reference points for the financial strategy and structure decisions described below.

Corporate Pro-forma Cash Flow Statements

The final step is the construction of cash flow statements for each year in the plan-ning period. Figure 20.4(C) presents an illustrative statement. Using the estimates contained in the pro-forma income statements and balance sheets, the additional requirements here are to include capital expenditures by year, proceeds from the maturity of marketable securities, the results from subsidiaries and joint ventures (if any), and the dividend payout using payout estimates that reflect the current dividend yield based on a forecasted stock price employing a normal price earnings multiple and the earnings estimates from Figure 20.4(A).

Sensitivity Analysis

The conservatively estimated profit and loss statements, the balance sheets, and the cash flow statements for each year in the planning period that have been pre-pared thus far can be considered the "most likely case." The next step is to repeat the process using two different set of assumptions . . . "worst likely case" and "best likely case." These additional estimates should be reasonable in the sense of hav-ing at least a 10–20 percent chance of occurring, as opposed to catastrophic situa-tions whose probability of occurring are very low.

Using these three sets of estimates, the purpose is to capture a "band of pos-sibilities" in terms of the financial consequences of the strategies and initiatives that have been developed.

Performance Analysis

Figure 20.5 presents an illustrative format for evaluating the financial conse-quences of the strategy and initiatives that have been developed as compared to the corporate objectives. The major types of objectives that were discussed in Chapter 14 are itemized down the left hand column. The years covered in the plan form the next grouping of columns, ending with a space for compound annual growth rate entries, where relevant. For each year, these separate entries are made: worst likely case, most likely case, and best likely case.

Figure 20.4(C) Pro-forma consolidated statements of cash flows

	Year				
	1	2	3	4	5
OPERATING ACTIVITIES:					
Net income	$	$	$	$	$
Adjustments to reconcile net income to net cash provided by (used for) operating activities					
Depreciation & amortization	$	$	$	$	$
Amortization of deferred compensation					
Deferred income taxes					
Loss or disposal of assets & impaired assets					
Minority interest					
Special & nonrecurring items					
Changes in assets & liabilities					
Accounts receivable					
Inventories					
Accounts payable					
Accrued expenses					
Income taxes payable					
Other assets & liabilities					
Net cash provided by operating activities	$	$	$	$	$
INVESTING ACTIVITIES:					
Capital expenditures	$	$	$	$	$
Investments in marketable securities					
Proceeds from maturity of marketable securities					
Proceeds from sales of subsidiaries					
Proceeds from sale of joint ventures					
Net cash used for investing activities	$	$	$	$	$
FINANCING ACTIVITIES:					
Repayment of long term debt	$	$	$	$	$
Proceeds from issuance of long term debt					
Repurchase of common stock, including transaction costs					
Dividends paid					
Proceeds from exercise of stock options & other					
Net cash provided by (used for) financing activities	$	$	$	$	$
Net increase (decrease) in cash & equivalents	$	$	$	$	$
Cash & equivalents (beginning of year)	$	$	$	$	$
Cash & equivalents (end of year)	$	$	$	$	$

Figure 20.5 Pro-forma performance analysis against objectives

	Unit	Year 1 WC*	Year 1 MLC*	Year 1 BC*	Year 2 WC	Year 2 MLC	Year 2 BC	Year 3 WC	Year 3 MLC	Year 3 BC	Year 4 WC	Year 4 MLC	Year 4 BC	Year 5 BC	Year 5 MLC	Year 5 BC	5 Year Compound Annual Growth Rate WC	MLC	BC
Scale:																			
Sales	$																		
Operating income	$																		
Net profit after taxes	$																		
Earnings per share	$																		
Cash flow	$																		
Cash flow per share	$																		
EVA	$																		
Growth:																			
Sales	%																		
Operating income	%																		
Net profit after taxes	%																		
Cash flow	%																		
Cash flow per share	%																		
EVA	%																		
Profitability:																			
Gross profit	%																		
Operating expenses	%																		
Net profit margin	%																		
Asset turnover	X																		
Return on assets	%																		
Financial leverage	X																		
Return on net worth	%																		
Return on invested capital	%																		
Cash flow return on assets	%																		
Cash flow return on net worth	%																		
Cash flow return on invested capital	%																		
Internal Efficiency:																			
Inventory turnover	X																		
Accounts receivable turnover	X																		
Working capital tunover	X																		
Plant /equipment turnover	X																		
Capacity utilization	%																		
Sales per employee	$																		
Operating profit per employee	$																		
Current ratio	X																		
Acid-test ratio	X																		
Debt/equity ratio	X																		

*WC= worst case, that has at least a 10% probability of occuring   MLC = Most likely case   BC= Best case, that as at least a 10% probability of occuring

Using the most likely case estimates, the question is: "Do the strategies and initiatives achieve the objectives?" If there are short-falls against the objective(s), the question becomes "why?" The alternatives are to recycle back to the appropriate point in the process and change the strategy and/or initiatives, or lower the objective(s).

FINANCIAL STRATEGY AND STRUCTURE

The starting point for this analysis is the pro-forma balance sheet (Figure 20.4(B)) and key balance sheet relationships presented in Figure 20.5. Using the figures presented in the "most likely case" scenario, and the "worst likely case" scenario, the issue is can the strategy and initiative agendas be financed comfortably? This involves a comparison against bank covenants, the company's credit rating, as well as key balance sheet relationships such as debt/equity, current ratio, acid-test ratio, and others that may be appropriate in specific situations. Comparisons of these relationships relative to what is considered normal and comfortable will lead to the judgment as to whether there is adequate capital, or whether additional capital is required, or whether excess capital is being generated.

Acquiring Additional Capital.   If additional capital is required, the issues become:

- How much additional capital is necessary?
- Can the company accommodate the additional capital or would it be in a position that is too risky from a financial perspective?
- What type of capital should be raised and when?

Answers to the first two questions involves analyses of the same metrics and relationships discussed above, namely the company's existing bank covenants and credit ratings, and the key balance sheet relationships including debt/equity, interest coverage, current ratio, acid-test ratio, and so on.

The type of capital that should be raised also involves an evaluation of these same factors, in addition to the company's existing capital structure, its cost of capital, and current financial market conditions, including the company's price-earnings multiple, interest rates, and the market's receptivity to the types of capital under consideration. Based on an evaluation of these factors, generally with the assistance of investment bankers, a decision can be made as to how much capital should be raised, and the mix between additional lines of bank credit, bank term loans, other debt, equity, or some type of debt/equity instrument such as a subordinated convertible debenture.

It may be that acquiring additional capital is not possible, or that it would put the company in a position that is judged too financially precarious. In this situation, it will be necessary to cycle back into the strategy formulation process and make the necessary adjustments including eliminating certain growth and strategic initiative, or, perhaps, delaying their implementation. In this case, the proforma financial statements and analyses presented here need to be revised and the entire process repeated.

Distributing Excess Capital.   In determining whether there is, or will be, excess capital, in addition to the analyses described above, it is important to keep a "cushion" to finance the business under the "worst likely case" scenario, and, perhaps, a fund for acquisitions beyond those currently contemplated in case a "blue bird" comes along.

Using the most likely case numbers for the years comprising the planning period, it is useful to compute the *intrinsic value* of the company, and compare it to current price of the stock.[146] Is the stock over or under valued? This is a useful benchmark for thinking about the excess capital distribution mix.

The other major factor to consider is the motivation of the shareholder base. What is the mix of stock ownership broken out by those interested primarily in growth, as opposed to those focused on value, and those focused on growth at a reasonable price?

Using this information, the decision can be made as to the distribution of excess cash via regular dividends, a special, one-time dividend and/or stock repurchase. In most cases, it is important to maintain the regular dividend yield as the price of the stock increases[147] In addition, it is usually a reasonable idea to maintain a stock repurchase program that, at a minimum, offsets increases in stock ownership resulting from the exercise of stock options by employees.

If additional cash exists beyond these amounts, it can be distributed by raising the regular dividend or increasing the stock repurchase program. From the company's perspective, the latter provides more flexibility than increasing the dividend, since reducing a regular dividend usually has negative connotations. The more undervalued the company's stock, the more aggressive the stock buyback program should probably be. There is no "right" answer; it depends on the facts of the specific situation. The only "right" answer is to distribute excess cash to shareholders in the form that is most meaningful to them.

FINANCIAL STATEMENTS, STRATEGY AND STRUCTURE AGENDA

The output of this, the final step in the strategy formulation process, should be profit and loss statements, balance sheets, and cash flow statements that reflect the financial results of the strategies, growth initiatives, and strategic initiatives, developed by the operating divisions and the corporate center under three scenarios: most likely case, worst likely case, and best likely case. These financial results should demonstrate the achievement of the corporate financial objectives, or these objectives should be adjusted.

Using these financial statements, particularly the balance sheets, decisions are made regarding financial strategy and structure. If additional capital is required, decisions as to the amount, type, and timing are made. If excess capital is generated, decisions as to the amount, mix between dividends and stock repurchases, and timing is made.

Having designed the long-range strategy for an enterprise with multiple operating divisions, it is now time to translate and integrate it into the annual planning and budgeting process. The long-range strategy *drives* the annual planning process.

PART IV

DEVELOPING
ANNUAL PLANS

Having developed a long range strategy, the next step is to translate that strategy into an annual operating plan (see Figures 1.1 and 1.2).

For too many companies there is no relationship between the long term strategy and the annual operating plan. In these companies, the long range strategy or plan is something that is done "ever so often" that has little or no relationship to the annual day to day activities of the business. In these companies some executives complain that working on the long term strategy is a "distraction from my job."

In sophisticated companies, there is a tight relationship between the long range strategy and plan, and the annual operating plan. The purpose of the annual operating plan is to implement year 1, or year 2, or whatever year is appropriate, of the long range strategy and plan. In other words, the long range strategy drives the annual operating plan.

The annual operating plan, in turn, forms the foundation for specific performance objectives for all senior executives in the business. Each executive then assigns some of his or her objectives, either in total or in part, to the executives reporting to them. The latter executives then assign some part of their objectives, or variations or sub parts of them, to those people reporting to them. This process cascades down the layers of the organization.

Finally, these objectives determine some or all, of each executive's incentive compensation, cash and equity. This process establishes a strong linkage between incentive compensation, the performance objectives of the annual operating plan, and the long range strategy and plan. This type of specific, direct, measurable linkage between long term strategy, annual operating plan, individual objectives, and individual incentive cash and equity compensation is extraordinarily important in helping the enterprise increase shareholder value.

The two chapters that comprise Part IV deal with developing annual plans. Chapter 21 focuses on developing an annual business plan for a single unit business or an operating division of a larger business. Chapter 22 is concerned with developing an annual business plan for a multi-division organization. In both cases, the long term strategy drives and shapes the annual business plan.

CHAPTER 21

DEVELOPING AN ANNUAL BUSINESS PLAN

"Press on. Nothing in the world can take the place of persistence."

Ray A. Kroc
Founder & Former Chairman
McDonald's

In 1961 a 52 year old mixer salesman bought a restaurant that he had been servicing since 1954 from the McDonald brothers for $2.7 million. At the time of the purchase, Mr. Kroc had lost his gall bladder and most of his thyroid gland, but was convinced that the best was ahead of him. Today McDonald's is the world's largest restaurant chain with over 31,000 restaurants in more than 115 countries. Last year the company earned $3.5 billion in net income on sales of $21.6 billion. Ray Kroc had, among other things, both vision and persistence.

For too many companies, there is a weak connection between vision and persistence. Companies may, or may not have a well thought out long term strategy. For those who do, many, unfortunately, treat it as a unique and bothersome exercise that has nothing particularly to do with "running the business."

Sophisticated companies, by contrast, have a strong linkage between their long-term strategy, their annual business plan, and their executive compensation structure. The long-term strategy drives the annual business plan, subject, of course, to any unusual environmental developments. The annual business plan deals with those parts of the long-term strategy that need to be implemented during the next fiscal year. Senior executives are compensated based on how well they achieve the results specified in the annual business plan, which, if achieved, will make the appropriate contributions to the achievement of the long-term strategy. Unless the long-term strategy drives the annual business plan, the strategy formulation discipline and process is substantially less useful.

This chapter presents a template for developing an annual business plan for a single division business, or an operating division of a multi-division business. Figure 21.1 presents one approach for translating the long-term strategy into the annual business plan. Using the concepts and processes described throughout this book, the template has been designed to be self-explanatory.

Figure 21.1 An illustrative template for developing an annual business plan for a single division business or an operating division of a multi-unit enterprise

Template	Description	Additional Comments
Current year's (CY) Financial Results A. Profit & loss statement B. Balance sheet C. Cash flow statement D. Other key financial metrics, measures & ratios	Include statements in appendix	Accompanying narrative should be confined to significant deviations from plan & the explanations for them
Next Year's Business Plan		
I. Executive Summary	One page summary of plan including sales, profit & profitability, objectives, growth & strategic initiatives, & key organizational development initiatives	
II. Strategic Audit		
A. Market growth rates & market share trends	Chart showing market share of business and key competitors over the past 3-5 years	Comment on growth rate of market, and why the business is gaining or losing market share, particularly *controllable* reasons for change
B. Key economic, technological, environmental, customer & consumer market trends	Confine discussion to those factors & developments that will impact the business, and/or require a response from the business	
C. Competence evaluation	Describe strengths & weaknesses of the business & each of its major competitors	
D. Competitors' likely moves	Discuss, by individual competitor, moves that are expected during the next year and how they relate to what the competitor is attempting to accomplish long-term	Identify response options & response requirements both long-term & next year
III. Vision / Mission / Values	A one paragraph statement of the vision/ mission & values of the business or operating division	
IV. Financial Objectives		
A. Long-term sales, profit & profitability objectives	A chart showing sales & profit objectives by year for the long-term planning period.	
B. Sales, profit, & profitability objectives for next year	Show $ numbers & % growth rates Show sales & profit dollar numbers for this year & next year, and the % growth	Comment on the relationship between next year's objectives & the long-term objectives if there is a significant difference in the growth rates
V. Value Proposition	State the value proposition of the brand/ product/division & compare it to each major competitor	

Figure 21.1 An illustrative template for developing an annual business plan for a single division business or an operating division of a multi-unit enterprise (*continued*)

Template	Description	Additional Comments
VI. Competitive Positioning		
A. Brand/product/division's competitive advantage(s)	• Identify the competitive advantage(s) of the company/product/brand & the advantages of all major competitors	Can not have more than three competitive advantages. Indicate which advantages (if any) are sustainable
B. Brand/product/division's competitive position to the customer and/or the consumer	• Identify positioning to both the customer & consumer of the company & compare each of its major competitors	
VII. Growth Initiatives		

A. Long-term growth initiatives
     • Market penetration
     • Market development
     • Reformulation/repositioning
     • Market extension
     • Replacement
     • Market segmentation/ product differentiation
     • Product line extension
     • Concentric diversification
     • Horizontal diversification
     • Conglomerate diversification
     • Integration
     • Divestiture
	• Describe the long-term growth initiatives & the sales, profit & other results expected from each initiative	

B. Next year's growth initiatives	Describe the activity & results, including financial results, expected from each initiative during the next year	Discuss reasons for degrees of emphasis on each initiative
VIII. Strategic Initiatives		

A. Long-term strategic initiatives
     • Margin enhancement
     • Economies of scale, scope, focus
     • Balance sheet productivity
     • Competitive advantage
     • Core competencies
     • Capabilities
	Identify long-term strategic initiatives to:
	   • Enhance margin, leverage expenses, achieve economies of scale & scope
	   • Strengthen or leverage competitive advantages
	   • Build new capabilities
	and the financial and other results expected from each	

B. Next year's strategic initiatives	Indicate the activity & results, including financial results, expected from each initiative during the next year	Explain the rationale behind the degree of emphasis & results expected from each initiative
IX. Organizational Design & Development Initiatives		

A. Executive evaluations
 	
   B. Executive development plans
     1. Long-term
     2. Next year
	One or two page chart showing evaluations & development plans for the direct reports of the CEO, and the direct reports of the direct reports, both long-term & next year	This section (IX) should be in a separate document distributed "as appropriate"

Template	Description	Additional Comments

C. Organization chart
   1. Long-term
   2. Next year
	Show organization charts with changes by year highlighted in different colors for each year	

D. Lateral linking mechanisms (communities of practice, liaisons, centers of excellence, task forces or teams, integrators)	Identify mechanisms to be used, the purpose of each, the results expected from each, and the senior executive in charge of each mechanism	

E. Compensation systems
   1. Recommended changes, if any
   2. Recommended bonus targets & other performance measures applicable to the compensation system
	These are suggested changes to the system, <u>not</u> salary & bonus recommendations for individual executives	

F. Governance system 1. Anticipated changes if any		

X. Pro-forma Financial Statements & Financial Strategy & Structure
A. Profit & Loss statement
   1. Long-term
   2. Next year
		• Highlight variances from objectives
		
		• Comment on differences in growth rates long-term vs. next year

B. Balance sheet		• Highlight variances from objectives
C. Cash flow statement		• Highlight variances from objectives
D. Capital structure recommendations (not applicable to operating divisions)		
E. Stock repurchase and dividend recommendations (not applicable to operating divisions)		

246

CHAPTER 22

DEVELOPING AN ANNUAL CORPORATE PLAN

"The toughest thing about success is that you have to keep on being a success. Talent is only a starting point in business. You've got to keep working that talent."

Irving Berlin
Composer & Lyrist

Mr. Berlin is perhaps the most prodigious and famous American songwriter. Although he never learned to read music beyond a basic level, he composed over 3000 songs, 17 film scores, and 21 Broadway scores. He formed his own publishing house, started ASCAP, owned a Broadway theatre, and, at age 94, had one of the top 100 selling songs in America. His skills bridged multiple music styles and he was successful professionally for over 80 years.

The long-term strategy should drive the annual plan. Corporate strategy is more than the sum of the strategies of the operating divisions of a multi-division enterprise. Similarly, the annual corporate plan is more than the addition of the annual plans of the operating divisions that comprise it. The annual corporate plan may have additional growth and/or divestiture initiatives; additional strategic initiatives including those focused on achieving or strengthening core competences and/or competitive advantages in more than one operating division; and organizational development initiatives, including organizational structure changes, horizontal linking mechanism improvements, compensation strategy modifications, and so on.

Figure 22.1 presents an illustrative template for developing an annual corporate plan for a multi-division enterprise. The template utilizes the concepts and processes presented throughout this book, and is designed to be self-explanatory.

Figure 22.1 An illustrative template for developing an annual corporate plan for a multi-division enterprise

Template	Description	Additional Comments
Current year's (CY) Financial Results A. Profit & loss statement B. Balance sheet C. Cash flow statement D. Other key financial metrics, measures & ratios	Include statements specified (in appendix) & short narrative	Confine comments to significant variances from plan and the reasons for them
Next Year's Corporate Plan		
I. Executive Summary	A one page summary of the plan including sales, profit & profitability, objectives, growth & strategic initiatives, & key organizational development initiatives	
II. Strategic Audit		Comment on growth rates of the various markets...which businesses are gaining share, which are losing share & why. Highlight reasons that are *controllable*. Can also superimpose profit & profitability measures on each business
A. Market growth rates & market share trends	Multi-year market share trends by brand, product category & operating division (if applicable)	
B. Key economic, technological, environmental, customer & consumer market trends	Describe key trends & identify which businesses & operating divisions are affected & how. Describe the actions that are required	Focus on those trends that present a threat or opportunity
C. Competence analysis	Brief description of the strengths, weaknesses & problems of the company & each of its major competitors	
D. Competitors' likely moves	Describe the most likely moves that competitors will make, the impact the moves will have, and what the company should do in anticipation of these moves.	
III. Vision / Mission / Values	Brief statement of the vision/mission & values of the enterprise	
IV. Financial Objectives		
A. Long-term sales, profit & profitability objectives	Sales, profit & profitability objectives by year for the long-term planning period. Show $ numbers & % growth rates	
B. Sales, profit, & profitability objectives for next year	Show sales, profit & profitability numbers for the current year & next year, and the % growth or change	Explain any significant differences in the long-term objectives and growth rates compared to those for next year

Figure 22.1 An illustrative template for developing an annual corporate plan for a multi-division enterprise (*continued*)

Template	Description	Additional Comments
V. Corporate Strategy		
A. Business portfolio	Describe the target business portfolio in terms of the desired sales & profits to be derived from each operating division/ product/brand vs. what exists currently, and the priority list for closing whatever portfolio gap that exists, with dates attached	
B. Redefining and/or repositioning existing business initiatives	List initiatives, if any, in priority order with dates attached	
C. Competitive advantage requirements	List requirements, in priority order, with actions required & timetable for implementation	Present rationale for priorities
D. Core competencies	List requirements, in priority order, with actions required & timetable for implementation	Discuss rationale for priorities
VI. Corporate Growth Initiatives		
A. Long-term growth initiatives • Market penetration • Market development • Business development • Diversification • Integation • White space	• Chart showing growth & divestiture initiatives by operating division with expected financial results by year • Chart showing *corporate* growth initiatives with expected financial results by year	
B. Next year's growth initiatives	• Separate chart highlighting growth & divestiture initiatives for the next year broken out by individual operating division & a separate corporate grouping	Explain why the priorities & rate of progress that are embedded in the plan are appropriate & reasonable in terms of achieving the long-term growth initiatives
VII. Corporate Strategic Initiatives		
A. Long-term strtegic initiatives • Margin enhancement • Economies of scale, scope, focus • Increasing balance sheet productivity • Competitive advantage requirements • Core competence requirements • New capabilities	• Chart showing strategic initiatives by operating division with anticipated financial results by year • Chart showing corporate strategic initiatives with expected financial results by year	
B. Next year's strategic initiatives	• Chart identifying strategic initiatives for next year broken out by individual operating division & a separate corporate grouping	Explain why the priorities & rate of progress are appropriate & reasonable in terms of achieving strategic initiatives

Figure 22.1 An illustrative template for developing an annual corporate plan for a multi-division enterprise (*continued*)

Template	Description	Additional Comments
VIII. Organizational Design & Development Initiatives		
A. Executive evaluations	• Summary chart showing evaluations & development plans for: • CEO direct reports	Section VIII should be in a separate document distributed to people "as appropriate"

B. Executive development plans
   1. Long-term
   2. Next year
	• Direct reports of direct reports
	   • CEOs of operating divisions
	   • High-potential executives
	 both long-term & for next year	

C. Organizational chart
   1. Long-term
   2. Next year
	• Show organizational charts with changes highlighted in different colors for each year	

D. Lateral linking mechanisms (LLM)
   • Communities of practice
   • Liasions
   • Centers of excellence
   • Task force or teams
	• Identify mechanisms to be used, the purpose of each, the results expected from each, and the senior executive in charge of each mechanism
	
	 • Most strategic initiatives that involve more than one operating division should have a lateral linking mechanism (LLM) and a sponsoring executive in charge
		• Provide rationale for strategic initiatives not having an LLM & sponsoring executive

E. Compensation systems
 	
   1. Recommended changes in the incentive compensation system, if any
 	
   2. Recommended incentive compensation targets & other performance measures applicable to the compenstion system
 	
   3. Governance system
 	
     1. Anticipated changes, if any
	These are changes to the <u>system</u>, not individual executive compensation recommendations	

IX. Pro-forma Financial Statements
 	
 A. Composite profit & loss statement for the enterprise
   1. Long-term
   2. Next year
	• Provide detail showing:
	   1. Results by operating division
	   2. Results by "profit-driver" (unit increases; unit volume increases; gross margin enhancement; operating expense leverage)
	   3. Results by geographic area (North America; Europe; Asia; etc.) for both long-term & next year	

Figure 22.1 An illustrative template for developing an annual corporate plan for a multi-division enterprise (*continued*)

Template	Description	Additional Comments

B. Composite capital expenditures for the enterprise
    1. Long-term
    2. Next year
	• Provide detail showing:
	  1. CAPEX by operating division
	  2. CAPEX growth rates vs. growth rates in sales & operating profits by operating division
	  3. Profitability measures by year for each operating division (return on assets employed; return on invested capital; economic value added)
	  4. Highlight operating divisions not earning the cost of capital for the enterprise both long-term & next year	

C. Balance sheet
    1. Long-term
    2. Next year		

D. Cash flow statement
    1. Long-term
    2. Next year
	• Provide detail showing:
	  1. Cash flow by operating division
	  2. Cash flow by geographic area (North America; Europe; Asia; etc.) for both long-term & next year	

E. Growth & profitability analysis	• Chart showing 3-5 years of historical data, next year's pro-forma expectations, & long term performance expectations:
	  1. Compare the enterprise with top 3-5 competitors in terms of:
	    a. Growth in sales, operating income & earnings per share
	    b. Profitability as measured by return on assets, return on invested capital and/or economic value added
	    c. Derivative measures of profitability as appropriate (eg: inventory turnover, day's sales outstanding, etc.)	

F. Capital structure policy & recommendations	• Recommended changes in equity & debt, if any, including timing & type(s) of instruments	
G. Shareholder return policies & recommendations including share repurchase & dividends	• Include form, timing & amounts	

PART V

EVALUATING STRATEGIES AND PLANS

The final step is to evaluate strategies and plans that have been developed, and make necessary changes and adjustments. As Figures 1.1 and 1.2 in Chapter 1 remind us, this evaluation occurs in many places. Functional heads of operating divisions have their plans evaluated by peers and superiors, including the CEO. Operating division CEOs have their strategies and plans evaluated and critiqued by their peers, various corporate staff, and the CEO of the enterprise. The CEO of the enterprise presents strategies and plans to the Board of Directors for their suggestions and final acceptance. Sometimes divisional CEOs will also present their strategies and plans to the Board, particularly if they are very large and/or extraordinarily critical to the success of the enterprise.

How should these strategies and plans be evaluated? What are the criteria that should be used? What questions should be asked? How do you know whether strategies and plans are good? Prudent? Will they increase shareholder value?

Part IV presents a framework and specific questions that can be asked, as appropriate in specific situations, in evaluating strategies and plans. Chapter 23 focuses on how to evaluate business strategies and plans. The final chapter, Chapter 24, presents a template for evaluating corporate strategies and plans.

Chapter 23

Evaluating Business Strategies and Plans

"Singleness of purpose is one of the chief essentials for success in life, no matter what may be one's aims."

John D. Rockefeller, Jr.

So far, we have presented a structure and process for developing a multi-year business strategy for a single-unit business, or an operating division of a multi-division enterprise. The components of this strategy have then been used to develop an annual business plan that is consistent with, and contributes to the achievement of the long-term strategy. Now the question is: *how good is this strategy and plan?* This chapter provides an illustrative framework and questions that can be used in making this assessment.

Evaluating Business Strategies

To maintain consistency, the evaluation will again utilize the generic system that has been used to develop business strategies.

Strategic Perspectives

- What stage of the life cycle is this business in?
- What is the profitability of the business? What is the trend? How does it compare with its competitors? Does it earn the cost of capital?
- What has been the recent history of this businesses' growth in operating income and, if appropriate, earnings-per-share? How does this compare with competitors?

- Is the planning horizon that the business uses appropriate? Is the business strategy addressing strategic issues for all three time frames: T1, T2, and T3?
- Is the business thinking of strategic growth options that are large enough given the size of the business, and other considerations?
- Does the business strategy have "functional myopia"? Which perspectives are over and under represented? What are the implications?
- Have the right people been involved in the strategic planning process? Which perspectives are over and under represented?
- Is the business strategy aggressive or conservative? Too aggressive? Too conservative? Why?
- What are the most significant risks with the strategic plan?
- What happens if the environment is less favorable than anticipated? More favorable? Are there contingency plans that are well thought out?
- Does the senior management team "buy into" the plan? Who does not, and why? What are the implications?

STRATEGIC AUDIT:

- Are the assessments of the strengths and weaknesses of the company and its competitors accurate?
- Does the company's strategy capitalize on its strengths?
- Are the appropriate things being done to deal with the company's weaknesses?
- Are new competitors likely to enter? Who? What is the significance? Should anything be done to minimize the impact of their entry?
- Has the company done the appropriate benchmarking and best practices analyses? Is appropriate follow-up action being taken?
- Have all relevant environmental trends been identified? Has the impact of these trends on the company been assessed appropriately? Are appropriate strategic responses included in the strategy?
- Is there a sound analysis of the impact of environmental and competitive trends on the supply chain? Is the impact assessment reasonable? Are appropriate strategic responses included in the strategy?
- Is there an insightful analysis of the future of distribution channels that are important to the company? Is the evaluation of the impact of these changes on the company reasonable? Is the company making appropriate strategic responses?
- Is there a useful review of consumption market trends and forecasts? Are appropriate strategic responses included in the strategy?

- Is there an analysis of the future strategies of major competitors? Do the conclusions seem reasonable? Is the company planning appropriate responses?
- Can you imagine a future that is significantly different from the one being presented? What are the implications?

MISSION, VISION AND VALUES

- Does the company have a mission, vision and values?
- Does it describe where the business is headed and what it wants to do?
- Is it inspirational? Motivational? Operational?
- Does the senior management team agree with it? What about other members of the organization?
- Are there standards of performance? Are they appropriate? Will they satisfy stakeholder expectations?
- Are the mission, vision and values consistent with the core competences of the business? If not, what new competencies need to be developed? Is this reasonable?
- What happens if the mission and vision are broadened? What are the strategic implications?
- What happens if the mission and vision are narrowed? What are the implications, strategically?
- Do the changes that are anticipated to occur in the consumption market, and/or environment, and/or competitive conditions suggest any changes in the mission, vision or values?
- What values of the company are inconsistent with societal and/or environmental values? Is this discrepancy appropriate?
- Is the business a good corporate citizen? What are the measures and metrics? What are the trends in each?
- Is the culture of the business enabling and uplifting to all associates? Does anything need to change?

OBJECTIVES:

- Does the company have objectives that are clearly stated and provide the direction that is needed?
- Are there earnings-per-share growth rate objectives? How do they compare with recent history, and what competitors have achieved? If the objectives were achieved, how would the company's profit growth rate compare with competitors: would it be among the top one or two companies? If not, why not?

- Is the earnings-per-share growth rate achievable? Is the organization capable of achieving it? If not, why not? How risky is this, and what are the risks? How can the risks be mitigated?
- Are there profitability objectives (some measure of return-on-investment and/or economic value added)? How do they compare with recent history, and what competitors have achieved? Is the rate of profitability improving at a reasonable rate? If not, why not? How will the company rank in the industry in terms of profitability?
- Does the company have other objectives? How do they compare with competitors? Are the levels of performance improving at a reasonable rate? Should the targets be increased?
- Should the company have objectives in addition to those that have been articulated? What should the levels of performance be?
- Is the company making the appropriate trade-off between increasing earnings-per-share growth and profitability?
- Are the objectives "stretched" appropriately? Too much? Too little? Are they stretched equally across all parts of the organization?
- Do all key executives "buy into" the objectives?

Business Strategy

- Is the company's product/market scope appropriate for the future? That is, are there any changes that the company should make in the products or services that it offers and/or the market segments and/or geographic markets it offers them to? If changes are recommended, do they make sense . . . are or will they earn a return greater than the cost of capital at an acceptable level of risk?
- For each product and service the company offers:
  - Is there a clearly stated value proposition that specifies the customer benefits that product will offer its customers? Is that benefit important and meaningful to the customer?
  - Does the company have a competitive advantage in providing that benefit to the customer? What, specifically, is it (are they)? Is it sustainable? Over what time period?
  - What are the specific competitive advantages of each competitor?
  - What is the company doing to strengthen its competitive advantage(s)?
  - Is there a clear understanding of what each functional area of the business must do so that the company can achieve its competitive advan-

tage(s)? Are these functional area requirements accurate and reasonable? Can they be achieved?

- ○ How does the company's supply chain compare with competitors? Are appropriate actions being taken to correct weaknesses and/or capitalize on strengths?
- ○ Has the company clearly identified the core processes that are most important in achieving and maintaining the competitive advantage(s) in delivering the value proposition? What are the strengths and weaknesses in each of these core processes? Are the appropriate actions being taken to maintain/strengthen the most critical core processes?

- Is the business adjusting the strategy appropriately to accommodate the changes that have been identified in the environment, customer/consumer markets, supply chain, distribution markets, and competitive dynamics?
- Are there other changes or developments that could impact the business strategy significantly? What are they, what would be the impact, and what, if any, preemptive adjustments should be made?
- Do all key executives "buy into" the strategy?

GROWTH INITIATIVES

- Do the growth initiatives being proposed close the strategic gap and enable the company to achieve its earnings growth and profitability objectives?
- What are the risks involved?
- Are the growth initiatives consistent with the company's core competences? If not, what are the implications?
- Will the business have a competitive advantage for each growth initiative being proposed? Is the advantage sustainable? Are the appropriate things being done to maintain or enhance the sustainability of the competitive advantage?
- Has the company evaluated each growth initiative in terms of its potential value as a growth platform?
- Has each growth option been evaluated in terms of its synergy characteristics? Are the evaluations reasonable?
- Have the growth initiatives been ranked in terms of their sales and profit potential by year? Are the estimates of sales and profits reasonable? Attainable?
- Does the strategic agenda reflect accurately the ranking of the growth initiatives?

- Have the growth platforms been ranked in terms of their sales and profit potential by year? Are the estimates reasonable and attainable? Does the strategic agenda reflect the ranking; that is do the priorities reflect the potential?
- Does the growth initiative agenda address T3 appropriately and adequately?
- Does the management talent exist to implement this portfolio of initiatives? If not, what is needed?
- Is the risk/reward relationship reasonable for each growth initiative and for the total agenda of initiatives?
- Do all key executives support the growth initiatives?

STRATEGIC INITIATIVES

- Are there margin enhancement initiatives for each product or service in the portfolio? Is the focus on lowering cost of sales or increasing prices or both? Are the price increases reasonable? What will be the impact of the price increases on the competitive structure? Are the margin enhancements prioritized? Is the priority reasonable?
- Are there strategic initiatives focused on strengthening core competences and competitive advantage?
- Are there initiatives focused on building new competitive advantages?
- Is the business achieving economies of scale and scope? If not, why not?
- Are there strategic initiatives that will deliver the needed economies of scale and scope in the future?
- How does the asset turnover of the business compare with industry leaders? Are there strategic initiatives focused on increasing balance sheet productivity?
- How will the asset turnover of the business compare with the industry leader at the end of the planning period? Can/should more be done to improve balance sheet productivity?
- Do all key executives support the strategic initiatives?

ORGANIZATIONAL DESIGN AND DEVELOPMENT:

- Is the organizational structure appropriate for the strategy? Have the necessary changes been made?
- Does the company have appropriate lateral linking mechanisms? Do they have appropriate mechanisms to coordinate and integrate those activities

and processes necessary to achieve and maintain a competitive advantage in solving customers' problems? Executing economies of scale and scope initiatives? Achieving additional balance sheet initiatives? Developing new capabilities that are critical to the future of the business?

- Is the structure of the incentive compensation system consistent with the company's strategy? Does it encourage/incentivize the right activities and behavior?
- Are all senior executives evaluated and reviewed in a reasonable way?
- Has a reasonable development plan been designed and implemented for each senior executive?
- Does the organizational development plan deal effectively with the organizational requirements necessary to execute the strategic plan in the future? Will the company have the right people in the right numbers with the right skill sets? For the T3 time period?
- Is the company's governance system appropriate to execute the strategy? Are the changes needed addressed?
- Is the company's leadership style(s) appropriate for the future? What changes are needed?

FINANCIAL STRATEGY AND STRUCTURE

- Does the company have pro-forma income statements, balance sheets, cash flow statements, and capital expenditure statements for each year in the planning period? Has it broken out these statements into appropriate detail: eg. by product line; geography, and so on?
- Has the company conducted a sensitivity analysis that considers "worst likely case" and "best likely case" and constructed each of the statements mentioned above for each of these scenarios?
- Does the strategic plan achieve the major objectives of the company? EPS growth objectives? Profitability objectives? Other objectives?
- If the strategic plan does not achieve the objectives, what are the reasons for the deficiency? Should the plan be changed? Should the objectives be relaxed?
- How will the company compare with its peers if the pro-forma results are achieved? Is this "good enough" or should the plan be revised? Should the company consider strategic alternatives?
- Does the company have adequate financial resources to achieve the plan?
- What options would there be if the company would find itself in the "worst likely case"? Would there be adequate financial resources?

- Is additional capital required or appropriate? What type of capital and when?
- If the company has a capital distribution strategy, is it appropriate? Is the stock buy back/ dividend mix appropriate? How does it compare with competitors? Leading companies? The preferences of major investors?

EVALUATING BUSINESS PLANS

There are two overarching issues in evaluating business plans for a single-unit business or an operating division of a multi-unit enterprise. First, will the annual plan generate the needed contribution to the longer term strategic plan? Secondly, does it exceed shareholder expectations in a way that has a reasonable risk/reward balance? Specific issues that should be addressed include:

STRATEGIC AUDIT

- Is the business gaining or losing market share? What are the reasons? Are the controllable reasons addressed satisfactorily in the plan?
- Have all significant economic, technological, environmental, customer and consumer market developments been considered and addressed in the plan?
- Is the plan making appropriate progress toward minimizing or fixing the company's competitive weaknesses?
- Is the business capitalizing on its competitive strengths?
- Does the plan identify the moves competitors are expected to make? Are the proposed responses to these competitive moves sensible?

VISION, MISSION AND VALUES

- Is there a clear, specific statement of vision, mission and values?
- Is it consistent with the statement of vision, mission and values in the long-term strategy?
- Is the plan consistent with the vision, mission and values?

FINANCIAL OBJECTIVES

- If achieved, would the earnings-per-share growth objectives and profitability objectives exceed shareholder expectations?
- Will the earnings and profitability objectives make the necessary contribution to the long-term objectives?

COMPETITIVE POSITIONING

- Does the plan articulate one to three competitive advantages for each product/service in the portfolio? Are these accurate and appropriate?
- Does the plan identify which of these competitive advantages are sustainable? Is this realistic?
- Does the plan identify the positioning to both the customer and consumer (if appropriate) of each of the company's products and compare them to competitor's positionings? Does this make sense? Does the plan address these strengths and weaknesses?

GROWTH INITIATIVES

- Does the plan identify the growth initiatives for the year?
- Are the growth initiatives consistent with those contained in the long-range strategy?
- Will the company make the progress needed this year so that the company can achieve the growth initiatives over the long-term?
- Have the growth initiatives been prioritized? Does the priority make good business sense?
- Does the degree of emphasis being placed on each initiative next year make sense?

STRATEGIC INITIATIVES

- Does the plan identify the margin enhancement initiatives for the year?
- Are the margin enhancements for the year consistent with the long-term strategy?
- Have the margin enhancement initiatives been prioritized? Does the priority make sense?
- Does the degree of emphasis being placed on each enhancement initiative next year seem appropriate? Where does that lead to a few years in the future?
- Are there strategic initiatives to:
  - Strengthen or leverage competitive advantage?
  - Leverage expenses and achieve economies of scale and scope?
  - Improve balance sheet productivity?
  - Build new capabilities that are needed?
- Are each of these strategic initiatives mentioned above consistent with those articulated in the long-term strategy? Do each of these have financial targets attached to them? Are they prioritized appropriately? If

achieved, will they make sufficient change/improvement so that required long-term results in these areas can be realized?

ORGANIZATIONAL DESIGN AND DEVELOPMENT

- Do the evaluations and assessments of senior executives make sense in terms of your exposure to them?
- Do the development plans for senior executives seen appropriate? Will they produce the talent and skills required for the business to achieve its objectives, both short and long term?
- Do the organizational changes being proposed (if any) make sense in terms of facilitating the achievement of the strategy and the annual plan?
- Are appropriate lateral linking mechanisms being used? Does the plan identify the results expected from each? Is there an executive in charge of each? Is there an opportunity for any additional ones, particularly in the functions and processes critical to the competitive advantages?
- Do the proposed changes (if any) to the incentive compensation system make sense? Will they promote the type of activity and behavior needed to achieve the strategy and plan?
- Are the proposed changes to the management governance system (if any) reasonable? Are they consistent with strategic requirements?

FINANCIAL STATEMENTS, STRATEGY AND STRUCTURE

- Do the income statements, balance sheets, cash flow statements, and capital expenditure schedule requirements, if achieved:
  - Exceed or satisfy stakeholder requirements?
  - Make the necessary contributions to the achievement of the long-term financial objectives, including T2 and T3?
  - Is the financial structure acceptable even under the "worst likely scenario"?
  - Is there a comfortable risk/reward relationship?
- Is the capital structure appropriate? Are the debt and equity amounts at the right levels? Is the mix of debt and equity appropriate? Are there opportunities to change the structure and gain a lower cost of capital, and/or distribute additional capital to shareholders?
- Are the dividend and stock buy back recommendations reasonable? Are they consistent with the long-term strategy and policy? Are there opportunities to leverage the business to gain a lower cost of capital, and/or distribute additional capital to shareholders with a capital structure that is prudent from a risk perspective?

CHAPTER 24

EVALUATING CORPORATE STRATEGIES AND PLANS

"The capacity to evolve is the greatest advantage."

Gary Hamel

The last chapter was concerned with evaluating business strategies and plans for a single-unit business, or an operating division of a multi-division organization. This chapter is focused on evaluating the long-term strategy and annual operating plan of an enterprise consisting of more than one operating division. Once again the central issue is *how good is the strategy and plan? Is it adequate and appropriate?* An illustrative framework and questions that can be used in making this assessment follow.

EVALUATING CORPORATE STRATEGIES

Chapters 12 through 20 presented a structure and process for developing a multi-year corporate strategy for a multi-division enterprise. The following evaluation will utilize the same generic system that has been developed in those chapters.

CORPORATE STRATEGIC PERSPECTIVES

- What has been the profitability of the corporation? What has been the trend in profitability? How does the level of profitability and trend compare with major competitors? Does the corporation generate economic value?
- What has been the recent history of growth in earnings-per-share? How does this compare with competitors?

- Is the corporate strategy addressing strategic issues for all three time frames: T1, T2, and T3?
- What is a realistic assessment of the management of the corporation? Are they doing a good job, a poor job, or something in between? Does the company have the management talent and depth to achieve its strategic plan?
- Is the company thinking of strategic growth options that are large enough given the size of the business and other considerations, including human and financial resources, economic and environmental trends, competitive conditions, etc.?
- Does the corporate strategy have a balanced perspective? That is, are the points of view of certain functions, or divisions, or people inappropriately overrepresented or influential?
- Have the right people been involved in developing the strategy? Bottoms up and top down? All divisions? Multiple management levels? All functions that are critical?
- Is the corporate strategy aggressive or conservative? Too aggressive or too conservative? Why? What are the implications? What should be done about it?
- What happens if external conditions are less or more favorable than anticipated? Are there contingency plans that have been well thought out?
- What are the most significant risks with the plan? Is there a reasonable risk/reward ratio?
- Is the strategy overly dependent on a few key people? What, if anything, should be done about this?
- Does the senior management team "buy into" the plan? Who does not, and why?
- Are there events or situations that have a reasonable probability of occurring that could have a catastrophic impact on the enterprise? Have these been identified, and have contingency plans been developed?

CORPORATE STRATEGIC AUDIT

- What are the growth rates (past and projected) of the industries in which the operating divisions participate? How do the growth rates of the company's businesses compare with the growth rates of their respective industries?
- What are the market shares and market share trends of each of the operating divisions? What are the reasons for these trends? Are the right weaknesses being addressed?

- Are new competitors likely in any of the operating divisions? What would be the impact? Has this been addressed?
- What is the market share and market share trends for the enterprise in total? What are the reasons for these trends?
- What is the expected composite growth rate for the industries that the company is involved in?
- Has the corporation correctly identified its strengths, weaknesses and problems? Is the assessment of competitor's strengths, weaknesses and problems comprehensive and objective? Do these evaluations include the supply chain, all functions, and all core processes?
- Does the long-term corporate strategy capitalize on the company's strengths? Are weaknesses and problems being addressed? Should they be?
- Has the company done an adequate job of financial benchmarking, including comparisons of income statements, balance sheets, and cash flow statements, numbers, ratios, and other metrics? Have the opportunities and issues been identified, and are they being addressed in the strategy?
- Has the enterprise done a financial best practices comparison of every income statement and balance sheet item, as well as every functional area and organizational process to identify improvement and innovation opportunities?
- Has the company done or obtained competent economic, environmental and market forecasts that are relevant to its space? Have significant trends, events, key threats and opportunities been identified correctly? Has anything important been omitted or overlooked?
- Has the company identified the most likely moves that competitors will make, when they will make them, and the impact they will have on the company? Is this assessment objective and reasonable?

CORPORATE MISSION, VISION AND VALUES

- Does the corporation have an accurate, appropriate and useful mission, vision and values?
- Do the mission and vision describe the "space" that the corporation is, or should be, in? Is the mission too narrow? Too broad?
- Do the mission and vision describe standards of performance that are exciting to investors and other stakeholders?
- Is the vision and mission motivational, and will it stretch the performance of all people in the organization?
- Does the company have a set of core values that are appropriate and understood throughout the organization?

- Are the core values motivational and uplifting? Do they encourage the right kind of behavior?
- Does the senior management team agree with the mission, vision and values? What about other levels in the organization?
- Are the mission, vision and values consistent with the core competences of the corporation? If not, what new competencies need to be developed? Is this possible and reasonable? Does the strategy address these issues?
- Do the changes that are anticipated to occur in the environment, consumer markets, customer markets, competition, and/or competitive conditions suggest any changes in the mission, vision, or values?
- Are there any values of the company that are inconsistent with societal and/or environments values and trends? Should theses discrepancies be addressed? Are they?
- Is the corporation a good corporate citizen? What are the measures and metrics, and the trends in each? What are the corporate commitments for the future and are they appropriate and adequate?

CORPORATE OBJECTIVES

- Does the enterprise have objectives that are clearly stated, provide direction, and measurable?
- Are there earnings-per-share growth objectives? How do they compare with recent history and what competitors have achieved? If the objectives were achieved, would the company be the first or second fastest growing company in the industry? Should it be? Can/should the enterprise grow its EPS at 15% or higher? If not, what are the constraints, and how could they be overcome?
- Is the earnings-per-share growth rate objective achievable? Are their adequate human and financial resources? What are the risks, and how can they be mitigated?
- Are there profitability objectives (some measure of return-on-investment and/or economic value added)? How do they compare with recent history and what competitors have achieved? If the company achieves the objectives, would it be first or second in its industry in terms of profitability? If not, what would it take to attain this level, and is it prudent to attempt it? Is the company improving its profitability at a rate that is acceptable? What would it take to earn an after-tax return on assets of more than 12% (if that is higher than the industry leader)? Why not try to achieve or exceed 12% ROA over some reasonable time period?

- Does the company's rate of return exceed its cost of capital? What is the trend in economic value added? How does it compare with competitors? Is the company doing the appropriate things and a reasonable pace in order to increase its EVA?
- Does the enterprise have other objectives? How do they compare with competitors in terms of the types of objectives, the quantitative scores on these objectives, the trends in these metrics, and the rate of improvement? Should the objectives be increased?
- Should the corporation have objectives in addition to those that it has articulated? What are they, and what should be the standards of performance?
- Is the company making the appropriate trade-off between earnings-per-share growth and profitability? Is this relationship well understood?
- Are the objectives "stretched" appropriately? Too much? Too little? Are they stretched equally across all operating divisions, functional areas of divisions, corporate staff, and others?
- Does senior management "buy into" these objectives? What about the rest of the organization?

CORPORATE STRATEGY

- Is the enterprise adding value to the operating divisions? How? Is it adding as much value as it should? How much value are competing enterprises adding to the economic value of their operating divisions, and how are they doing it? Are there any useful insights here?
- Is the enterprises' business portfolio appropriate? Has a reasonable target business portfolio been identified? Is the corporation making reasonable progress toward the attainment of this portfolio?
- Has the enterprise identified operating divisions and/or existing businesses that need to be redefined and/or repositioned? Are these strategies reasonable?
- Has the company identified the sustainable competitive advantages for each product in each of its operating divisions? Has it identified businesses and operating divisions that have competitive advantages that are unique and out of the range of most divisions' competitive advantages? Are these businesses being considered for divestiture? Should they be?
- Has the company identified corporate core competencies that elevate the performance of operating divisions? Do you agree that these are, in fact, core?

- Has the enterprise identified its strategic priorities correctly? Do you agree with management's choice of growth businesses and operating divisions? Do you agree with the businesses and companies slated for divestiture? Is the allocation of human and financial resources consistent with the priority?

CORPORATE GROWTH INITIATIVES

- Do the growth initiatives being proposed close the strategic gaps and enable the enterprise to achieve its earnings growth and profitability objectives? Is there a reasonable cushion of 10 to 20%?
- Have the best growth initiatives been selected from the growth option agendas of the operating divisions of the business?
- Are their additional, corporate growth initiatives being proposed? How do these initiatives compare with the *core* of the enterprise? Are the adjacencies reasonable, or are they a substantial departure from what the enterprise has proved it knows how to do profitably?
- Have the growth options been evaluated rigorously? Have competitive advantage requirements been identified correctly, and does the business already have them or can it develop them? Have the options been evaluated in terms of their growth platform potential? Have sales and operating income, and capital expenditure projections been made, and are they reasonable? Have appropriate profitability calculations been made, and do they meet or exceed the "hurdle rates"? Have synergies been identified correctly and estimated conservatively?
- Has the company identified "white space" opportunities? Are there opportunities that have not been proposed that should be pursued?
- Are there any growth initiatives that should be made for defensive purposes in order to protect existing businesses, preclude additional competition, and/or for other reasons?
- Is the divestiture agenda inclusive enough?
- Does the corporate growth initiative agenda address the T3 time period appropriately and adequately?
- Does the management talent and depth exist to implement this portfolio of growth initiatives? Are the needed actions, if any, included in the organizational development plan?
- Is the risk/reward relationship reasonable for each growth initiative and for the total agenda of initiatives?

CORPORATE STRATEGIC INITIATIVES

- Are there, or should there be, strategic initiatives designed to improve and strengthen margin enhancement opportunities across several operating divisions, particularly with respect to activities and programs designed to reduce cost of sales through joint purchasing, transportation, sourcing, warehousing, methodologies such as lean six sigma, and so on? Have all the opportunities in these areas been exploited?
- Are there competitive advantage requirements that are common to a significant number of businesses/operating divisions? If so, are there corporate strategic initiatives designed to strengthen and enhance these capabilities? Are these initiatives leveraging the opportunities?
- Are there core competence requirements that are common to a significant number of businesses/operating divisions? Are there, or should there be, corporate initiatives designed to improve and enhance these common core competence requirements? If some are proposed, do they really leverage the situation?
- Are there, or should there be, corporate strategic initiatives designed to leverage economies of scale, scope and focus initiatives across the operating divisions?
- Are there opportunities to implement shared services programs that have not been implemented, or not implemented effectively?
- Are there opportunities to initiate, coordinate or integrate initiatives focused on improving balance sheet productivity across operating divisions?
- Are there, or should there, be corporate strategic initiatives focused on developing new capabilities that will be needed to maintain or enhance competitive advantage and/or achieve corporate objectives across several operating divisions?

CORPORATE ORGANIZATIONAL DESIGN AND DEVELOPMENT

- Have the appropriate organizational changes been made, or are they going to be made, in order to execute the corporate strategy, growth initiatives and strategic initiatives?
- Does the enterprise have appropriate lateral linking mechanisms to coordinate, integrate, and leverage those activities and processes necessary to achieve and maintain a competitive advantage that is common to several operating divisions? Does the corporation have appropriate organizational coordination and oversight for initiatives designed to achieve economies of scale, scope, and focus, and balance sheet productivity that

are common to several operating divisions? Are there new capabilities that are common to several divisions that could be facilitated with some type of lateral linking mechanism?

- Is the structure of the corporate incentive compensation system consistent with the company's strategy and strategic priorities? Does it reward the right activities and behavior?
- Are all senior corporate executives and senior operating division executives, evaluated and reviewed in a reasonable and timely way?
- Has an appropriate and effective development plan been designed and implemented for each senior executive at the corporate and operating division level?
- Have high potential executives been identified and appropriate development plans developed and implemented for them?
- Does the corporate organizational development plan deal effectively with the organizational requirements necessary to execute the strategic plan in the future? Will the company have the right people in the right numbers with the right skill sets? Have the general requirements for the T3 time period been identified and included in the plan?
- Is the enterprise's corporate governance system appropriate to execute the strategy? Have the changes that are needed been addressed?
- Does the company have an effective organizational and governance structure to manage all the strategic activities of the enterprise?
- Is the enterprise's leadership style appropriate for the future? What changes are needed?

CORPORATE FINANCIAL STRATEGY AND STRUCTURE

- Does the company have pro-forma income statements, balance sheets, cash flow statements, and capital expenditure estimates for each year in the planning period? Has it broken out these statements by operating division, provided separate analyses by functional area or EPS driver, by geographic area, and/or by other classifications that are appropriate and meaningful for the enterprise?
  - Are sales volume and operating income requirements for each division reasonable?
  - Is the business overly dependent on a few operating divisions? If so, are steps being taken to reduce this dependency?
  - How does the sales and operating profit by geographic area look? Is the enterprise too dependent on one geographic area? Is it overly dependent on areas with geo-political risk?

- Are the relative growth rates of the operating divisions consistent with the corporate strategy?
- What about operating divisions that are losing money, or not adding any economic value? Is the strategy moving toward a satisfactory resolution of the issues affecting these businesses?
- Are any operating divisions, or is the enterprise in total, too dependent on price increases? Are the assumptions and strategies realistic?

- Has the enterprise prepared a sensitivity analysis that considers the "worst likely case" and the "best likely case" and constructed each of the statements mentioned above (income statements, balance sheets, cash flow statements, and capital expenditure estimates) for each of these scenarios?
- Does the strategic plan as proposed achieve the major objectives of the enterprise? EPS growth objectives? Profitability objectives? Other objectives?
- If the strategic plan does not achieve the objectives, what are the reasons for the short fall? Should the plan be changed so that it meets the objectives? Should the objectives be relaxed?
- How will the enterprise compare with its peers if the pro-forma results are achieved? Is this "good enough" or should the plan be revised?
- Is, or should, the business considering strategic alternatives for any of its operating divisions, or the enterprise in total?
- Does the company have adequate financial resources to achieve the plan, and still have a comfortable margin for error?
- What options would there be if the company would find itself in the "worst likely case"? What would be its financial condition and would there be adequate financial resources to respond effectively?
- Is additional capital required or appropriate? What type of capital and when?
- Is the company's proposed stock repurchase and dividend policy appropriate given the corporate strategy, the investor base, and the investment environment including capital availability, interest rates, hedge funds, and so on? How does it compare with competitors? With leading companies?
- Does the enterprise have a process that it would implement in the event of an unsolicited offer to buy the company? Have the appropriate things been done so that it would be possible to implement that process?

EVALUATING CORPORATE ANNUAL PLANS

An effective corporate annual plan will incorporate the annual plans of its operating divisions with the additional plans for the enterprise in total. Long-term business and corporate strategies should drive the annual plans for the operating divisions and the total enterprise. So, in evaluating corporate annual plans, the first issue is will the annual corporate plan generate the needed contribution to the achievement of the longer term corporate strategic plan? Secondly, does the corporate annual plan exceed shareholder and other stakeholder expectations in a way that has a reasonable risk/reward balance? Questions that may be useful in making these judgments are listed below.

CORPORATE STRATEGIC AUDIT

- Are the operating divisions gaining or losing market share? Are the controllable reasons being addressed in the annual plan? If applicable, is the enterprise in total gaining or losing market share? Are these issues being addressed in the plan?
- What are the industry growth rate projections for the respective operating divisions? For the enterprise in total? Is the company in a slow growth, average growth, or fast growth situation?
- What stage in the life cycle are each of the operating divisions in? What about the enterprise as a whole?
- Is the corporation in the right industries? Are there any that should be exited? When?
- Have all significant economic, technological, environments, consumer and customer trends affecting operating divisions and the enterprise been considered and addressed satisfactorily in the plan?
- Does the plan include actions designed to minimize or fix the competitive weaknesses of the operating divisions and the enterprise? If achieved, will the rate of progress be adequate?
- Are the operating divisions, and the enterprise, pursing strategies that capitalize on their competitive strengths?
- Does the plan identify the moves that competitors of the operating divisions and the enterprise are expected to make? Are the proposed responses to these competitive moves sensible?
- What other things, that have a reasonable chance of occurring, could have a serious impact on operating divisions or the enterprise? Should any preparatory and/or preventive actions be taken?

CORPORATE VISION, MISSION AND VALUES

- Is there a clear, specific, operational statement of vision, mission and values for each operating division and for the enterprise?

- Are the VMV statements in the annual plans consistent with those in the long-range strategy?
- Are the annual plans for the operating divisions and the enterprise consistent with the vision, mission and values?

CORPORATE FINANCIAL OBJECTIVES

- If achieved, would the earnings-per-share growth objectives and profitability objectives exceed shareholder and other stakeholder expectations?
- If achieved, would the earnings growth objectives and the profitability objectives make the necessary contribution to the long-term corporate objectives?

CORPORATE STRATEGIES

- Is the annual corporate plan making reasonable progress toward the target business portfolio? Where are the issues, if any?
- Are the initiatives outlined in the corporate plan making enough progress in redefining and repositioning those businesses and operating divisions that require it?
- Does the annual plan make adequate progress in strengthening and/or enhancing the competitive advantages of each of the operating divisions and the enterprise in total? Are the priorities correct?
- Does the annual plan make sufficient progress in developing/strengthening core competencies of each of the operating divisions and the enterprise in total? Are the priorities reasonable?
- Do new core competences need to be developed? Are they?

CORPORATE GROWTH INITIATIVES

- Does the plan include growth and divestiture initiatives by operating division with expected financial results by year for each year of the long-term strategic plan?
- Does the plan show corporate growth initiatives with expected financial results for each year of the strategic plan?
- Will the plans for next year achieve the required financial results to satisfy stockholder and other stakeholder expectations, as well as make the necessary contribution to the achievement of the long-term growth initiative?

- Is the plan too dependent on any single initiative, or executive, or operating division, or is it as balanced as can be expected?
- Are the priorities consistent with the long-term strategic plan? Are they reasonable?

CORPORATE STRATEGIC INITIATIVES

- Does the plan include strategic initiatives by operating division with anticipated financial results by year for each year of the long-term strategic plan?
  - Margin enhancement initiatives?
  - Competitive advantage requirements?
  - Core competence requirements?
  - Economies of scale, scope and focus financial targets?
  - Balance sheet productivity improvement targets?
  - Developing new capabilities?
- Does the plan include corporate strategic initiatives with expected financial results for each year of the corporate strategic plan?
- Does the plan identify strategic initiatives for next year broken out by operating division and with a separate grouping for corporate initiatives? Does each initiative have the expected financial results?
- Will the plans for next year achieve the required financial results, as well as make the necessary contribution to the achievement of the long-term strategic initiatives?
- Is the plan too dependent on any single initiative, or operating division, or management team, or is it as balanced as can be expected?
- Are the priorities consistent with the long-term strategic plan? Are they reasonable?
- How do the financial results that are forecasted compare with what competitor's are achieving?

CORPORATE ORGANIZATIONAL DESIGN AND DEVELOPMENT

- Do the evaluations and assessments of senior corporate and operating division executives seem accurate based on your exposure to them?
- Do the development plans for the next year for senior corporate and operating division executives seem appropriate? Will they produce the needed improvement so that the enterprise can achieve its long-term objectives? Are they consistent with the long-term role anticipated for each executive?

- Are the organizational changes being proposed for next year (if any), consistent with the long-term organization plan? Do they facilitate it? Do they make sense in terms of facilitating the achievement of the long-term strategy and the annual plan?
- Are appropriate lateral linking mechanisms being used? Are they promoting the types of activities, behavior, coordination, and integration necessary to achieve the long-term strategy as well as the annual plan? Does the plan identify the results expected from each? Is there an executive in charge of each? Is there an opportunity for any additional ones, particularly in the functions and processes critical to the competitive advantages corporately and at the operating divisions? Are these mechanisms being used to help develop the right executives?
- Do the proposed changes (if any) to the incentive compensation systems make sense? Will they promote the type of activity and behavior needed to achieve the long-term strategy as well as the annual plan?
- Are the proposed changes to the management governance system (if any) reasonable? Will they promote the type of activity and behavior needed to achieve the long-terms strategy as well as the annual plan?

CORPORATE FINANCIAL STATEMENTS, FINANCIAL STRATEGY AND STRUCTURE

- Do the income statements, balance sheets, cash flow statements, and capital expenditure schedule requirements, if achieved:
  - Exceed or satisfy "street" expectations?
  - Exceed or satisfy shareholder and other stakeholder requirements and expectations?
  - Make the necessary contributions to the achievement of the long-term financial objectives in the long-term strategy, including T2 and T3?
- If achieved, how will the company compare with competitors in terms of EPS growth rates, profitability measures, and other financial metrics?
- Will the capital structure be adequate, even under the "worst likely scenario"? Will the debt/equity mix be acceptable? Is there any significant danger of violating covenants? Are there opportunities to change the structure and gain a lower cost of capital, and/or distribute additional capital to shareholders?
- Are the dividend and stock buy-back recommendations reasonable? Are they consistent with the long-term strategy and policy?
- Are there opportunities to leverage the business and gain a lower cost of capital, and/or distribute additional capital to shareholders with a resultant capital structure that is prudent from a risk perspective even if a significant downturn occurs?

Appendix A

Financial Metrics and Formulas

Metric or Ratio	Formula	Description/Use
Accounts receivable turnover	$\dfrac{\text{Annual credit sales}}{\text{Accounts receivable}}$	Average time required to collect money on credit sales.
After-tax cost of debt	(1-marginal tax rate) cost of debt[1]	Used to calculate the cost of capital & return on invested capital [1]Based on the quality of the company's debt as measured by *Moodys* or *Standard & Poors*.
Asset turnover	$\dfrac{\text{Net sales}}{\text{Average assets}}$	The rate at which investments in assets generate sales. For example, an asset turnover of 3x means that each dollar invested in assets produces $3 in sales.
Average collection period	$\dfrac{\text{Accounts receivable}}{\text{Average daily sales}}$	Average number of days required to receive payment following a sale.
Cash flow	Profit after taxes + depreciation	A measure of funds available to finance expenses above the current level of expenses and asset investments.
Cash flow return on assets (CFROA)	$\dfrac{\text{Profit after taxes + depreciation}}{\text{Average assets}}$	The rate at which investments in assets generate cash flow. For example, a CFROA of 17% means that every dollar invested in assets generates 17¢ in cash flow.
Cash flow return on equity (CFROE)	$\dfrac{\text{Profit after taxes + depreciation}}{\text{Average shareholder equity}}$	The rate at which shareholder investments generate cash flow. A 25% CFROE means that every dollar invested by shareholders generates 25¢ in cash flow.
Cost of equity	Risk free rate + β (market rate - risk free rate)	Where: Risk free rate = interest rate on government securities; Market rate = rate of return on S&P 500 or a more appropriate index.

Metric or Ratio	Formula	Description/Use
Cost of equity (cont'd)		$\beta = Rj,t = aj + bjRm,t + ej,t$ Where: Rjt = the actual return of company j's securities at time t; aj = a constant equal to $(1-bj) RFR_t$; bj = an estimate of βj; Rm,t = rate of return on a diversified portfolio of securities at time t; ej,t = the error estimating Rj,t (The value of bj is estimated through regression analysis, and is the estimate of βj).
Current ratio	$\dfrac{\text{Current assets}}{\text{Current liabilities}}$	A measure of the ability to pay current liabilities with assets that can converted into cash reasonably quickly.
Debt to assets	$\dfrac{\text{Total debt}}{\text{Total assets}}$	The proportion of asset investment funded by debt.
Debt to equity	$\dfrac{\text{Total debt}}{\text{Total equity}}$	A measure of the relative use of debt and equity to finance the asset investment in the business.
Dividend payout	$\dfrac{\text{Dividends}}{\text{Profits after taxes}}$	The percentage of after-tax profits paid out in dividends to shareholders.
Dividend yield	$\dfrac{\text{Dividend per share common stock}}{\text{Market price per share common stock}}$	The dividend as a percent of the market price. For example, if the dividend is $2 per share and the price per share is $100, the dividend yield is 2%.
Earnings per share	$\dfrac{\text{Profit after taxes - preferred stock dividends}}{\text{Shares of common stock outstanding}}$	A measure of earnings available to owners of common stock.
EBIT	Net sales - (cost of goods sold + operating expenses)	A measure of profit before interest and taxes. Commonly used to measure operating profit of a division and/or a highly financially leveraged organization.
EBITDA	Net sales - (cost of goods sold + operating expenses + depreciation & amortization)	A measure of profit before interest, taxes, depreciation & amortization. Sometimes used to measure the operating profit of a division and/or the operating performance of a highly financially leveraged division or business.
Economic value added	EVA = NOPAT - C% (TC) NOPAT=Net operating profit after taxes C= % cost of capital TC=Total capital	EVA is a superior measure of profit because it reduces operating profit by the cost of all the capital a company employs, including debt and equity. EVA charges a business or operating division for the cost of the assets they employ.
Financial leverage	$\dfrac{\text{Total assets}}{\text{Shareholders equity}}$	The amount or proportion of total assets funded by shareholders as opposed to other sources of capital. For example, a leverage ratio of 2x means that shareholders are financing 50% of the investment in assets.
Gross margin rate	$\dfrac{\text{Sales - cost of goods sold}}{\text{Net sales}}$	The amount (or rate) available to pay for operating expenses and profit before taxes.

Metric or Ratio	Formula	Description/Use
Inventory turnover	$$\frac{\text{Cost of goods sold}}{\text{Average inventory (at cost)}}$$	A measure of the number of times the inventory is sold per year.
Invested capital	Operating current assets + book value of fixed current assets - net other operating assets + non-interest bearing current liabilities	The denominator in a popular measure of return on investment...return on invested capital.
Intrinsic value	$$\frac{\text{After-tax cash flows before debt service}}{\text{Weighted average cost of capital}}$$	A method to estimate the value of a business or an operating division of a business.
Operating expense rate	$$\frac{\text{Operating expenses}}{\text{Net sales}}$$	The dollars or percent of sales required to pay operating expenses. The remaining percentage is available to pay for the products or services (cost of goods sold) and provide a profit before taxes.
Operating income	Sales - (cost of goods sold - operating expenses)	Operating income includes a charge for depreciation but not interest or taxes. A common measure of profit performance of a business, particularly an operating division of a multi-unit enterprise.
PEG ratio	$$\frac{\frac{\text{Current market price per share} \div}{\text{After tax earnings per share}}}{\text{Forecasted growth rate in earnings per share over next 3-5 years}}$$	The PE ratio relative to the anticipated EPS growth rate. For example, a PEG ratio of 2.0 means that a stock is selling at a PE ratio twice as fast as its anticipated earnings growth rate.
Plant & equipment productivity	$$\frac{\text{Sales and/or some measure of profit}}{\text{Dollar investment in plant and/or equipment}}$$	A measure of the efficiency of a physical asset such as plant and/or equipment in generating sales and/or profits. Various profit measures can be used including gross profit, operating income, EBIDTA, net profit before and after taxes. These metrics can be used to measure trends over time and/or compare the company with competitiors and others of interest.
Price/earnings multiple	$$\frac{\text{Current market price per share}}{\text{After-tax earnings per share}}$$	Price of the stock compared to the earnings of the stock. For example, a PE ratio of 15 means that a stock is selling at 15 times its earnings. Sometimes, earnings are those during the past 12 months (historical); other times, earnings are over the next 12 months (forward).
Productivity	$$\frac{\text{Some measure of output}}{\text{Some measure of input}}$$	Productivity measures can be used to measure the efficiency of an organization at a point in time, trends in efficiency, and comparisons to other organizations.
Profit-margin	$$\frac{\text{Profits after taxes}}{\text{Net sales}}$$	The efficiency of generating profits on sales volumes.
Profit per employee	$$\frac{\text{Some measure of profit}}{\text{Number of employees or full-time equivalents}}$$	A measure of the efficiency of employees in generating profits. Various profit measures can be used including gross profit, operating income, EBIDTA, net profit before & after taxes. These metrics can be used to measure trends over time and compare the company with competitors and others of interest.

Metric or Ratio	Formula	Description/Use
Quick ratio	$\dfrac{\text{Current assets - inventory}}{\text{Current liabilities}}$	A measure of the ability to pay liabilities without selling inventory.
Return on assets (ROA)	$\dfrac{\text{Profit after taxes}}{\text{Average assets}}$	The rate at which investments in assets generate profit after taxes. For example, an ROA of 15% means that every dollar invested in assets generates 15¢ in profit after taxes.
Return on equity (ROE)	$\dfrac{\text{Profit after taxes}}{\text{Average shareholder equity}}$	The rate at which shareholders' investment generates net profit after taxes. For example, an ROE of 20% means that every dollar shareholders invest in the business generates 20¢ in profit after taxes.
Return on invested capital	$\dfrac{\text{Net operating profit after taxes}}{\text{Average invested capital}}$ Where: Net operating profit after taxes = operating income + amortization + implied lease interest expense - taxes Average invested capital = total assets - non-interest bearing current liabilities + present value of lease obligations (average of this year & last year) + operating current assets + book value of fixed current assets - net operating assets + non-interest bearing current liabilities (average of this year & last year)	The efficiency with which invested capital generates operating profit after taxes. For example, a return on invested capital of 20% means that every dollar of invested capital generates 20¢ in net operating profit after taxes.
Sales per employee	$\dfrac{\text{Sales}}{\substack{\text{Number of employees or}\\ \text{full-time equivalents}}}$	A measure of the efficiency of employees in generating sales. Can be used to analyze trends over time, and for comparisons with competitors and other organizations of interest.
Times interest earned	$\dfrac{\text{Profit before interest \& taxes}}{\text{Total interest charges}}$	A measure of the amount profits can decline and the company will still be able to meet interest costs.
Weighted average cost of capital	Weighted average cost of debt: $\dfrac{\text{Market value of debt}}{\text{Company's market value}}$ x (after tax cost of debt) Weighted average cost of equity: $\dfrac{\text{Market value of equity}}{\text{Company's market value}}$ x (cost of equity)	Weighted average cost of capital = weighted average after-tax cost of debt + weighted average cost of equity. The percentage cost of the capital that is employed in a business or operating division. The return on invested capital must exceed the cost of capital for there to be economic value added (EVA).

ENDNOTES

1. Some insightful work on corporate strategy can be found in: Gary Hamel, *Leading the Revolution*. (New York: Penguin Group, 2002); Gary Hamel & C.K. Prahald, *Competing for the Future*. (Boston: Harvard Business School Press, 1996); Michael Porter, *Competitive Strategy: Techniques for Analyzing Industries and Competition*. (New York: The Free Press, 1980); Michael Porter, *Competitive Advantage: Creating and Sustaining Superior Performance*. (New York: The Free Press, 1985); Jim Collins, *Good to Great*. (New York: Harper Collins, 2001); David A. Aaker, *Developing Business Strategies*. (New York: John Wiley & Sons, Inc., 1995); H. Igor Ansoff, *Corporate Strategy*. (New York: McGraw-Hill, Inc., 1965); Alfred D. Chandler, Jr., *Strategy and Structure*. (Cambridge: The M.I.T. Press, 1962); Peter F. Drucker, *The Practice of Management*. (New York: Harper & Row, 1954).

2. For some textbooks used at leading business schools see: David Besanko, David Dranove, Mark Shanley and Scott Schaefer, *Economics of Strategy*. 3rd. Edition. (New York: John Wiley & Sons, Inc. 2004); Garth Saloner, Andrea Shepard and Joel Podolny, *Strategic Management*. (New York: John Wiley & Sons, Inc., 2001); Robert M. Grant, *Contemporary Strategy Analysis*. 4th Edition. (Oxford, UK.: Blackwell Publishers, 2002); Phillipe Lasserre, *Global Strategic Management*. (New York: Palgrove Macmillan, 2003); Jay B. Barney, *Gaining and Sustaining Competitive Advantage*. 3rd Ed. (Upper Saddle River, New Jersey: Pearson Prentice Hall, 2007).

3. Some classic insights in this area are contained in: Theodore Levitt, "Exploit the Product Life Cycle," *Harvard Business Review*, Vol. 43 (November-December, 1965), pp. 81–94; and Robert D Buzzell, "Competitive Behavior and Product Life Cycles," in J.S. Wright and J. Goldstacker, eds., *New Ideas for Successful Marketing*. (Chicago: American Marketing Association, 1966), pp. 46–67.

4. Some original thoughts are contained in: Seymour Tilles, "Strategies for Allocating Funds," *Harvard Business Review*, Vol. 44 (January-February, 1966), pp. 72–80; and Donald K. Clifford, Jr., "Leverage in the Product Life Cycle," *Dun's Review and Modern Industry*, May, 1965, pp. 62–70.

5. Michael Porter, "How Competitive Forces Shape Strategy," *Harvard Business Review*, (March-April, 1979), pp. 137–145; Michael Porter, *Competitive Advantage: Creating and Sustaining Superior Performance*. (New York: The Free Press, 1985).

6. David T. Kollat, Roger D. Blackwell and James F. Robeson. *Strategic Marketing*. (New York: Holt, Rinehart & Winston, Inc., 1972), pp. 18–19.

7. Dave Ulrich and Norm Smallwood, "Capitalizing on Capabilities," *Harvard Business Review*, (June, 2004), pp. 119ff.

8. David Aaker, *op. cit.*, p. 111.

9. Michael Porter, "How Competitive Forces Shape Strategy," *loc. cit.*

10. Ibid.

11. Nelson D. Schwartz, "Has Nokia Lost It?" *Fortune*, (January 24, 2005), pp. 98–106.

12. David Aaker, *op. cit.*, pp. 65–72.

13. Gary Hamel, *Leading the Revolution.*, *op. cit.*

14. For additional perspectives see Warren Bennis and Burt Nanus, *Leaders: The Strategies for Taking Charge.* (New York: Harper and Row, 1985).

15. Theodore Levitt, "Marketing Myopia," *Harvard Business Review*, (July-August, 1960).

16. Jim Collins, *Good to Great. op. cit.*

17. Some refer to this as "strategic intent." See Gary Hamel and C.K. Prahalad, "Strategic Intent," *Harvard Business Review*, (May-June, 1989).

18. Stuart L. Hart, "Beyond Greening: Strategies for a Sustainable World," *Harvard Business Review*, (January-February, 1997).

19. For additional insights see: C.K. Prahalad and Gary Hamel, "The Core Competence of the Corporation," *Harvard Business Review*, (May-June, 1990). For an interesting compilation of business and corporate mission statements and value statements see Jeffrey Abrahams, *101 Mission Statements From Top Companies*, (Berkeley: Ten Speed Press, 2007).

20. John Helyar, "Will Harley Davidson Hit the Wall?" *Fortune*, (August 12, 2002), pp. 120–124.

21. Fred Vogelstein, "The Cisco Kid Rides Again," *Fortune*, (July 26, 2004), pp. 132–140.

22. Amy Barrett, "Hershey: Candy is Dandy, But . . . ," *Business Week*, (September 29, 2003), pp. 68–69.

23. See Garth Saloner, *et. al.*, *Strategic Management*, *op. cit.*, p. 88 & pp. 589–91; Jeffrey Abrahams, *op. cit.*

24. Tom Chappell, *The Soul of a Business.* (New York: Bantum Books, 1993), p. 32.

25. Jim Collins, *Good to Great.*, *op. cit.*; and Jim Collins, *Built to Last.*, *op. cit.*

26. Richard S. Tedlow, "The Education of Andy Grove," *Fortune*, (December 12, 2005), pp. 117ff.

27. Bing Cao, Bin Jiang, and Timothy Kolley, "Balancing ROIC and Growth to Build Value," *McKinsey on Finance*, (Spring, 2006), p. 12ff.

28. See, for example, Al Ehrbar, *EVA.*, (New York: John Wiley & Sons, Inc., 1998).

29. Cao, *et. al.*, "Balancing ROIC and Growth to Build Value," *loc. cit.*, p. 12.

30. N.J. Mass, "The Relative Value of Growth," *Harvard Business Review*, (April, 2005), pp. 102–112.

31. *Ibid.*

32. Bruce D. Henderson, "Strategy Planning," *Business Horizons*, (Winter, 1964), pp. 21–24.

33. This distinction and relationship is made by many observers. See, for example, Robert M. Grant, *Contemporary Strategy Analysis*, *op. cit.*, pp. 123–125.

34. In addition to the sources noted in endnotes 1 and 2, see: Kenneth Andrews, *The Concept of Corporate Strategy.* (Homewood Illinois: Richard D. Irwin, 1971);

Robert S. Kaplan and David P. Norton, "Having Trouble With Your Strategy?" *Harvard Business Review*, (September-October, 2000), pp. 167ff; George Stalk, Philip Evans, Laurence Shulman, "Competing on Capabilities," *Harvard Business Review*, (March-April, 1992); David J. Collis and Cynthia A. Montgomery, "Competing on Resources," *Harvard Business Review*, (July-August, 1995).

35. Stephanie Mehta, "Virgin's Territory Spawns Imitators," *Fortune*, (September 20, 2004), pp. 50–52.

36. Al Ehrbar, "Breakaway Brands," *Fortune*, (October 31, 2005), pp. 153–170.

37. Carol Loomis, "The Big Surprise is Enterprise," *Fortune*, (July 24, 2006), pp. 141–150.

38. Robert S. Kaplan, *et. al.* "Having Trouble with Your Strategy? Then Map It," *loc. cit.* For additional perspectives on value propositions see: Sydney Finkelstein, Charles Harvey, and Thomas Lawton, *Breakout Strategy.* (New York: McGraw-Hill, 2007).

39. Robert S. Kaplan, *et. al.,* Having Trouble with Your Strategy? Then Map It," *loc cit.* For some additional insights into value propositions, customer benefits, and brand positioning see: David A. Aaker, *Developing Business Strategies, op. cit.;* David A. Aaker, *Building Strong Brands.* (New York: The Free Press, 1996); Michael J. Silverstein and Neil Fiske, *Trading Up.* (New York: The Penguin Group, 2003); William J. McEwen, *Married to the Brand.* (New York: Gallup Press, 2005); Sergio Zyman, *The End Of Marketing As We Know It.* (New York: Harper Business, 1999); Sergio Zyman, *The End of Advertising As We Know It.* (New York: John Wiley & Sons, Inc. 2002).

40. Christopher Palmeri, "How Guess Got It's Groove Back," *Business Week*, (December 18,2006), p. 126.

41. David Kirkpatrick, "Dell in the Penalty Box," *Fortune*, (September 18, 2006), pp. 70–78.

42. Jena McGregor, "Customer Service Champs," *Business Week*, (March 5, 2007), pp 52ff.

43. Betsy Morris, "Charles Schwab's Big Challenges, *Fortune*, (May 30, 2005), pp. 89–99.

44. Robert D. Hof, "The Wizard of Web Retailing," *Business Week*, (December 20, 2004), p. 18.

45. Mark Gottfredson, Rudy Pieryear, and Steven Phillips, "Strategic Sourcing From Periphery to the Core," *Harvard Business Review*, (February, 2005), pp. 132 ff.

46. Much of this section is adapted from the pioneering work of Douglas Lambert. See Douglas M. Lambert, (ed.) *Supply Chain Management.* (Sarasota, Florida: Supply Chain Management Institute, 2004).

47. For more discussion of this see Michael Hammer, "The Super Efficient Company," *Harvard Business Review*, (September-October, 2001).

48. See Michael Beer and Russell A. Eisenstat, "How to Have an Honest Conversation About Your Business Strategy," *Harvard Business Review*, (February, 2004); and George Stalk, *et. al.,* "Competing on Capabilities," *loc. cit.*

49. Michael Porter, "How Competitive Forces Shape Strategy," *loc. cit.*

50. Diane Brady, "Unsung CEO," *Business Week*, (October 25, 2004), pp. 74–84.

51. The value chain concept was popularized by Michael Porter, *Competitive Strategy, op. cit.* For other variations see Sydney Finkelstein, *et. al., Breakout Strategy, op. cit.*

52. Robert Grant, *Contemporary Strategy Analysis, op. cit.*, p. 281.

53. W. Chan Kim and Renee Manborgne, "Value Innovation: The Strategic Logic of High Growth," *Harvard Business Review*, (January-February, 1997).

54. Jay B. Barney, *Gaining and Sustaining Competitive Advantage. op. cit.*, pp. 150–151.

55. This strategy matrix was developed by the writer and has been used extensively in consulting work. Some of the original influences on the development of the matrix were: Samuel C. Johnson and Conrad Jones, "How to Organize for New Products," *Harvard Business Review*, (May-June, 1959; Led Adler, (ed) *Plotting Marketing Strategy, op cit.*, and I. Ansoff, *Corporate Strategy, op. cit.*

56. See, for example, Chris Zook and James Allen, *Profit from the Core*. (Boston: Harvard Business School Press, 2001).

57. Katrina Brooker, "Masterpiece Theatre," *Fortune*, {May 15, 2006), pp. 120–129.

58. Christopher Steiner, "Entrepreneurs: Peter Van Stolk," *Forbes*, (April 11, 2005), p. 75.

59. Monte Burke, "Unlikely Dynasty," *Forbes*, (September 19,2005), pp. 122–128.

60. Jena McGregor, "The World's Most Innovative Companies," *Business Week*, (April 24, 2006), pp. 63–74.

61. William C. Symonds, "Thinking Outside The Big Box," *Business Week*, (August 4, 2003), pp. 62–63.

62. David Whitford, "The People's Owner," *Fortune*, (October 13, 2003), pp. 181–186.

63. Al Ehrbar, "Breakaway Brands," *Fortune*, (October 31, 2005), pp. 153–170.

64. Christopher Palmeri, "The $600 Million Circus Maximus," *Business Week*, (December 13, 2004), pp. 81–82.

65. William C. Symonds, David Kiley, and Stanley Homes, "A Java Jolt for Dunkin' Donuts," *Business Week*, (December 20, 2004), pp. 61–63.

66. Robert Berner, "Extreme Makeover," *Business Week*, (November 1, 2004), pp. 105–106.

67. Marc Gunther, "MTV's Passage to India," *Fortune*, (August 9, 2004), pp. 117–125).

68. David Welch, "The Second Coming of Cadillac," *Business Week*, (November 24, 2003), pp. 79–80.

69. Joseph Weber, "Public TV's Identity Crisis," *Business Week*, (September 30, 2002), pp. 65–66.

70. Aude Lagorce, "Spice for Your Smile," *Forbes.com* (October 27, 2003.

71. Spencer E. Ante, "A Software Vets' Growth Spurt," *Business Week*, (April 4, 2005), p. 72.

72. Louise Lee, "Jean Therapy, $23 a Pop," *Business Week*, (June 28, 2004), pp. 91–93.

73. Janet Guyon, "Jimmy Choo Tries to Sell Its Sole," *Fortune*, (November 29, 2004), p. 58.

74. David Stires, "Taxing Times At H&R Block," *Fortune*, (March 21, 2005), pp. 181–184.

75. ———, "50 Best Performers," *Business Week*, March 26,2007, pp. 74ff.

76. *Ibid.*

77. Matthew Boyle, "Best Buy's Giant Gamble," *Fortune*, (April 30, 2006), pp. 69–75.

78. Catherine Holahan, "Going, Going . . . Everywhere," *Business Week*, (June 5, 2006), pp. 42–44).

79. Jack Ewing, "Otto the Modest," *Business Week*, (June 5, 2006), pp. 42–44.

80. Anne Fisher, "America's Most Admired Companies," *Fortune*, (March 6, 2006) and company annual reports.

81. Peter Kafka, "Bean Counter," *Forbes*, (February 28,2005), pp. 78–80.

82. ———, "Feature Marketer of the Year," *Advertising Age*, (December 12, 2005), p. 5.

83. Chana R. Schoenberger, "House Call," *Forbes*, (September 6, 2004), pp. 93–94; and Brian Grow, "Renovating Home Depot," *Business Week*, (March 6, 2006), pp. 50–58.

84. Donald L Laurie, Yves L. Doz, and Claude P. Sheer, "Creating New Growth Platforms," *Harvard Business Review*, (May, 2006), pp. 80ff.

85. David Besanko, *et. al.*, *Economics of Strategy, op. cit.*, pp. 74–76.

86. Michael Hammer, "Deep Change: How Operational Innovation Can Transform Your Company," *Harvard Business Review*, (April, 2004), pp. 85ff.

87. Rita Gunther McGrath and Ian C. Macmillan, "Market Busting Strategies for Exceptional Business Growth," *Harvard Business Review*, (March, 2005), pp. 81–89.

88. *Ibid.*, p. 87.

89. David J. Collis and Cynthia A. Montgomery, "Competing on Resources," *loc. cit.*

90. Alfred Chandler, *Strategy and Structure, op. cit.*

91. This section was adapted from Philippe Lassere, *Global Strategic Management, op. cit.*, pp. 72–91.

92. For additional insights see Dave Ulrich, *et. al.*, "Capitalizing on Capabilities," *loc. cit.*

93. Peter F. Drucker, *The Effective Executive*. (New York: Harper Business Essentials, 2002).

94. Jim Collins, *Good to Great, op. cit.*

95. Ruth L. Williams and Joseph P. Cothrel, "Building Tomorrow's Leaders Today," *Strategy and Leadership 26*. (September-October, 1997).

96. Arie De Geus, "The Living Company," *Harvard Business Review*, (March-April, 1997).

97. Robert M. Grant, *Contemporary Strategy Analysis, op. cit.*

98. *Ibid.*

99. T. Copeland, T. Koller, and J. Murrin, *Valuation: Measuring and Managing the Value of Companies*. 3rd ed. (New York: Wiley, 2000).

100. Gary Hamel and C.K. Prahalad, "Strategic Intent," *loc. cit.*, and Jim Collins, *Good to Great, op. cit.*

101. Gary Hamel and C. K. Prahalad, "The Core Competence of the Corporation," *loc. cit.*

102. Garth Saloner, *et al.*, *Strategic Management, op. cit.*, p. 88.

103. Jim Collins, *Good to Great, op. cit.*

104. N.J. Mass, "The Relative Value of Growth," *loc. cit.*

105. *Ibid.*

106. See, for example, Michael E. Porter, "From Competitive Advantage to Corporate Strategy," *Harvard Business Review,* (May-June, 1987); Andrew Campbell, Michael Goold and Marcus Alexander, "Corporate Strategy: The Quest for Parenting Advantage," *Harvard Business Review,* (March-April, 1995); and Garth Saloner, *et. al., Strategic Management, op. cit.*

107. *Ibid.*

108. Some of these distinctions have been articulated in Michael E. Raynor and Joseph L. Bower, "Lead From The Center: How to Manage Divisions Dynamically," *Harvard Business Review,* (May, 2001). Also, see Robert Grant, *Contemporary Strategy Analysis, op. cit.*

109. Lee Dranikoff, Tim Koller and Anton Schneider, "Divestiture: Strategies Missing Link," *Harvard Business Review,* (May, 2002).

110. *Ibid.*

111. David J. Collis and Cynthia A. Montgomery, "Creating Corporate Advantage," *Harvard Business Review,* (May-June, 1998).

112. C.K. Prahalad and Gary Hamel, "The Core Competence of the Corporation," *loc. cit.;* Gary Hamel and C.K. Prahalad, "Strategic Intent," *loc. cit.;* Andrew Campbell, *et. al.,* "Corporate Strategy: The Quest for Parenting Advantage," *loc. cit.;* and Robert Grant, *Contemporary Strategy Analysis, op. cit.*

113. For definitions of these financial metrics see Appendix A.

114. Thomas J. Waite, "Stick to the Core . . . or Go For," *Harvard Business Review,* (February, 2002), pp. 31ff.

115. Chris Zook and James Allen, "Growth Outside the Core," *Harvard Business Review,* (December, 2003), pp. 66ff.

116. Chris Zook and James Allen, *Profit From The Core.* (Boston: Harvard Business School Press, 2000), pp. 18 and 148.

117. Youngme Moon, "Break Free From the Product Life Cycle," *Harvard Business Review,* (May, 2005), pp. 87–93.

118. Arlene Weintraub and Christine Tierney, "Can Nestle Resist This Morsel," *Business Week,* (September 2, 2002), pp. 61–62.

119. Monte Burke, "Ski, Fish and Pitch," *Forbes,* (March 28, 2005), pp. 81–82.

120. Robert M. Grant, *Contemporary Strategy Analysis, op. cit.,* pp. 470–471.

121. David Besanko, *et. al., Economics of Strategy, op. cit.,* pp. 195–197.

122. Constantinos C. Markides, "To Diversify or Not to Diversify," *Harvard Business Review,* (November-December, 1997).

123. Patricia Sellers, "It Was A No-Brainer," *Fortune,* (February 21, 2005), pp. 97–102.

124. Chester Dawson, "Buy A Toyota, Get a Mortgage," *Business Week,* (September 13, 2004), p. 56.

125. Chris Zook with James Allen, *Profit From the Core, op. cit.,* p. 148.

126. Lee Dranikoff, *et. al.,* "Divestiture: Strategy's Missing Link," *loc. cit.*

127. Kathryn Kranhold, "The Immelt Era, Five Years Old, Transforms GE," *Wall Street Journal,* (September 11, 2006), p. B1.

128. Arie De Grus, "The Living Company," *loc. cit.*

129. See Michael Goold and Andrew Campbell, "Desperately Seeking Synergy," *Harvard Business Review*, (July-August, 1998); and Michael Porter, "From Competitive Advantage to Corporate Strategy," *loc. cit.*

130. Robert M. Grant, *Contemporary Strategy Analysis, op. cit.*; Michael Goold and Andrew Campbell, "Desperately Seeking *Synergy*," *loc. cit.*

131. Rita Gunther McGrath, *et. al.*, "Market Busting Strategies for Exceptional Business Growth," *loc. cit.*

132. Philippe Lassere, *Global Strategic Management, op. cit.*, pp. 72–91.

133. Christopher A. Bartlett and Sumantra Ghosal, *Managing Across Borders: The Transnational Solution.* (Cambridge: Harvard Business School Press, 1998).

134. Garth Saloner, *et. al.*, *Strategic Management. op. cit.*

135. E. C. Wenger and W. M. Snyder, "Communities of Practice: The Organizational Frontier," *Harvard Business Review*, (January-February, 2000).

136. I. Nonada and H. Takeuchi, *The Knowledge-Creating Company.* (New York: Oxford University Press, 1995).

137. Dave Ulrich, *et. al.*, "Capitalizing on Capabilities," *loc. cit.*

138. Larry Bossidy and Ram Charan, *Execution.* (New York: Crown Business, 2002). Mr. Bossidy was a senior executive at GE.

139. Robert S. Kaplan, *et. al.*, "The Office of Strategy Management," *loc. cit.*

140. Peter F. Drucker, *The Effective Executive, op. cit.*

141. Jim Collins, *Good to Great, op. cit.*

142. ———, "GE's New Set of Leadership Traits," *Business Week*, (August 1, 2005), p. 68.

143. Ruth L. Williams and Joseph P Cothrel, "Building Tomorrow's Leaders Today," *Strategy and Leadership.* 26 (September-October, 1997).

144. D. Goleman, "What Makes a Leader," *Harvard Business Review*, (November-December, 1995).

145. Insights from the following sources have also been useful. Garth Saloner, *et. al.*, *Strategic Management, op. cit.*; Robert Grant, *Contemporary Strategy Analysis, op. cit.*; David Bosanko, *et. al.*, *Economics of Strategy, op. cit.*; and Philippe Lassere, *Global Strategic Management, op. cit.*

146. See Appendix A for definition.

147. See Appendix A for definition.

INDEX

operating divisions (*cont.*)
   lateral linking mechanisms, 216–217
   long-term corporate strategy, 6–9
   organizational design and development initiatives, 211
   performance measurement, 218
   strategic initiatives, 202–203
operating expenses, 109–111, 181–182, 281
operating income, 179–180, 229, 281
operating synergy, 103
Oracle, 71
organizational culture. *See* culture, organizational
organizational design and development, for business, 117–128, 260–261, 264. *See also* corporate organizational design and development
organizational structure, 119–120, 121, 122, 123, 212–216
Otto Group, 100

P

Patagonia, 70
PBS, 97
Peet's, 195
PEG (price/earnings to growth) ratio, 52, 159, 281
PE (price/earnings) multiple, 52, 159, 281
PepsiCo, 3, 152, 154–155, 171, 174
performance analysis, 133, 135, 235, 237
Performance Food Group, 190
Peterson, Wilferd A., 157
plans, annual business, 5, 241, 243–246, 262–264
plans, annual corporate, 8–9, 241, 247–251, 273–277
plant & equipment productivity, 281
portfolio analysis, 144–147
portfolios, business, 168–170, 187, 196
positioning, 71–72, 190, 263
price component, of value proposition, 68–69
price increases, 109

privately-held companies, 49
Procter & Gamble (P&G)
   balance sheet productivity, 206–207
   competitive advantages, 203
   core competencies, 173–174
   corporate objectives, 163
   Crest, 97
   Gillette acquisition, 194, 212
   market penetration, 189–190
   Old Spice market extension, 96
   strategic priorities, 175
product availability component, of value proposition, 69
product component, of value proposition, 68
product differentiation, 28, 97–98
product innovation, 14–15, 30
productivity, 281
product life cycle model, 12–14, 113
product line extension, 98–99
product reformulation/repositioning strategies, 95
product replacement strategies, 96–97
product scope, 81–82
profitability
   accounting perspective vs. requirements for, 15
   of business growth initiatives, 104
   business objectives, 53–56, 57, 262
   corporate objectives, 160, 162–163
   by operating division, 230
   organizational orientation toward, 126
profit and loss statements, 104, 129–131, 232–233
profit-margin, 57, 281
profit model, 76–78
profit orientation, 221
profit per employee, 281
pro-forma balance sheets, 131–132, 233–234
pro-forma cash flow statements, 133, 134, 235, 236
pro-forma profit and loss statements, 104, 129–131, 232–233
Progressive Group of Insurance Companies, 43